Employment Policy in Emerging Economies

Employment is a critical part of the macro-economy and a key driver of economic development. India's employment policy over the past three decades provides an important case study for understanding how government attitudes to the labour market contribute to an emerging economy's growth and development. This study contains important insights on the policy challenges faced by one of the world's most populous, labour abundant economies in securing employment in a context of structural change.

The book considers India's approach to employment policy from a national and global perspective and whether policy settings promote employment intensive growth. Chapters in the first half of the volume evaluate India's approach to employment policy within the national and international context. This includes the ILO Decent Work program, the national agenda for inclusive growth, and national regulatory frameworks for labour and education. Chapters in the second half of the volume focus on how employment policy works in practice and its impact on manufacturing workers, the self-employed, women, and rural workers. These chapters draw attention to the contradictions within the current policy regime and the need for new approaches.

Employment Policy in Emerging Economies will interest scholars, policy makers and students of the Indian economy and South Asia more generally. It will support undergraduate and postgraduate academic teaching in courses on economic development, global political economy, the Indian economy and global labour.

Elizabeth Hill is a Senior Lecturer in the Department of Political Economy at the University of Sydney, Australia.

Amitendu Palit is Senior Research Fellow and Research Lead (Trade and Economic Policy) at the Institute of South Asian Studies (ISAS) in the National University of Singapore.

Routledge Studies in Development Economics

For a complete list of titles in this series, please visit www.routledge.com/series/SE0266

131 The Economics of Child Labour in the Era of Globalization
Policy Issues
Sarbajit Chaudhuri and Jayanta Kumar Dwibedi

130 International Taxation and the Extractive Industries
Resources without Borders
Edited by Philip Daniel, Michael Keen, Artur Świstak and Victor Thuronyi

131 Fiscal Policy and the Natural Resources Curse
How to Escape from the Poverty Trap
Paul Mosley

132 Sustainable Growth in the African Economy
How Durable Is Africa's Recent Performance?
Jeffrey James

133 Fair Trade and Organic Initiatives in Asian Agriculture
The Hidden Realities
Rie Makita and Tadasu Tsuruta

134 Economic Transformation for Poverty Reduction in Africa
A Multidimensional Approach
Edited by Almas Heshmati

135 Employment Policy in Emerging Economies
The Indian Case
Edited by Elizabeth Hill and Amitendu Palit

136 Inequality in Economics and Sociology
New Perspectives
Edited by Gilberto Antonelli and Boike Rehbein

Employment Policy in Emerging Economies

The Indian Case

Edited by Elizabeth Hill and Amitendu Palit

LONDON AND NEW YORK

First published 2018 by Routledge

2 Park Square, Milton Park, Abingdon, Oxfordshire OX14 4RN
52 Vanderbilt Avenue, New York, NY 10017

Routledge is an imprint of the Taylor & Francis Group, an informa business

First issued in paperback 2019

British Library Cataloguing in Publication Data
A catalogue record for this book is available from the British Library

Library of Congress Cataloging in Publication Data
A catalog record for this book has been requested

ISBN: 978-1-138-91870-2 (hbk)
ISBN: 978-0-367-87353-0 (pbk)

Typeset in Bembo Std
by Swales & Willis Ltd, Exeter, UK

Contents

Figures

Tables

Contributors

Homagni Choudhury is a Lecturer in Economics and is the Director of Research for Accounting, Finance and Economics at the Aberystwyth Business School, Aberystwyth University (UK). Having completed his first degree in Economics at the University of Delhi (India), Homagni proceeded to do a Master's program at Lancaster University (UK) and then obtained a PhD in Economics at the University of Dundee (UK). He has a strong background in academia with professional research and teaching experience in a wide range of topics in economics and related areas. His broad research interests lie in the areas of Development Economics and Applied Economics with particular interests on aspects of International Trade, Labour, Productivity, Industrial and Regional economics. He has been associated with the World Bank's 'Jobs and Development' program at ICRIER (India) since it started in 2013–14.

Elizabeth Hill is Senior Lecturer in the Department of Political Economy at the University of Sydney. Her research interests focus on women and employment in India and Australia. Elizabeth is the author of *Worker Identity, Agency and Economic Development: Women's Empowerment in the Indian Informal Economy* (Routledge 2010). She has published on the issue of women's work and care in a number of edited volumes including *Women, Work and Care in the Asia Pacific* (Routledge 2017); *Inclusive Growth and Development in the 21st Century: A Structural and Institutional Analysis of China and India* (World Scientific Publishing 2014); and *The Global Political Economy of the Household in Asia* (Palgrave Macmillan 2013).

Deb Kusum Das teaches at the Department of Economics, Ramjas College, University of Delhi and is an external consultant with ICRIER, New Delhi. His research focuses on the economics of labour markets, industrial economics, especially growth and productivity change at industry level, and applied trade policy. He has been one of the lead researchers in labour regulations and manufacturing performance research in the World Bank's Jobs for Development project at ICRIER. He is also associated with compiling the India KLEMS dataset. He holds a PhD from the Delhi School of Economics and is the founder of South Asia Economics Students Meet (SAESM) – a knowledge sharing platform for undergraduate students of economics of South Asian colleges and universities.

Jayan Jose Thomas is an Associate Professor of Economics at the Indian Institute of Technology, New Delhi. His research deals with various aspects of Indian development, especially issues related to labour, industrialisation and the macro economy.

Salim Lakha is Honorary Senior Fellow in the School of Social and Political Sciences at the University of Melbourne. He was formerly the Coordinator of Development Studies Program at Melbourne University, and in 2011 a Visiting Senior Research Fellow at the Asia Research Institute, National University of Singapore. His research interests include social protection, decentralisation, migration, transnational identities, and the international division of labour. His current research project examines the capacity constraints and governance aspects of Mahatma Gandhi National Rural Employment Guarantee Scheme which was enacted in 2005. This research was funded by the Australia India Institute, University of Melbourne.

Amitendu Palit is Senior Research Fellow and Research Lead (Trade and Economic Policy) at the Institute of South Asian Studies (ISAS) in the National University of Singapore. He is an economist specializing in international trade policies and regulations, political economy of international trade, comparative economic studies and public policies. His current research is on trade and regional architectures in the Asia-Pacific, trade regulations and governance, China-India comparative economic developments, and political economy of economic reforms.

Supriya RoyChowdhury is Professor at the Centre for Political Institutions, Institute for Social and Economic Change (ISEC), Bangalore. She holds a PhD in Politics from Princeton University. Her research interests are in the areas of globalisation, trade unions, informal labour and urban poverty. Her articles have appeared in the *Journal of Development Studies*, *Third World Quarterly*, *Economic and Political Weekly*, as well as in several edited volumes.

Catherine Saget is a Chief of Unit with the Research department of the International Labour Office (ILO). She has also contributed to the setting up of a unit on wages within the ILO and has worked on employment policy at times of economic crisis. She was the Senior Employment Specialist in Delhi at the time of writing this book. As an Economist with the Organisation for Economic Cooperation and Development (OECD) between 2006 and 2007, she participated in the OECD thematic review on youth employment policies. She holds a PhD in Economics from the European University Institute in Florence (Italy).

Jaivir Singh is Professor at the Centre for the Study of Law and Governance, Jawaharlal Nehru University, having previously taught at the University of Delhi. Trained as an economist at the Delhi School of Economics, University of Delhi, his research work is oriented towards an interdisciplinary exploration of the interaction between the law and the economy. He has published on diverse topics that include the Indian constitution, regulation, labour law, competition law, corporate law and international investment treaties. Currently he is involved with survey-based research on the impact of the law on Indian labour markets.

Ratna M. Sudarshan was a National Fellow at National University of Educational Planning and Administration from 2013–15, Director of the Institute of Social Studies Trust, New Delhi from 2003–2011, and Principal Economist, National Council for Applied Economic Research prior to this. Her research and publications have addressed women's work in the informal economy and social protection; education and social change; research, action and policy linkage; gender and evaluation.

B. P. Vani is an Assistant Professor at the Centre for Economic Studies and Policy (CESP), Institute for Social and Economic Change, Bangalore, India. She holds a Master's in Statistics from the Bangalore University. She has published papers in journals of international repute and her research focuses on poverty and income distribution.

Sher Singh Verick is Deputy Director of the ILO Decent Work Team for South Asia and Country Office for India. Prior to this position, he was Senior Employment Specialist in the Delhi office, leading the ILO's support to governments in South Asia on employment policy formulation and related research, and Senior Research Economist for the ILO in Geneva. He has also worked for the United Nations Economic Commission for Africa and various research institutions in Europe and Australia. He holds a Master's degree in development economics from the Australian National University and a PhD in economics from the University of Bonn. Since December 2004, he is a Research Fellow of the Institute for the Study of Labor (IZA). Through various roles, he has led and undertaken policy-oriented research to promote the formulation and implementation of more effective policies. He has published in a range of journals and has authored or edited a number of volumes including *Transformation of Women at Work in Asia: An Unfinished Development Agenda (2016)*, *Perspectives on Labour Economics for Development* (2013), and the *Labour Markets of Emerging Economies* (2013).

Preface

Employment is one of the fundamental objectives of economic development. In his famous 1969 paper 'The Idea of Development', Dudley Seers argues that the elimination of poverty, inequality and unemployment are the primary goals of development. Economic growth is the means to this end, but employment has a special role to play in reducing poverty and limiting inequality.

Much of the scholarship on employment issues in emerging economies has focused on the labour experience. This has been of enormous value, highlighting the overwhelmingly informal, precarious and exploitative nature of work in these contexts. However to fully understand the labour experience in emerging economies our analysis must also pay attention to the prevailing policy frameworks that define labour markets and employment. This volume looks beyond the labour experience to focus on various dimensions of employment policy and its impact on the structure and growth of employment. The volume brings together scholarship that evaluates whether India has effective employment policies consistent with its development goals. These research findings are particularly relevant at a time when emerging economies are struggling to address the mounting challenge of unemployment.

Preparation of this volume required scholars from around the globe to meet and deliberate on the role of employment policy in economic growth and development. We are grateful to the University of Sydney Office for Global Engagement for its financial support through the International Program Development Fund. This allowed us to bring contributing authors together at the Institute for South Asian Studies at the National University of Singapore in February 2014 for a preliminary workshop. We also thank the International Labour Organisation South Asia Regional office, New Delhi for their organisation and support for a supplementary symposium on employment policy in India in December 2016. At the event a number of contributors along with other academics, policy makers and union delegates discussed the current state of Indian employment policy and its direction. We also thank the contributing authors for their work and patience in preparing the volume for publication.

Elizabeth Hill and Amitendu Palit
March 2017

Part I

Employment policy in the global and national context

1 Re-thinking employment in the Indian economy

Inclusive growth and well-being

Elizabeth Hill

In September 2015 the state government of Uttar Pradesh in northern India advertised 368 jobs for peons at the Uttar Pradesh Secretariat with a starting salary of Rs. 16,000 per month. The minimum qualification required was school level education of at least grade five and the ability to ride a bicycle. More than two million people applied for the 368 jobs on offer. Amongst the applicants around 200,000 were reported to have graduate degrees and 255 had a PhD (Sharda 2015). This story is not unique: mass applications by overqualified candidates for government jobs are a regular event in many states in India. The tabloid nature of these reports makes for captivating headlines. But the stories are important because they focus attention on some of the systemic problems confronting the contemporary Indian labour market and highlight the urgent need to make employment policy a national priority.

Employment policy in developing economies like India has been strongly influenced by Arthur Lewis's pioneering theory of economic growth with unlimited supplies of labour (1954). Lewis argued that as economies grew the labour market would be transformed, with labour from agriculture and "traditional" modes of petty production smoothly reallocated to more productive forms of formal industrial employment. This normative approach has left an explicit focus on employment policy sidelined in macro-economic planning, even as traditional modes of petty production, informal employment, and under-employment flourish—often in high growth economies. This laissez-faire approach to employment policy is not delivering decent work or efficient labour markets. Unskilled workers entering the Indian labour market for the first time or shifting out of subsistence agriculture are rarely absorbed into formal employment in high productivity jobs. Instead most find employment in the informal economy where the absence of a formal employment contract leaves workers unprotected by formal labour laws and social protection legislation. Many educated workers also face problems accessing formal employment and likewise find themselves working in informal jobs.

Employment in a global perspective

At the global level the importance of employment as both an economic and social goal has begun to gain traction in policy circles. Employment has been the focus of a number of recent reports by large international economic and development institutions such as the United Nations Development Programme, the International Labour Organization and the World Bank. These reports highlight the specific role that employment plays in promoting inclusive patterns of growth and development (UNDP 2015; ILO 2015; World Bank 2012). In recent years, concerns regarding deepening inequality and the capacity for decent work to promote social and economic inclusion and growth have seen employment policy brought centre stage (Stiglitz 2015). The positive relationship between decent work and economic growth has been recognised in Goal 8 of the new Sustainable Development Goals agreed to by the global community in 2015 (United Nations 2016). Policy that delivers regular, secure and safe employment is increasingly understood to be essential for global growth, prosperity and well-being.

The demand for decent work has also made it onto the national agenda in emerging and developed economies. Rapid economic growth across many emerging economies has delivered a new class of aspirational young people with expectations of decent employment, prosperity and well-being. Many of these economies have a very young demographic profile and burgeoning working age populations—key ingredients in the much vaunted "demographic dividend". Sub-Saharan African nations have the youngest populations, with South Asian countries not far behind. In India the working age population is growing by around 1 million every month, equating to a projected overall rise in the working age population of 33 per cent by 2050 (UN DESA 2015). A steady stream of quality jobs is required to meet this emerging demand, and failure to deliver risks turning the demographic dividend into a demographic disaster.

In the rich OECD economies the issues are different, but the focus on employment is the same. In many developed economies the proportion of the population that is of working-age has peaked and debate centres on how governments can intervene to maintain economic productivity and living standards as the population ages and dependency ratios increase.[1] Middle-income China also has a rapidly aging profile on account of its one-child policy: by 2050 the working-age population is projected to decline by 212 million and the proportion of citizens over 60 years of age to more than double (UN DESA 2015). In these economies with rapidly aging populations and high dependency ratios employment policy is understood to be an essential tool for securing well-being and ongoing prosperity. Policy initiatives include raising the retirement age and redesigning work so people can remain in the workforce longer.

The employment challenges that define the economies of the global south and the global north on account of their demographic profiles are also being shaped by rapid change in the industrial and consumer landscape. Increased automation and outsourcing opportunities in both manufacturing and services have changed the structure of the labour process. Global value chains and production networks in particular highlight the close link between the structure and quality of employment opportunities in the global south and those in the global north. New regimes of global capital accumulation have fundamentally changed the conditions of employment in complex and often contradictory ways. When "old economy" manufacturing in the USA, Australia or Europe is moved off-shore to Mexico, the Caribbean or China, global poverty is reduced as poor, often rural, people access new employment opportunities that pay more than subsistence agriculture or casual day labour. The hours of work may be long, the work dangerous and low-paid by global standards, but these jobs often provide a stepping stone for the rural poor to improved well-being. Meanwhile middle-class male breadwinners in the global north and their households confront a decline in employment opportunities and rising unemployment. For many men in the manufacturing sector, the new service jobs in retail, communications, banking and finance do not easily accommodate their skills, interests or sense of masculinity. And many of these jobs—particularly those focused on back office support—are increasingly outsourced to call centres in the Philippines and India, providing in turn, new employment opportunities for educated English-speaking workers in these countries.

The employment challenges that define the economies of the global south and the global north in the early twenty-first century are complex and connected. It is a multifaceted story shaped by class, gender, race and ethnicity, and globalisation has rendered workers both winners and losers. However one clear outcome of the restructuring of the labour process and international trade that is evident in all economies has been the global shift toward precarious non-standard forms of employment that are not covered by national labour laws, do not provide workers with basic social protection and have limited or no security of tenure (Standing 1999, 2011). In the USA, this global shift has seen the rise of a new class of the working poor (Shipler 2004). In emerging economies global production chains have underwritten the prevalence and even growth of the informal economy and vulnerable forms of low-skilled employment such as home-based work, which are essential to the production of cheap consumer durables for the global middle-class (Barrientos and Kritzinger 2004; Phillips 2011, 2013). This particular structure of global production and accumulation has supported global growth for several decades. But whether or not the model is sustainable under emerging economic and political conditions is unclear.

Political sentiment in the USA and the United Kingdom is turning against globalisation, partly on account of concerns about adequate and decent employment. Faltering global growth since 2008 and concern that structural problems in the Chinese economy will deliver further contraction have seen increased competition between individual countries for foreign investment and market share. The prevailing conditions mean that the labour-intensive and export-oriented manufacturing model that proved so successful in East Asia and China is now more difficult to sustain than in previous decades, creating new challenges for the low-wage labour surplus economies in South Asia, Africa and Latin America.

In many economies where wages are low and labour is abundant, manufacturing is not providing the expected level of economic activity and growth in employment is declining, even as Chinese wages rise and China's dominance in global manufacturing begins to recede. Dani Rodrik labels this shifting and shrinking profile of manufacturing "premature deindustrialisation" (Rodrik 2016). While the forces of deindustrialisation are varied and are driven by both global and national economic dynamics, the failure of many emerging economies to develop a large manufacturing sector creates serious problems for governments with millions of unskilled workers in need of decent employment opportunities to secure their future. The lack of regular low-skilled manufacturing jobs has seen a critical rung on the traditional ladder to economic development kicked away. And in many cases the dearth of regular employment opportunities has underwritten the prevalence and even growth in informal employment—particularly self-employment.

Debate about the role of informal employment in economic development is conflicted. Some scholars argue that informal employment provides an essential safety net and a basic livelihood for the impoverished masses, even though it is unproductive and prone to excessive rates of exploitation (Portes, Castells and Benton 1989). Other scholars see informal employment as a vibrant sphere of economic entrepreneurship and innovation that can be deployed by individuals wishing to build their own futures (De Soto 1989). Empirical evidence shows that for some, informal employment can deliver economic prosperity. However, for the majority, the conditions of informal work do not support capital accumulation and for most informal workers this type of employment is closely correlated with poverty, vulnerability and inter-generational inequality (Breman 2013, 2016; Chen 2012; Hill 2010; Sanyal 2007).

The global response to these employment challenges has been led by the International Labour Organization and its Decent Work agenda. Since 2000 the ILO has been at the vanguard of research and policy development on decent work, defined as employment that delivers a fair income, provides respect for rights at work and social protection for workers and their families. The rationale is that decent work is an essential component of sustainable, inclusive economic growth and the elimination of poverty (ILO 2016b). The Decent Work agenda deploys existing ILO conventions, protocols and recommendations on wages and conditions, such as the minimum wage, working hours, right to association, maternity leave and social protection. In addition a number of new conventions have been developed to support decent work for the hundreds of millions of workers, particularly women, who are employed in the informal sector of emerging economies as home-based workers (C177) and domestic workers (C189). ILO tools are used to support governments working to improve employment opportunities and develop alternative approaches to employment policy.

In recent years the ILO's research and policy agenda has been complemented by World Bank (2012) and United National Development Program (2015) reports on the critical role that employment plays in national economic development. The case for decent work was reiterated in the aftermath of the global financial and economic crisis of 2008 and has been progressively embedded in a range of international and human rights agendas. In 2015 decent work was adopted as a universal objective in the UN's 2030 Agenda for Sustainable Development.[2] The International Monetary Fund has also addressed the importance of employment as a critical contributor to global economic prosperity, arguing forcefully for "the need to counteract waning potential growth through structural reforms to boost labor force participation, better match skills to jobs, and reduce barriers to market entry" (IMF 2016).

How these global trends play out in emerging economies and how national policy regimes are responding to the demands of their increasingly well-educated and aspirational working age population is the focus of this volume. We use the case study of the Indian economy and employment policy environment to explore some of the challenges posed by a large underutilised working age population in which the majority are still rural-based and the informal economy is dominant. In this socio-economic environment, what role does employment policy play in the extension of decent work for all?

Employment in the Indian economy

India faces many challenges in the area of employment—particularly around the expansion of decent work opportunities. With a very large informal economy and a majority of the population defined as working poor, it is surprising that employment policy has not been at the top of the economic policy agenda. Instead, employment concerns have been cast within debates and policy initiatives focused on livelihoods, poverty alleviation and micro-enterprise development. In the Economic Survey that accompanies the annual Union Budget, the discussion on employment has, until recently, been located in the chapter on social infrastructure and human development rather than as a stand-alone economic category. In part, this is a reflection of India's experience as a poor developing nation with a policy focus on the livelihoods of the very poor. However, in the post-1990 era of a liberalised economy and high growth rates, employment slowly made its way into the five year planning process. This was particularly the case in the 11th and 12th Five Year Plans that focused increasingly on the idea of "inclusive growth". In these documents the creation of productive and decent employment was identified as a fundamental pathway to inclusive growth.

But in spite of the emerging focus on employment in policy and planning documents, total employment has essentially stagnated during the high growth era, as India has failed to undergo the same structural transformation of the labour market as other countries with similar levels of GDP per capita. Just under half of all Indian workers continue to be employed in low productivity agricultural work that contributes an ever-declining share of GDP and for which they receive very low wages. The majority of India's economic growth is generated by the highly productive services sector. But while employment in services is growing, many of these sectors, such as finance, insurance, real estate and public utilities, do not generate large numbers of jobs for unskilled and semi-skilled workers. And where new employment opportunities are available, they are concentrated in urban centres. In urban India 58.7 per cent of employment is located in the service sector, compared to just 16.1 per cent in rural regions (ILO 2016a). Manufacturing employment in the high growth era has also failed to be a major driver of employment creation, providing only between 10.5 and 13 per cent of employment (ILO 2016a). In India, the sectoral composition of economic growth has not supported employment-intensive growth and development, leaving the majority of people without access to productive decent work. This has created a number of employment challenges for India. The discussion below provides a snapshot of India's labour force profile and these employment challenges.

Labour force profile

The World Bank reports that in 2014, India had almost 497 million workers aged 15 years and above. However the massive scale of India's labour force deflects attention from the very low participation rates. Since economic reforms were introduced in 1991, total labour force participation rates for those above 15 years have fallen from 60.9 per cent to 54.2 per cent in 2014. This is almost 10 percentage points lower than the global average of 63.5 (see Table 1.1).[3] The low total participation rate is driven primarily by India's extremely low female participation rate, which currently stands at around 27 per cent, almost half the world average. Indian men, in comparison, have higher participation rates than the global average, at 80 per cent.

The vast majority of workers, just under half the total labour force, are employed in the agricultural sector. The next largest employment sectors are manufacturing (12.8 per cent), trade, hotels and restaurants (11.4 per cent) and construction (10.6 per cent) just a few percentage points ahead of community, social and personal service (8.2 per cent). These numbers reflect a steady shift out of agriculture since the 1991 reforms, and large gains in construction work, which has more than tripled its share of employment (see Table 1.2).

Table 1.1 Labour force participation rates: India and the world

	India			*World*		
	women	*men*	*total*	*women*	*men*	*total*
1991	35	85	60.9	52.2	80.4	66.3
2014	27	80	54.2	50.3	76.7	63.5

Source: World Bank (2016) http://data.worldbank.org/

Table 1.2 Share of employment by industries: 1990–2012

Industrial sector	*1993–94*	*2004–05*	*2011–12*
Agriculture, Forestry & Fishing	64.8	58.5	48.9
Mining & Quarrying	0.7	0.6	0.5
Manufacturing	10.5	11.7	12.8
Electricity, Gas & Water	0.4	0.3	0.4
Construction	3.1	5.6	10.6
Trade, Hotels & Restaurants	7.4	10.2	11.4
Transportation, Storage & Communications	2.8	3.8	4.4
Finance, Real Estate, Business Services	0.9	1.5	2.6
Community, Social and Personal Services	9.4	7.7	8.2
TOTAL	100.0	100.0	100.0

Source: IHD (2014, 2008), Employment & Unemployment Survey, NSS various rounds.

Table 1.3 Industrial structure of the workforce: 2011–12

Industrial sector	*Male %*	*Female %*
Agriculture, Forestry & Fishing	43.6	62.8
Mining & Quarrying	0.6	0.3
Manufacturing	12.5	13.5
Electricity, Gas & Water	0.5	0.2
Construction	12.3	6.1
Trade, Hotels & Restaurants	14.0	4.9
Transportation, Storage & Communications	5.9	0.3
Other services	10.4	12.0
TOTAL	100.0	100.0

Source: IHD (2014, 209), Employment and Unemployment Survey, NSS 68th round.

The gendered pattern of employment shows women are more likely than men to be employed in agriculture, but much less likely than men to be employed in construction, trade, hotels and restaurants, or transportation, storage and communications (see Table 1.3). As a proportion of the working population women and men share similar rates of employment in manufacturing and other services.

Employment challenges

In the context of this general employment profile there are a number of specific employment challenges facing India: the demographic challenge, the decent work challenge, and the challenge to increase women's workforce participation. Each of these issues points to serious underlying limitations in the structure of the Indian economy and its capacity to promote the inclusive growth identified as the goal of both the 11th and 12th Five Year Plans.

The demographic challenge

Demographic trends in India exacerbate the negative impact of sluggish employment growth and leave many people of working age without access to decent employment. The era of strong economic growth coincided with a period of rapid population growth that saw the Indian population pass the one billion mark, putting the country on track to overtake China as the most populous nation on earth. This demographic trend delivered a parallel increase in the proportion of the population of working age—an increase of 7.36 percentage points over a 25 year period, to a high of 65.6 per cent in 2015 (see Table 1.4).

Such a hike in the proportion of the population of working age should be good news for the economy as it increases the proportion of economically active people relative to those requiring support—the young, the old and the incapacitated. This is called the dependency ratio. Between 1990 and 2015 a rapid rise in the working age population led to a dramatic fall of 19.26 percentage points in the dependency ratio.[4] This trend is expected to continue. In 2020 the average Indian citizen is expected to be just 29 years old, much younger than in other economies such as China or the US, where the average age will be 37 years, or Western Europe where the average will be 45. Half of India's current population is under 25 years and 65 per cent of the population is under 35 years.[5] These demographic trends mean that an estimated 300 million people will be added to India's working age population between 2010 and 2040, delivering on average around 10 million potential new workers every year, or nearly 1 million every month (Aiyar and Mody 2011, 5). Demographers call this a "youth bulge".

Whether the youth bulge translates into a demographic dividend or disaster depends entirely on the capacity of the economy and the labour market to deliver the requisite number of jobs.[6] Where decent work is available, economic growth and well-being is likely. However, the absence of adequate employment opportunities has significant economic and social costs. Unemployed and underemployed educated youth can experience confusion and be demoralised by a hostile labour market (C. Jeffrey, P. Jeffrey, and R. Jeffrey 2008; Jeffrey 2010). Events such as the Arab Spring of 2011 show how a lack of employment opportunities can fuel economic and political instability (Miller 2013). This is a challenge India currently faces.

Evaluation of the structure of economic growth post-1991 has led many economists and commentators to conclude that the Indian economy is marked by "jobless growth" (Chandrashekar and Ghose 2011; EPW 2010; Kannan and Raveendran 2009). Employment elasticity to total output has decreased over time, suggesting that the capability of the Indian economy to generate employment is limited. And even as newly created jobs in the service sector have provided decent employment opportunities for several million people, the absence of expanded labour-intensive manufacturing means that the majority of workers remain engaged as informal workers, often as urban self-employed or in agriculture.

Table 1.4 Population and workforce

	1990	*1995*	*2000*	*2005*	*2010*	*2015*
Annual GDP Growth %	5.533	7.574	3.841	9.285	10.26	7.57
Population[1]	870,601,776	960,874,982	1.053 billion	1.144 billion	1.231 billion	1.311 billion
Working Age Population (15–64 yrs) as % Total Population[2]	58.24	59.3	60.86	62.44	63.99	65.6
Dependency Ratio[3]	71.71	68.62	64.31	60.16	56.27	52.45
Size of Labour Force 15yrs+[4]	329,095,256	368,396,898	406,359,368	467,648,895	471,277,041	496,960,163 (2014)
Labour Force Participation Rate, Total (% of Total Population 15yrs+)[5]	60.9	60.5	59.1	60.8	55.4	54.2 (2014)

Source: World Bank Indicators http://data.worldbank.org/indicator

1 Source: World Bank Indicators http://data.worldbank.org/indicator/SP.POP.TOTL?locations=IN
2 Source: World Bank Indicators. http://data.worldbank.org/indicator/SP.POP.1564.TO.ZS?locations=IN&view=chart
3 Age dependency ratio is the ratio of dependants—people younger than 15 or older than 64—to the working-age population, those aged 15–64. Data is shown as the proportion of dependants per 100 working-age population. Source: World Bank Indicators http://data.worldbank.org/indicator/SP.POP.DPND?end=2015&locations=IN&start=1960&view=chart
4 Total labour force comprises people aged 15 and older who meet the International Labour Organization definition of the economically active population, i.e. all people who supply labour for the production of goods and services during a specified period. It includes both the employed and the unemployed. While national practices vary in the treatment of such groups as the armed forces and seasonal or part-time workers, in general the labour force includes the armed forces, the unemployed, and first-time job-seekers, but excludes homemakers and other unpaid caregivers and workers in the informal sector. Source: World Bank Indicators http://data.worldbank.org/indicator/SL.TLF.TOTL.IN?locations=IN
5 Source: World Bank Indicators http://data.worldbank.org/indicator/SL.TLF.CACT.ZS?locations=IN

Stagnant jobs growth has meant that the decline in the formal dependency ratio has not produced the surplus economic output and demographic dividend anticipated. The size of the actual labour force for 15 year olds and above has grown, but it has not kept pace with the growth in the proportion of the population of working age. In addition, labour force participation rates for Indian citizens 15 years and older have plummeted during the high growth era, from 61 per cent to only a fraction more than 54 per cent (Table 1.4). With fewer people working than could be the case, productivity and economic growth has been constrained and the much vaunted demographic dividend has been compromised.

The quality challenge: decent work for all

The quality of work is the second major employment challenge facing the Indian economy. In India, informal work has always dominated the economy, much more so than in the case of other economies at a similar stage of development. Recent labour surveys report that around 92.5 per cent of the Indian workforce is informally employed (IHD 2014,57).[7] The dominance of informal employment has not changed in the high growth era, posing a serious problem for the "inclusive growth" agenda and thwarting the aspirations of the increasingly aspirational lower-middle and middle-classes.

Informal employment is defined by the lack of a formal employment contract. This means the work is unprotected by labour law, does not include basic social security services and typically has low levels of productivity. It also pays very low wages. The declining quality of the employment experience is acutely reflected in data from the *Informal Sector and Conditions of Employment in India* report, based on the employment and unemployment survey conducted in the 68th NSSO round (GOI 2014). This report showed that the percentage of workers across India who did not have a written contract of employment or paid leave had increased from 63 per cent of workers in 2004–05 to 68.8 per cent in 2011–12. The number of workers with no access to social security also increased slightly over the same period, from 71 to 72 per cent. No lack of access to union representation was another feature of the majority of Indian workers, with the report finding that 80 per cent of workers are employed in activities with no union representation. In all cases, employment insecurity and vulnerability was found to be more extreme among rural workers compared to their urban counterparts.

Clearly, the need for jobs that are secure, with conditions protected by law and delivering a living wage is particularly acute in India. Jobs that meet the ILO "decent work" standard are required if economic growth is to translate into the well-being of citizens. However the policy framework has moved in the opposite direction. The new economic policy of 1991 ushered in an era of open liberalised markets, the privatisation of government utilities and outsourcing in both domestic and international production. These changes produced a general rise in the use of contract labour and new forms of non-standard and insecure employment contracts. Numerous studies of the structure of employment since the 1991 reforms show that the majority of new jobs created in the high growth era have been informal, with many of these increasingly located in the formal sector (GOI 2009; IHD 2014).[8] Figures for 2011–2012 show that 58 per cent of workers in the formal economy (46 million workers) are informally employed, 17 percentage points higher than the 41 per cent of workers informally employed in 1999–2000. This deterioration in formal job quality in the post reform era is largely a result of the decline in public sector employment and a rise in the use of contract labour in the private sector (IHD 2014, 58).

In terms of employment status, more than half of all workers are self-employed, almost one third are casual labourers and less than one in five are regular salary or wage earners (see Table 1.5). These relative proportions have not changed significantly in the post-reform high growth era, although there has been a five percentage point increase in the proportion of people employed in regular waged work. Casual work has declined slightly, with women less likely to be employed as casual workers than they were in the early 1990s. There was no change for men. And while wages in general have increased over this time, casual workers continue to receive the lowest wages, at only one third those of regular wage earners (IHD 2014, 96).

The quality of work available matters enormously in an economy of more than a billion people. Employment that assures security of tenure, decent pay and basic social protection measures is fundamental to an inclusive model of economic growth and well-being. In an economy overwhelmed by informal employment practices and structural changes that have enhanced economic informality in new and emerging industries, the provision of decent work remains a significant challenge.

The gender challenge: women's low participation in paid labour

India's third employment challenge is the very low rate of women's workforce participation. Numerous official economic reports, including the Government's Economic Survey, highlight women's low participation in paid employment as a significant problem for the Indian economy (GOI 2016, 197). Historically, official rates of labour market participation for Indian women have been low.

Table 1.5 Distribution of workers by employment status: 1993–94 to 2011–12

	1993–94			*2004–05*			*2011–12*		
	Women	*Men*	*Total*	*Women*	*Men*	*Total*	*Women*	*Men*	*Total*
Self-Employed	56.8	53.7	54.7	61.4	54.7	56.9	56.1	50.7	52.2
Regular Wage/ Salaried Employees	6.2	16.7	13.2	8.3	17.2	14.3	12.7	19.8	17.9
Casual Labour	37.0	29.6	32.0	30.3	28.1	28.9	31.2	29.4	29.9

Source: IHD (2014, 213) employment and unemployment survey, various rounds.

Table 1.6 Women's labour force participation 2014: India compared

	Labour force participation for women[1]	*% of total labour force who are women*
India	27	24.2
South Asia	31	26.5
Lower-Middle Income Countries	39	32.5
East Asia & Pacific	61	43.5

Source: World Development Indicators, World Bank.

1 Percentage of female population aged 15+ modelled ILO estimate using World Bank population estimates.

Currently women's participation sits at around 29 per cent, lower than the average rate of 32 per cent for women across South Asia, much lower than the 37 per cent participation rate for women in other lower-middle income countries, and half the East Asian and Pacific average (see Table 1.6).[9]

Low participation rates mean that women make up only about a quarter of all Indian workers, with rates varying across the urban/rural divide.[10] Since 1990 rural women have participated in paid employment at twice the rate of urban women, with the most recent figures reporting rural women's labour force participation at 36.4 per cent compared with urban women's rate of 19.7 per cent.[11] Men, both urban and rural, have much higher workforce participation rates than women, at close to 75 per cent. Women's participation has been unresponsive to high growth and has not changed significantly relative to men's. The quality of women's work also remains poor, due to their disproportionate concentration in informal employment. The National Commission for Enterprises in the Unorganised Sector reported that 91.3 per cent of working women were employed in the informal/unorganised economy (GOI 2009, 23). Women's informal employment is highly heterogeneous. It includes small scale producers, vendors, daily labourers and industrial outworkers or home-based workers, located across all industry sectors. Women's informal work status results in economic insecurity and vulnerability to gendered forms of exploitation by middle-men and public officials (Hill 2010). Where women do find employment in the public sector it is often on reduced terms in highly feminised jobs such as anganwadi[12] workers and helpers, or Accredited Social Health Activists (ASHAs) who are paid an "honorarium" at a fraction of the prevailing minimum wage.

Strong economic growth has seen the advent of new service sector jobs. Expansion in the information technology and business processing industries in particular has delivered new jobs in call centres and high-end software and engineering development. Many of these new employment opportunities have been filled by women, as the IT/BPO sector has explicitly prioritised the recruitment of English-speaking educated women (Hill 2014; Palit 2008).

Some jobs in the IT/BPO sector have been for highly skilled professional women who can demand global wages and conditions. But for the majority who work in call-centres wages are much less and conditions onerous (Patel 2010). National growth in per capita income has also brought with it the rise of a new "servant-employing middle class" (Palriwala and Neetha 2009, 17). Since the early 1990s employment in this type of low-paid informal service work has become increasingly feminised, with many young women, often from poor rural regions, engaged as paid domestic workers in private households (Neetha and Palriwala 2011).

Gender inequality in the Indian labour market is a reflection of the gendered division of all labour, both paid and unpaid. In an effort to value unpaid work a National Classification of Activities for Time Use Studies (NCATUS) was developed and piloted in Bihar and Gujarat in 2013. It is due to be extended across all states and will provide a national data platform against which policies to support women's employment and value unpaid work can be developed. In the meantime policy initiatives to support women's employment are focused on implementing the women's quota of 30 per cent in the Mahatma Gandhi National Rural Employment Guarantee Act (MNREGA) and ongoing support for women's self-help groups as part of the National Rural Livelihoods Mission (NRLM) (GOI 2016, 197). However neither of these official approaches is expected to result in any significant improvement in women's labour force participation rate in decent work, leaving the challenge of women's economic insecurity largely unresolved.

Employment policy in the high-growth era

In India, the assumption that strong economic growth would produce employment growth has not been met. In the post-reform era the economic policy agenda focused on the capital intensive sectors. While this approach successfully generated a rise in GNP, it failed to deliver broad-based employment growth in labour-intensive industries. "Jobless growth" became a regular catch phrase used by both economic commentators and some economists. By the mid-2000s the union government had begun to identify the critical role that productive employment plays in national well-being and prosperity. Seeking inclusive and sustainable growth, the 11th and 12th Plans of the Planning Commission were focused on the need to promote the quantum and quality of employment opportunities and social protection for the poorest workers. Since then, employment has gained increased attention in policy circles and is now seen as a critical domain in need of urgent support and reform.

For many years the focus of the employment debate has been on the restrictive nature of labour law and the urgent need to reform and modernise the legal framework (Sharma 2006). The orthodox view is that the Industrial Disputes Act 1947, written in pre-independent India, is outdated and out of step with the new globally-integrated and services-oriented Indian economy. In a bid for increased flexibility, employers have argued that existing labour laws limit the employment capacity of businesses operating in the global context. On the other side of the debate are those who argue that while Indian labour law might be outdated, it is not the main cause of sluggish employment growth. Scholars and commentators have shown that business has devised multiple methods of getting around problematic laws. While the formal debate continues there is widespread consensus on the need to modernise Indian labour laws (NLC 2002, 6).

Historically the politics of labour law reform at the national level has been fraught. However since 2014 reform has gathered pace. In its first year of tenure the new Bharatiya Janata Party (BJP)-led government simplified 16 of the 44 national labour laws and streamlined regulatory and compliance reporting. State governments also become proactive. Rajasthan was the first state to initiate comprehensive labour law reform. In 2014 laws were passed to relax the Trade Union Act, Industrial Dispute Act, Contract Labour Act, the 1948 Factories Act and the 1961 Apprenticeship Act. Under the reforms, companies in Rajasthan can lay off up to 300 workers without government permission, a three-fold increase in the previous 100-employee threshold. In order to be formally recognised, trade unions now require membership of at least 30 per cent of a company's workers—up from 15 per cent—and factory laws now only apply to sites that employ 20 or more workers, instead of the previous 10. In 2015 Madhya Pradesh and Gujarat introduced similar reforms when amendments to the labour laws in these states were given Presidential assent.[13] Other states are now looking to follow suit. The aim of the new laws is to spur economic development, attract foreign investment, improve the ease of doing business, and increase employment. Some advocates of the changes argue that these labour law reforms will increase the share of formal employment in the national economy from around 10 to nearly 40 per cent (PTI 2016). The labour movement is sceptical, arguing the changes will dramatically erode workers' rights and conditions in the interests of corporate welfare.

Outside of formal labour law reform, employment-related policy for informal workers has in large part been pursued via social policy, first with the Mahatma Gandhi National Rural Employment Guarantee Act 2005, then the Unorganised Workers' Social Security Act 2008 and finally through the National Skill Development Corporation (NSDC) and National Skills Mission 2008. The Right to Education Act 2005 could also be included as a measure supporting employment in the future. These insurance, employment, education and skills policies were made under the United Progressive Alliance (UPA) Congress-led government with some positive outcomes for the livelihoods of rural workers and human capital formation, but with no significant shifts in the quantum, quality and returns to employment.

"Come, Make in India": employment policy since 2014

The election of the BJP-led National Democratic Alliance government in April 2014 brought renewed focus on employment and its importance for national growth and prosperity. In the 2014 BJP election manifesto Narendra Modi identified jobless growth as the most serious political issue after food price inflation. Detailing the party's economic agenda, the manifesto made a clear argument for job creation and entrepreneurship, advocating the development of labour-intensive manufacturing, retail, agricultural employment, investment in infrastructure, youth self-employment and a new approach for job search infrastructure (BJP 2014, 3). A commitment to human capital formation, credit and social protection for unorganised sector workers also formed part of the employment policy objectives (BJP 2014, 28) as did the need to make labour laws efficient, and to smooth relations between industry and labour (BJP 2014, 31). Once in government these election priorities were rolled out in the form of a number of high profile national policy initiatives, including *Make in India*, *Skill India*, and more recently, *Start-Up India* and *Stand Up India*.

Make in India has been the mantra of the first few years of the NDA government. It has provided the policy framework within which labour-intensive manufacturing has been positioned at the centre of the government's economic strategy to make India the world's fastest growing emerging market economy. India has been declared "open for business", with foreign investment welcome and facilitated by a number of new policy initiatives designed to improve the ease of doing business. Detractors have argued that the *Make in India* campaign is no more than a marketing strategy to relaunch much of the content of the national manufacturing policies of previous governments and add momentum to liberalisation strategies in the areas of land, labour, tax and governance. More substantive reviews of *Make in India* argue that the government's vision of India as the world's new low-wage unskilled manufacturing hub is unlikely to be successful given India's de/non-industrialisation and the capital and skill intensive profile of Indian manufacturing and services (GOI 2015, 102–116). Together with global concerns about the fragmentation of global value chains and a general slowdown in global growth, the *Make in India* strategy faces significant challenges.

The *Skill India* campaign is a re-badging of the previous government's National Skill Policy. The NDA Policy for Skill Development and Entrepreneurship 2015 aims to train 402 million people by 2022. While challenges regarding the scale of the need for new educational institutions abound, concern remains about growing inequality if low-skilled labour-intensive employment is not part of the future structure of growth. Two other campaigns aim to address this problem. The *Start-Up India* initiative promotes bank finance and a favourable regulatory environment for start-up ventures, and an allied programme, *Stand Up India*, is designed to provide smaller bank loans, between 1 million and 10 million rupees to women and members of the scheduled castes or scheduled tribes who initiate new micro businesses. The hope is that these programs will boost entrepreneurship and encourage the creation of new jobs and employment opportunities.

So far, these new and rebranded government policies have not produced widespread growth in employment opportunities. Reports that government data shows employment creation was the slowest on record in 2015, with just 135,000 net new jobs in the formal sector of the economy against the estimated 12 million new entrants to the workforce, has seen a growth in popular protest and the demand for decent work (Chaudhary and Marlow 2016).

The policy debate and employment outcomes

An overview of the relationship between economic growth post-1991 and employment outcomes demonstrates that there is an obvious disconnect between the Indian growth process and adequate employment generation. The extent to which the policy environment has exacerbated this disconnect is a contentious area of debate which the chapters included in this volume address. Active labour market policies, in addition to financial and social protection measures introduced by successive governments, do not appear to have bolstered employment generation or economic security. Macro-economic policy also appears limited, as it has been explicitly deployed to manage inflation, using monetary policy to keep interest rates higher than the global norm and exercise tight control over fiscal policy.

The distrust of proactive fiscal policy and deficit financing espoused by global financial institutions, even when economically justified, has limited the policy choices available to Indian governments and underwritten fiscal contraction during the high growth era (Chandrashekar 2016). A conservative approach to fiscal policy has kept public debt at modest levels and in rupees, with the expectation that foreign investors will supply much-needed investment finance. Foreign credit has made a significant impact since 1991, but largely in terms of support for a private spending boom that has been debt-financed. Foreign credit has been used as retail loans for houses, cars and consumption. This has produced a certain kind of growth, but one that is not employment-intensive (Chandrashekar 2016). With the government caught between managing inflation and keeping a tight grip on fiscal policy, the chronic and growing underutilisation of labour within the Indian economy has in many respects been left to fester.

The chapters assembled in this volume provide a critical evaluation of the policy framework and the underutilisation of labour that is so pronounced in the macro-economic data. The opening chapters provide an analysis of India's employment policy ecosystem within the national and global context. In Chapter Two Catherine Saget discusses the contemporary global framework for decent work promoted by the International Labour Organization. The ILO's Decent Work agenda and global labour conventions are presented as instruments that could be deployed to improve employment outcomes for informal workers in India. ILO conventions on vulnerable forms of home-based work (C177) and domestic work (C189) along with the convention on minimum wages (C131) are of particular relevance to employment policy in India.

In Chapter Three Deb Kusam Das, Jairvir Singh and Homagni Choudhury evaluate the role of legal institutions and the ways in which they shape employment trends and outcomes. This chapter provides a detailed analysis of how contract labour law has been interpreted by the courts in the post-reform era in ways that *de facto* support the extension of flexible labour in the manufacturing sector. The focus on the role of the judiciary in industrial regulation provides a fruitful line of investigation into some of the unexpected domains of influence over the production of decent and productive work opportunities, particularly in the manufacturing sector. The following chapter, on education policy, provides additional insight into the ways in which the broad national policy framework impacts on employment outcomes and informs current challenges. In Chapter Four Ratna M. Sudarshan develops a critical analysis of the relationship between human capital formation, employment and productivity. The chapter shows that under current settings education and skills policies are not well aligned with the structure and needs of a labour market dominated by informality. Systemic misalignment in education and skills policy underwrites much of the mismatch and problems of employability raised by industry and job seekers. Sudarshan argues that the context of overwhelming economic informality demands a work-centred approach to education and skills development.

The second half of the volume looks at employment policy form the point of view of specific sectors and types of workers. In Chapter Five Jayan Jose Thomas evaluates India's failure to establish a manufacturing sector dynamic enough to absorb a large portion of the nation's working age population. Thomas discusses the policy settings that shape the manufacturing sector in order to develop an explanation for the limited role of manufacturing in India's development since 1991. The failure of the Indian economy to generate a labour-intensive manufacturing sector has left hundreds of millions of people with no option but to be self-employed. In Chapter Six Supriya Roy Chowdhury and B. P. Vani show how policy settings premised on orthodox economic assumptions that economic growth will deliver formal jobs for the masses have left the self-employed unprotected and trapped in low wage, insecure work. Inadequate and misplaced policy, they argue, leave the self-employed excluded from the mainstream economy and poor. Class, caste, gender and religion are critical dimensions of self-employment that shape the politics of policy reform in this part of the economy.

Chapter Seven directly addresses the experience of women in the Indian labour market. Sher Singh Verick explores Indian women's very low rates of workforce participation and the systemic problems this raises for inclusive growth and development. Women's concentration in informal employment is of particular concern due to the lack of protective policy, poor work conditions, low wages and insecurity. The chapter evaluates the policy settings that have reinforced women's dismal participation rate and outlines policy options to improve women's opportunities for decent work. Some of these concerns apply to women in rural areas. Rural employment is specifically addressed in Chapter Eight by Salim Lakha. This chapter assesses the contribution of the Mahatma Gandhi National Rural Employment Guarantee Act

(MNREGA) to employment growth, economic security, social inclusion and skills development in rural India. Lakha evaluates some of the limitations of the MNREGA when it is viewed primarily as an employment policy and discusses the measures required to create more effective and sustainable employment capable of delivering greater economic security. The chapter argues that greater emphasis on skills training as part of the MNREGA will enhance both the quality of the projects implemented and the employment prospects of MNREGA beneficiaries.

The volume concludes on a somewhat pessimistic note. Summarizing the employment policy framework to date, Amitendu Palit argues that growth in the Indian economy and the well-being of the population are hamstrung by a policy ecosystem that is failing to deliver enough jobs of adequate quality to meet the demand of a burgeoning working age population in an era of technological change: there is a crisis of "less and loss". In part this is due to structural challenges associated with the pattern of services-led growth, but it is also the result of increasing automation in industries that have traditionally been labour-intensive. Increasing automation poses a new set of policy challenges for India, as new global production and capital accumulation strategies shape patterns of national economic development.

Building a responsive policy framework to these challenges will be demanding. The chapters in this volume suggest that in the case of India, established ways of thinking about employment in emerging economies are redundant. New approaches that move beyond economic theory to recognise how labour markets actually operate in a context of rapid global change are urgently required. Attention to securing the macro economic conditions that support adequate employment generation for a burgeoning working age population is essential. But employment must be of a decent quality, with adequate conditions and protection for workers. Dynamics in the global economy mean that national policy frameworks must be agile, configured to deal with both the pressures of increased automation and the uneven spread of economic opportunities across urban and rural regions. Social protection policies will be required to support economic transition. Getting employment policy right is more urgent than ever.

Notes

1 Among advanced countries, the working-age population will shrink by 26 per cent in South Korea, 28 per cent in Japan, and 23 per cent in both Germany and Italy by 2050 (UN DESA 2015).
2 Goal 8 http://www.un.org/sustainabledevelopment/economic-growth/
3 World Bank (2016). http://data.worldbank.org/indicator/SL.TLF.CACT.ZS?locations=IN
4 The World Bank defines the dependency ratio as the ratio of dependants (people younger than 15 or older than 64) to the working-age population (those aged 15–64).
5 2015 Revision of World Population Prospects. See https://esa.un.org/unpd/wpp/

6 A demographic dividend is the accelerated economic growth that may occur when a change in the age structure of the population results in a large working age population relative to the very young and the elderly. Economic growth is not automatic but depends on the availability of adequate and decent employment opportunities for this burgeoning group.
7 This includes workers employed in the informal or unorganised sector of the economy—about 392 million workers—plus another 46 million workers employed informally but in the formal sector of the economy.
8 The trend toward growing informalisation of employment was highlighted by the National Commission for Enterprises in the Unorganised Sector (GOI 2009). The downgrading of employment quality occurred at a rapid rate between 1999 and 2005, during which time there was a 42 per cent increase in the number of unorganised jobs located within the organised sector. (GOI 2008: Table 4.1, 3.2 and 3.4)
9 India is classified by the World Bank as a lower middle income country. These are countries with $1,006–$3,975 GNI/capita 2010.
10 Workforce participation rates are based upon the number of employed people as a proportion of the total population. This is different from labour force figures which include employed and unemployed people looking for work as a proportion of the total population.
11 Figures are for "usual status". This is the most generous measure of workforce participation and includes primary plus subsidiary workforce status.
12 A typical anganwadi centre provides basic health care, nutrition and some childcare in Indian villages. The centres are part of the national Integrated Child Development Services programme.
13 Labour laws fall under the Concurrent List of the Constitution, which specifies matters on which states can legislate, but the final approval rests with the Centre, making Presidential assent essential.

References

Aiyar, S and A. Mody. 2011. "The Demographic Dividend: Evidence from the Indian States" IMF Working paper no.38, http://www.imf.org/external/pubs/ft/wp/2011/wp1138.pdf

Barrientos, S., and A. Kritzinger. 2004. "Squaring the Circle: Global Production and the Informalization of Work in South African Fruit Exports." *Journal of International Development* 16: 81–92.

BJP. 2014. *Sabka Saath, Sabka Vikas*. BJP Manifesto 2014. http://www.bjp.org/images/bjp_manifesto_an_abridged_version_english_26.04.14.pdf.

Breman, Jan. 2013. *At Work in the Informal Economy of India: A Perspective from the Bottom Up*. New Delhi: Oxford University Press.

Breman, Jan. 2016. *On Pauperism in Present and Past*. New Delhi: Oxford University Press.

Chandrashekar, C.P., and J. Ghose. 2011. "The Latest Employment Trends from the NSSO". *Macroscan* http://www.macroscan.net/index.php?&view=article&aid=1122

Chandrashekar, C.P 2016. "Macroeconomic policy, employment and decent work in India" Employment Policy Department EMPLOYMENT Working Paper No. 205, International Labour Office, Employment Policy Department, Employment and Labour Market Policies Branch. - Geneva: ILO. http://www.ilo.org/wcmsp5/groups/public/---ed_emp/documents/publication/wcms_542029.pdf

Chaudhary, A., and I. Marlow. 2016. "Modi's Reelection Faces Voter Backlash because of Jobless Growth." *Livemint*, November 16. http://www.livemint.com/Politics/hreg8bhLafTjtsSz3KMgDN/Modis-reelection-faces-voter-backlash-because-of-jobless-g.html

Chen, M. 2012. *The Informal Economy: Definitions, Theories and Policies*. Cambridge, MA: WIEGO. [Working Paper 1] http://wiego.org/sites/wiego.org/files/publications/files/Chen_WIEGO_WP1.pdf

De Soto, Hernando. 1989. *The Other Path: The Invisible Revolution in the Third World*. London: I. B. Tauris.

EPW. 2010. "Jobless Growth." *Economic and Political Weekly* 45 (39): 7–8.

GOI (Government of India, National Commission for Enterprises in the Unorganized Sector). 2008. *Task Force Report on Definitional and Statistical Issues*, New Delhi.

GOI (Government of India). 2009. *The Challenge of Employment in India: Report of the National Commission for Enterprises in the Unorganised Sector*. New Delhi: Academic Foundation of India.

GOI (Government of India). 2014. *Informal Sector and Conditions of Employment in India, NSS 68th Round (July 2011–June 2012)*. National Sample Survey Office (NSSO), Ministry of Statistics and Programme Implementation. [Report 557] http://mospi.nic.in/Mospi_New/upload/nss_report_557_26aug14.pdf

GOI (Government of India, Ministry of Finance). 2015. "What to Make in India? Manufacturing or Services?" *Economic Survey 2014–15*, 1: 107–116. http://indiabudget.nic.in/es2014-15/echapter-vol1.pdf

GOI (Government of India, Ministry of Finance). 2016. *Economic Survey 2015–16*, 9:192–213. http://indiabudget.nic.in/budget2016-2017/vol2_survey.asp

Hill, E. 2010. *Worker Identity, Agency and Economic Development: Women's Empowerment in the Indian Informal Economy*. London: Routledge.

Hill, E. 2014. "Women's Employment as a Barometer of 'Inclusive Growth': How Well is India Doing?" In Dilip Dutta (Eds.), *Inclusive Growth and Development in the 21st Century: A Structural and Institutional Analysis of China and India*, Series on Economic Development and Growth: Volume 9, (pp. 219–242). Singapore: World Scientific Publishing.

IHD (Institute for Human Development) 2014. *India Labour and Employment Report 2014*. New Delhi: IHD.

ILO (International Labour Organization). 2015. *World Employment and Social Outlook—Trends 2015*. Geneva: ILO.

ILO (International Labour Organization). 2016a. *India Labour Market Update*. ILO Country Office for India. http://www.ilo.org/wcmsp5/groups/public/---asia/---ro-bangkok/---sro-new_delhi/documents/publication/wcms_496510.pdf

ILO (International Labour Organization). 2016b. *Decent Work Program*. http://www.ilo.org/global/topics/decent-work/lang—en/index.htm

IMF (International Monetary Fund). 2016. *World Economic Outlook—Subdued Demand: Symptoms and Remedies*. Washington DC: IMF. http://www.imf.org/external/pubs/ft/weo/2016/02/pdf/text.pdf

Jeffrey, Craig, Patricia Jeffrey, and Roger Jeffrey. 2008. *Degrees without Freedom? Education, Masculinities and Unemployment in North India*. Stanford: Stanford University Press.

Jeffrey, Craig. 2010. *Timepass: Youth, Class, and the Politics of Waiting in India*. Stanford: Stanford University Press.

Kannan, K.P., and G. Raveendran. 2009. "Growth Sans Employment: A Quarter Century of Jobless Growth in India's Organised Manufacturing." *Economic and Political Weekly* 44 (10): 80–91.

Lewis, A.W. 1954. "Economic Development with Unlimited Supplies of Labour." *The Manchester School* 22: 139–91.

Miller, Steven. 2013. "Achieving Full, Productive and Freely Chosen Employment for Young People." in *The Twin Challenges of Reducing Poverty and Creating Employment*, 159–174. New York: UN/DESA. http://www.un.org/esa/socdev/documents/employment/twinchallenges.pdf

Neetha N., and R. Palriwala. 2011. "The Absence of State Law: Domestic Workers in India." *Canadian Journal of Women and the Law* 23: 97–119.

NLC (National Labour Commission II). 2002. *Report of the National Commission on Labour.* http://www.prsindia.org/uploads/media/1237548159/NLCII-report.pdf

Palit, A. 2008. *Evolution of Global Production Systems and their Impact on Employment in India.* New Delhi: ILO.

Palriwala, R., and N. Neetha. 2009. *Paid Care Workers in India: Domestic Workers and Anganwadi Workers.* Geneva: UNRISD.

Patel, Reena, 2010, *Working the Night Shift: Women in India's Call Centre Industry.* Stanford: Stanford University Press.

Phillips, N. 2011. "Informality, Global Production Networks and the Dynamics of 'Adverse Incorporation'." *Global Networks* 3: 380–397.

Phillips, N. 2013. "Unfree Labour and Adverse Incorporation in the Global Economy: Comparative Perspectives from Brazil and India." *Economy and Society* 42 (2): 171–196.

Portes, A., M. Castells and L. Benton, Eds. 1989. *The Informal Economy.* Baltimore: Johns Hopkins University Press.

PTI 2016. "Changes in Labour Laws Can Raise Formal Employment to 40 per cent." *Economic Times,* December 19. http://economictimes.indiatimes.com/industry/jobs/changes-in-labour-laws-can-raise-formal-employment-to-40-per-cent/articleshow/56064287.cms

Rodrik, Dani. 2016. "Premature Deindustrialization." *Journal of Economic Growth* 21 (1): 1–33.

Sanyal, K. 2007. *Rethinking Capitalist Development: Primitive Accumulation, Governmentality and Post-colonial Capitalism.* New Delhi: Routledge India.

Sharda, Shailvee. 2015. "Over 23Lakh in Race for 368 Peons' Posts." *Times of India,* September 17. http://timesofindia.indiatimes.com/city/lucknow/Over-23Lakh-in-race-for-368-peons-posts/articleshow/48993012.cms

Sharma, A.N. 2006. "Flexibility, Employment and Labour Market Reforms in India." *Economic and Political Weekly* 41 (21): 2078–85.

Shipler, David. K. 2004. *The Working Poor: Invisible in America.* New York: Vintage.

Standing, Guy. 1999. *Global Labour Flexibility: Seeking Distributive Justice.* UK: Palgrave Macmillan.

Standing, Guy. 2011. *The Precariat: The New Dangerous Class.* London: Bloomsbury Academic.

Stiglitz, Joseph. 2015. *Rewriting the Rules of the American Economy: An Agenda for Shared Prosperity.* New York: Roosevelt Institute. http://rooseveltinstitute.org/wp-content/uploads/2015/10/Rewriting-the-Rules-Report-Final-Single-Pages.pdf

UN DESA (United Nations Department of Economic and Social Affairs Population Division). 2015. *World Population Prospects: The 2015 Revision.* Volume I:

Comprehensive Tables (ST/ESA/SER.A/379). https://esa.un.org/unpd/wpp/Publications/Files/WPP2015_Volume-I_Comprehensive-Tables.pdf

UNDP (United Nations Development Program). 2015. *Work for Human Development* New York: UNDP [Human Development Report 2015] http://hdr.undp.org/sites/default/files/2015_human_development_report_1.pdf

United Nations. 2016. *2015–2030 Sustainable Development Goals* http://www.un.org/sustainabledevelopment/economic-growth/

World Bank. 2012. *World Development Report 2013: Jobs*. Washington, DC: World Bank. http://econ.worldbank.org/external/default/main?contentMDK=23044836&theSitePK=8258025&piPK=8258412&pagePK=8258258

World Bank Group. 2016. *Global Monitoring Report 2015/2016: Development Goals in an Era of Demographic Change*. Washington, DC: World Bank.

2 Employment policy in the International Development Agenda and its relevance in India

Catherine Saget

For most of the post-war era, economic development theory treated employment as a kind of residual category of macro-economic policy. Only in recent years has this begun to change, with international development institutions, planners and practitioners starting to consider the critical role that employment plays in the development process. Policy recommendations designed to deal with high and persistent unemployment in the late 1980s and mid 1990s through an emphasis on "growth first" were exemplified in the Organisation for Economic Co-operation and Development (OECD) 1994 Jobs Strategy. This strategy included maximizing non-inflationary growth, encouraging innovation, enhancing product market competition and promoting flexibility in the labour market. It encompassed flexibility of working time, low minimum wages – especially for youth, financing social protection through consumption tax rather than income tax, lower unemployment benefits and active labour market policies. However, this approach met with limited success and it was reassessed in 2006. Persistently high levels of non-participation in the labour market, high rates of under-employment and unemployment, alongside the apparent inability of labour market institutions to generate adequate jobs growth underscored the need for change. In response, a new approach that incorporated policy initiatives – such as part-time work and family-friendly initiatives – designed to address the needs of specific and often vulnerable groups began to supplant the earlier growth-oriented priorities. While the new approach made some headway, the OECD Re-assessed Jobs Strategy continued to view high tax wedges and unemployment benefits as the main obstacles to high employment rates (OECD 2006).

More recently, the conventional wisdom was challenged by the World Bank in the 2013 *Development Report on Jobs*. In this report, the World Bank started from the observation that the impact of growth on the creation of quality employment varied enormously from one country to another, and that a "job strategy" rather than a "growth strategy" could be the appropriate policy response. In addition, the report presented the "plateau" theory of labour market regulations. While neither very strict nor overly flexible regulations are conducive to efficiency gains and productivity increases, the Bank argued that in between these extremes lies a "plateau" where the effect of labour market regulations are mostly redistributive. The report concluded: "Overall, labour policies and institutions are neither the major obstacle nor the magic bullet for creating good jobs for development in most countries" (World Bank 2012, 258).

Changes in approach to thinking about employment by mainstream international organisations such as the OECD and the World Bank have in many respects been supported by ongoing work at the International Labour Organisation (ILO). Since the end of the 1990s, the ILO has developed and implemented the concept of "decent work", an initiative that culminated in 2008 with the adoption of the ILO Declaration for Social Justice for a Fair Globalisation. This declaration reflected a wide consensus among members of the ILO on the need for a strong social dimension to globalisation that would support improved and fair employment outcomes for all. The declaration defined employment, social protection, social dialogue and rights at work as the four pillars of decent work. At the same time, the declaration stressed the need for a holistic and integrated approach recognising that each of the objectives are "inseparable, interrelated and mutually supportive". The implementation of international labour standards play a central role in each of these areas.

This chapter maps the evolution of global approaches to employment policy and how they relate to the employment conditions and challenges that are particular to the Indian economy and development experience. This discussion raises the critical issue of employment data and the development of labour force survey tools that meet the demands of very large and highly informalised labour markets. India has been at the centre of innovation in the design and implementation of labour force surveys and monitoring. The chapter then looks specifically at three categories of highly vulnerable workers – domestic workers, home-based workers and minimum wage workers – focusing on the global and national legal frameworks that apply to each of them. Finally the chapter examines the idea of the "on-demand economy" and how this idea might affect the terms of employment and working conditions of millions of Indian workers.

Global approaches and employment policy in India

After the progressive achievement of macro-economic stability in many countries in the mid-1990s (IMF 2000), the global development agenda increasingly came to focus on the factors behind "jobless growth", seeking to turn high rates of growth combined with low inflation and (more) moderate budget deficits towards the creation of employment. However, the employment outcomes of these new development frameworks were mostly disappointing (ILO 2014a). In some countries, development strategies have focused on free trade and export markets as a way to promote employment. More broadly, the idea that national development agendas should mainstream employment creation in a coordinated way has gained prominence. This has been the approach taken by the ILO in its support for governments and social partners, and in some cases it has resulted in the implementation of a national employment policy or some type of alternative coordination mechanism (ILO 2014b).

Employment policy can be defined as a coherent and broadly accepted vision of employment objectives and the way to achieve them.[1] Under ILO principles, the goals of an employment policy are twofold: first, employment creation should be promoted actively, as a major goal of the policies pursued by ratifying member states; second, employment creation should follow the ILO approach to the policy process, informing social partners of government policies and involving them as informants in policy design. On the implementation side, the ILO principles imply that there needs to be a coordination mechanism across ministries and institutions responsible for sector-level policies and vocational training, as well as employment programmes to integrate intervention or support systems.

At the global level, development strategies have adopted a similar emphasis on "inclusive growth strategies". This is embodied in goal eight of the UN Sustainable Development Goals (SDG 8) to promote sustained, inclusive sustainable economic growth, full and productive employment and decent work for all.[2] In China inclusive growth has been promoted through rural development programmes, modernisation of agriculture and more recently, an increase in urban wages in the export-led sectors, through adjustments in the minimum wages. These interventions were further supported through social security policies, especially the provision of universal health care and the old age pension.

The spirit in which the ILO approaches support for member states and social partners seeking to achieve SDG 8 is twofold. With regard to content, the ILO facilitates the coordination of employment policies, social protection measures, fundamental principles and rights at work, so that they contribute to an inclusive growth strategy in mutually supportive ways. With respect to process there is an expectation that constituents will be consulted on policy design. The benefits of this coordinated approach are evident in Bangladesh, where national growth rates of between six and seven per cent were achieved through the development of the ready-made garment export market – a labour intensive strategy (ADB and ILO 2016).

Two additional developments spearheaded by the ILO which have supported or complemented the agenda on employment policy and inclusive growth were the development of labour market indicators to inform policy makers, and the attempt to give more protection to vulnerable workers, for example, domestic workers and home-based workers.

Gaps in the employment policy and inclusive growth framework in India

India's record with respect to full and productive employment and decent work, the computation and use of labour statistics for policy making, and the protection of vulnerable groups of workers is mixed. India ratified the ILO

Convention 122 on Employment Policy in 1998, and as such has an obligation to report on the implementation of the provisions of the Convention and how it is adopting a policy promoting full, productive and freely chosen employment. This goal is important in the context of India, where jobless growth, or a mismatch between growth and employment, is currently a structural feature of the labour market.

The performance of the Indian labour market has been weaker than expected over the past two decades. Employment-to-population ratios have decreased almost linearly from 58 per cent in 1991 – a low level by international standards – to 52 per cent in 2013. This is partly due to the low and declining labour force participation of women, most of which is the result of the lack of work opportunities (Chaudhary and Verick 2014). Women's share of employment in the formal sector never rose above 10 per cent, with a high proportion (43 per cent in 2004–05 in non-agricultural activities) being contract work (Institute for Human Development 2014). Employment of women in the manufacturing sector has oscillated between 11 and 13 per cent of total employment in the past fifteen years. At the same time, GDP growth has been very strong, averaging consistently above five per cent in the 1990s and accelerating further to average more than seven per cent per annum in the 2000s. It was this mismatch between high growth, falling employment ratios and degraded forms of work that led to the "jobless growth" thesis. The reason for the lack of decent employment during the high growth era lies partly in the prevailing macro-economic settings and sectoral policies which have tended to overlook labour market issues. The government of India is aware that one of the biggest challenges it faces is the labour market, and it has placed a high priority on job creation, especially for youth. The need to increase female labour force participation is also on the agenda (Ghose 1996).

Jobless growth and the low quality of employment generated can also be attributable to supply side factors in the education and skills formation domains. India has the largest youth population in the world. The rapid increase in the working-age population – the "demographic dividend"– has potential benefits in terms of economic growth. But many young people in India, especially women, struggle to acquire the skills needed by employers to successfully navigate the transition from school to work. On the whole, the employment strategy followed by the government with respect to the provisions of ILO Convention 122 has been assessed: "As indicated by the ILO on the technical advice provided to the Government in recent years, the Committee notes that for an employment strategy to be effective, it is important to mainstream employment in the country's development strategy. The Government might consider going beyond special programmes and integrating employment concerns into policy-making at the macroeconomic as well as sectoral level. The Government and the social partners might wish to identify sectors that are more employment-friendly and pursue policies and programmes conducive to their growth based on an analysis of the employment impact of growth of such sectors."[3]

Labour statistics

International standards of labour statistics

Identifying relevant measures of labour market indicators in a given country depends on the nature of its economy and society, as well as the needs of users. There are challenges in collecting labour statistics related to emerging economies, especially those where the informal economy plays a significant role in generating employment and income. In this case, statistics should be collected with the objective of contributing to the progressive formalisation of the whole economy. This includes estimating the contribution of the informal economy to growth, total income and employment creation to support the design and implementation of macro-economic policies. Labour statistics in developing countries also need to contribute to the development and evaluation of targeted policies to strengthen the productive capacities of informal enterprises and improve the working conditions of informal workers. Two indicators are needed in this process: (1) the total number of informal sector enterprises (unincorporated firms, producing goods for sale or barter, below a certain size, usually five workers, and engaged in the production of non-agricultural activities), and (2) informal employment, including own-account workers, contributing family workers, and employees holding informal jobs. This dual approach aligns with the 2003 definition of informal workers as those "who, in law or in practice, [are] not subject to national labour legislation, income taxation, social protection or entitlement to certain employment benefits whether employed by formal sector enterprises, informal sector enterprises, or as paid domestic workers by households" (ICLS 2003).

Methods of data collection and reporting frequency should follow international standards, to promote comparability and for evaluation purposes. There has been widespread progress across the globe in this domain and in 2016 labour force survey data was available for about 127 countries. Some countries that do not have dedicated labour force surveys often rely on household surveys and include a special module to cover labour statistics, although the sample size might limit the number of indicators. There are also other groups of statistics that can complement labour statistics, for example, surveys on economic establishments, jobs per sector, job vacancies, wages and labour costs, population censuses, various administrative records covering beneficiaries of social benefits, and training programmes. International standards regarding statistics also recommend the computation of indicators for the population as a whole disaggregated by sex, age groups, regions, and urban and rural areas. Evaluation, communication and dissemination measures should include information on the source, coverage and methodologies used and quality control procedures in place. Statistics should be made publicly available and publicised to inform public policy debate.

The most recent standard on labour statistics concerns the measurement of employment. The contribution "of all persons in all forms of work and in all sectors of the economy", in particular own-use production of goods or services, unpaid trainee work and volunteer work related to economic development, needs to be measured so that the right policy mix of support for paid and unpaid work can be implemented (ICLS 2013, 2–3). To understand the decline in female labour force participation in India and Sri Lanka, and more recently also in Bangladesh, it is also important to measure all work performed within the household, and avoid gender bias in the recognition of forms of work (Chaudhary and Verick 2014). Other limitations of the traditional labour market statistics, with their focus on employment, unemployment and inactivity became clear during the global financial crisis, when estimates of labour underutilisation could have helped determine the scope of sector policy if they had been available. Standard measures of unemployment do not provide for the monitoring of labour market behaviour and have also been criticised for their lack of relevance as a labour market indicator in developing countries, where the coverage of unemployment benefits and unemployment assistance is low. Only five per cent of the unemployed in developing countries have access to unemployment benefits from social insurance or social assistance (ILO 2014c). To adapt labour statistics to the new standard will take time: according to a review covering the period 2000–11, only 40 per cent of countries in Asia and the Pacific cover own-use of production of goods in labour force surveys (ILO 2013).

The Resolution on Work Statistics adopted by the International Conference of Labour Statisticians in 2013 recognises all productive activities as work, including care work and volunteer work: "[Work is] any activity performed by persons of any sex and age to produce goods or provide services for use by others or for own use" (ICLS 2013, Paragraph 6).[4] The Resolution also provides guidelines for measurement of labour underutilisation, defined as "mismatches between labour supply and labour demand, which translates into an unmet need for employment amongst the population" (paragraph 40) on the basis of four indicators. The first is the familiar concept of the unemployment rate, while the second indicator extends unemployment to underemployment, defined as employed persons who want to work more hours, whose combined working time in all jobs is lower than the threshold, and who are available to work additional hours. The third indicator of labour underutilisation is essentially the unemployment rate and includes the unemployed, those not employed who are seeking work for pay or profit but are not available for work in the reference period, and those not employed who do not seek work for pay or profit but want to work and are available (formerly "discouraged workers"). The fourth indicator is a composite measure of labour underutilization: (Persons in underemployment + persons in unemployment + those not employed who are seeking work for pay or profit and are not available for work in the reference period + those note employed who do not seek work for pay or profit but want to work and are available) / (Labour force + those not employed who are seeking work for pay or profit and are not available for work in the reference period + those not employed who do not seek work for pay or profit but want to work and are available).

This 2013 Resolution on Work Statistics is expected to provide the global definitions that will be used to measure work and labour market statistics for the immediate future. The changes are particularly important on account of their capacity to better capture and quantify household members' production of goods and services for own final use. This data is critical for the effort to improve gender equality. The new computation of all those who work for pay or profit, and all others by categories will also enhance the international comparability of labour statistics, and support the SDG process.

Labour market statistics in India

In India there are several sources of labour market statistics with differences in coverage, frequency and quality. The quinquennial surveys conducted by the National Sample Survey Office (NSSO) on Employment and Unemployment (EUS) provide data on labour force estimates, individual characteristics, occupation and wages at the national and state/union territory level. In 2010, Employment-Unemployment Surveys (EUS) were introduced, conducted on a roughly annual basis. By February 2016, four EUS surveys had been undertaken. However, the quality of the EUS has been questioned and wage data based on these surveys is yet to be published. It is understood that the EUS is to be discontinued, and replaced with quarterly labour force surveys, including wage statistics. Quarterly labour force data will facilitate economic and social policy monitoring but a downside of the forthcoming survey is that it is based on the urban sector only. Wage indicators for the broad labour force will continue to be published only every five years, as part of the quinquennial surveys.

In terms of comparability, labour market statistics from India do not follow all international standards. First, data provided for employment, unemployment and labour force refers to "usual principal status". Relying on status during a specified brief period (such as a week, or a day) this concept deviates from the international definitions, and can limit comparability with other countries. Second, there is no lower age limit, and the age coverage deviates from the usual "working-age" concept (age 15 and above). In addition to ensuring international comparability, labour market indicators can also be strengthened in other ways, such as establishing an agreed method of extrapolation for wage statistics, and examining the effective coverage of internal migrants within the NSSO.

Robust data on vulnerable groups of workers has historically been difficult to access, however three recent global recommendations could improve the coverage, quality and usability of labour statistics in this regard (Papola 2014). Globally, and in India in particular, data on the informal economy and the size of the informal workforce has been difficult to generate. However the implementation of regular Time Use Surveys (TUSs) would help capture many invisible and informal forms of work. India has run a pilot TUS in several states and is due to implement it more broadly. Data on contract labour also needs to be collected and compiled systematically. One way of improving collection of this type of data would be to add a module to the EUS to capture the working conditions of workers on labour contracts. Finally, data on labour migration, which is currently only available from the population census run every ten years, needs to be collected at more regular intervals.

Employment and social protection for vulnerable categories of workers

While social protection can help individuals cope with major risks in life, it can also have many broader benefits. Social protection measures can be designed to support sectors of the economy and enterprises to adjust to shocks more rapidly, while also facilitating the acceptance of change by workers. In an initial report designed to monitor coverage of social protection policies, the ILO found that one third of countries, accounting for 28 per cent of the world's population, had access to comprehensive social protection, including health and unemployment benefits, family allowance, employment injury and old age insurance and pensions (ILO, 2010a). Recognition that the Millennium Development Goals (MDGs) could not be reached without comprehensive strategies for the progressive extension of social protection to all culminated in 2012 with the adoption of the ILO Recommendation concerning National Floors of Social Protection. This was endorsed by a range of UN agencies and the World Bank. It was agreed by these agencies that the types of policies that should be prioritised included: (1) Essential health care, including maternity care, which meets the criteria of availability, accessibility, acceptability and quality; (2) Basic income security for children; (3) Basic income security for the unemployed and those on maternity and disability leave; and (4) Basic old age pensions. It was also agreed that countries should formulate and implement national social security extension strategies, based on national consultations through effective social dialogue and social participation, and provide higher levels of protection to as many people as possible.

With the implementation of the MDGs (2005–15) and growing acceptance of the reality of the "working poor", regulatory frameworks directed at workers outside the framework of traditional employment relations have begun to be embraced. Below, three examples are discussed: ILO Convention 189 on domestic workers; ILO Convention 177 on home-based workers and ILO Convention 131 on minimum wages. These three ILO Conventions play a valuable role in protecting disadvantaged groups of workers and are of direct relevance to the development of robust employment policy in India.

Domestic work

In countries where data on domestic work exists, this form of labour is found to represent a significant proportion of total employment. In developing countries, domestic or household labour accounts for between four and 10 per cent of total employment; for women, who represent the overwhelming majority of domestic workers, the proportion is much greater (ILO 2010b). In parts of Europe, the Gulf countries and Middle East, a majority of domestic workers are migrant workers (ILO 2010b). In many countries, including industrialised countries, domestic workers fall outside the scope of the labour code or are excluded from the protection of specific labour laws. For example, in the United Kingdom, domestic workers are placed outside the scope of working time regulation and are excluded from the protection of health and safety legislation (Einat and Mantouvalou 2012).

Convention 189 regulating the terms and conditions of work for domestic workers was adopted by the ILO in 2011. This was the first ILO Convention to recognise domestic labour as a form of remunerated work and address the particular disadvantage of domestic workers. The main provisions of the Convention oblige member states ratifying the Convention to provide domestic workers with clear information on their terms and conditions of employment and the same basic rights as other workers, including a weekly day of rest, limits on hours of work, the right to be paid in cash, minimum wage coverage, and overtime compensation.[5] Recognising the vulnerabilities of domestic workers, the ILO standard also provides for protection of domestic workers from abuse and violence, and the regulation of private employment agencies that act as intermediaries between the employer and domestic workers. According to the terms of the Convention, migrant domestic workers should be entitled to a written contract. So the key provisions of Convention 189 provide for workers to receive information on their conditions of work and protection from abuse and violence, as well as the regulation of private employment agencies.

Domestic workers are particularly vulnerable in India where they are one of the few groups of unorganised sector workers that are not covered by the Minimum Wage Act (1948). In 2011, the government of India extended the Rashtriya Swasthya Bima Yojana (RSBY) health insurance scheme to domestic workers, and in 2012 issued guidelines on how this provision was to be implemented. By March 2016, the only three states to have responded were Kerala, Jharkhand and Chhattisgarh. Challenges facing the successful extension of health insurance schemes to domestic workers are related to the registration of domestic workers, and their certification as eligible for the measure. On both matters, state governments have not been adequately informed as to the guidelines for implementation.

In 2013, domestic workers were brought under the protection of a new law prohibiting sexual harassment in the workplace. Nonetheless, Indian domestic workers remain vulnerable to abuse and subject to exploitation primarily due to the absence of a law regulating the recruitment of domestic workers both in India and abroad. Amongst migrant domestic workers, an ILO study of female workers from Kerala working as domestics in the Arab states found that most migrants were prone to abuse and even to forced labour (ILO 2015). The same study also reported that most female domestic workers who migrated from rural Jharkhand to Delhi to work as domestic helpers experienced physical and verbal abuse, restriction of movement, long hours of work and lack of clear information on actual wages.

Home-based workers

Home-based workers are defined as those working on contract for others but in their own homes. They are essentially dependent workers who lack the autonomy and economic independence necessary to be considered self-employed. Home-based workers are usually excluded from the protection of the labour code, and hence from minimum wage regulations, regulations governing working hours, and social security benefits. They are normally paid on a piece rate basis and occupational health and safety standards in their home-based work places tend to be very low. Home-based work is very common in sectors like garment making, jewellery, shoe-stitching, embroidery, carpet weaving, electronics, and the production of a variety of other consumer goods. Some home-based workers provide clerical services such as data processing and invoicing (ILO 1996).

The main provisions of ILO Convention 177 (1996) on home work are intended to promote equality of treatment between homeworkers and other wage earners. The Convention states that equality of treatment shall be promoted, in particular, in relation to:

(a) the homeworkers' right to establish or join organisations of their own choosing and to participate in the activities of such organisations;
(b) protection against discrimination in employment and occupation;
(c) protection in the field of occupational safety and health;
(d) remuneration;
(e) statutory social security protection;
(f) access to training;
(g) minimum age for admission to employment or work;
(h) maternity protection.

As of June 2016 this Convention had only been ratified by 10 member countries, not including India.

Since the beginning of the 21st century, the number of home-based workers in India has increased dramatically, from 23.3 million in 1999–2000 to 31.0 million in 2004–05 and 37.4 million in 2011–12. Home-based workers represented 18 per cent of workers in urban employment in 2011–12, while the proportion of women in the sector varied between 41 and 46 per cent over the same 12-year period (WIEGO 2013). The increase in the number of home-based workers reflects the efforts of firms to reduce production costs and the development of economic sectors which are more likely to use home work. A mix of measures could improve the working conditions of home-based workers (Unni and Rani 2005). These include access to the minimum wage if the workers are wage earners, access to credit if they are self-employed, cluster-based approaches to improve their position in global value chains, skills upgrading, and opportunities to organise and make their voices heard. In one innovative measure, India has attempted to develop welfare funds for beedi/cigarette workers, most of them home workers. A tax fee is levied on the final product and its revenue is used to finance basic social security for these workers. However, there are gaps in the implementation of this interesting initiative.[6]

Minimum wages

The legal framework of minimum wage setting encompasses: the institutional setting and whether the minimum wage is defined at the national or at the sectoral level; the degree of consultation of the social partners, which can vary from no consultation to collective bargaining; the use of social and economic criteria to fix or adjust the level; the frequency of adjustment, which is not always specified in the legislation; the coverage and whether all workers are entitled to at least the minimum wage or whether some sectors (services) or workers (e.g. domestic, migrants) are excluded.

The Minimum Wage Fixing Convention 131 provides for ratifying member states to commit to the establishment of a system of minimum wages which "covers all groups of wage earners" and protects them against "unduly low wages". Subject to justification, it is possible to exclude some groups from coverage, for example, youth benefiting from on-the-job training. Minimum wages should be adjusted "from time to time", and social partners should be fully consulted (not just informed). Criteria for fixing or adjusting the minimum wage should include:

a) "the needs of workers and their families, taking into account the general level of wages in the country, the cost of living, social security benefits, and the relative living standards of other social groups"; and
b) "economic factors, including the requirements of economic development, levels of productivity, and the desirability of attaining and maintaining a high level of employment".

Turning to minimum wage trends, a number of countries have adjusted their minimum wage in real terms, including during the 2008 global financial and economic crisis. An inventory of policy responses to the financial crisis in 77 countries from all income groups showed that 32 of these countries increased their minimum wage over the period from mid-2008 to end 2010, including 19 in real terms (ILO and World Bank 2012). There were several explanations as to why minimum wages were increased at a time of slowdown or even recession, including commitments made by the United States in 2007 that were to be implemented subsequently, fear of deflation, and the need to maintain social peace and give protection to the lowest-paid workers. Incentives to join the labour force and remain in employment also played a role. In addition, many meta-analyses found that the impact of the minimum wage on employment is very small and sometimes positive, and that most of the effect is redistributory, resulting in a (modest) increase in wages for minimum wage earners (Broecke, Forti, and Vandeweyer 2016).

In India wages in the formal organised sector are determined through negotiations and settlements between employer and employees. In the informal unorganised sector, where labour is vulnerable to exploitation due to illiteracy and the absence of any effective bargaining power, minimum wage rates are fixed and revised both by central and state governments. The occupations to which these provisions apply are known as the "scheduled employments" that fall under their respective jurisdictions. Wage setting is guided by the provisions of the Minimum Wages Act 1948 (Ministry of Labour, Department of Labour Annual Reports).

The minimum wage system for the unorganised sector is complex, with multiple rates, unusual adjustment rules, gaps in coverage and an almost complete lack of awareness by the workers concerned (Saget 2005). The central government sets minimum wages for workers it employs across India, covering about 45 different unskilled occupations. Additionally, the states have set minimum wages for more than 1,000 different occupations, or scheduled employments, in their respective regions. Minimum wages fixed by the central government are higher than those fixed by the states. Broadly speaking, occupations covered by these provisions include construction and road maintenance workers, agricultural workers, workers in mines, railway workers, and stone crushing workers. Coverage is on the rise: every year new scheduled employments are added by states. In particular, agricultural workers are now covered in most states. Among uncovered occupations, the most noticeable is probably domestic work. In terms of implementation, a review of compliance with minimum wage regulations in developing countries found that in India, 50 per cent of casual rural workers were paid less than the state-level minimum wage; this was also the case for 30 per cent of rural salaried workers (Rani et al. 2013).

Regarding revisions, the minimum wages are often composed of two elements: a basic rate and a "variable dearness allowance" (VDA). The most noticeable exceptions are often agricultural sector jobs and a few other low paid occupations for which there is only a basic rate in many Indian states. As the name indicates, the level of the VDA is linked to inflation. Increasing the VDA has become the major channel for revising minimum wage rates. In many instances, the VDA is increased by the same amount for all scheduled occupations. As a result, the span of wages tends to reduce over time.

There has been much debate on the scope and feasibility of the minimum wage in India. Some early studies drew attention to the potentially negative effects of an enforced minimum wage on female labour force participation (Ghose 1996). More recent studies emphasise the increase in earnings and reduction in poverty that a compulsory national minimum wage or extension of the coverage of state-level minimum wages could achieve for low-paid workers (Belser and Rani 2011). A simpler and more effective minimum wage system would make this possible, and long-term trends and the international experience suggest that this might be the right time for India to move in this direction. As discussed earlier, a national minimum wage would support domestic workers and (waged) home-based workers, and would be easier to monitor – in terms of both compliance and effectiveness – than the current piecemeal system. A commonly accepted minimum wage which acts as a floor for entry-level wages could reduce inequality and also support improved bargaining procedures between workers and employers. This is an important side-effect in a society faced with significant labour market inequalities. In 2011–12, a rural casual worker earned less than seven per cent of the wage of a public-sector employee (Institute for Human Development 2014). The NFLMW (National Floor Level Minimum Wage) which is fixed as a minimum wage for the majority of informal workers has been adjusted from Rs 137 (USD 2) to Rs 160 (USD 2.40) per day with effect from July 1, 2015.

The future of work

The world of work is being transformed across the globe. Full-time permanent employment contracts with the associated forms of social protection and insurance are being replaced by a myriad of non-standard and informal forms of work. Demographic change, the need for environmental sustainability, technological progress, persistent poverty and growing inequality work together to maintain downward pressure on employment protection and conditions. The ILO has addressed these issues through the adoption of international labour standards for specific forms of informal and non-standard employment, in particular part-time, home-based work and domestic labour. Informal employment has been the norm in many developing economies, and this is particularly the case in India. However, economic growth is not producing the expected improvements in employment conditions. Employment challenges are heightened in the Indian context and while there have been some opportunities to respond at the policy level, these initiatives have met with only limited success. Among the many issues requiring attention in addressing the decent work deficit in India are the challenges posed by the increasing casualisation of work in the private and public sector due to technological change. In general, innovation, falling prices and infrastructure development have generated high growth in Information and Communication Technology (ICT) access; in Asia and the Pacific, 39 per cent of households had internet access in 2015, compared to just 11 per cent in 2005 (ITU 2015; ITU 2013). ICT offers consumers many opportunities, including the ability to match jobs to workers via technology platforms (mobile "apps"). However the result may be the creation of new forms of precarious labour, as in the case of the mobile app "Uber".[7] Connecting suppliers of cars or flats with consumers, or employers with workers willing to work on demand, raises questions about how decent work can be promoted in the "on-demand economy".

The business model of firms in the on-demand economy is characterised by the shift of the business risk from the firm to the workers. Workers in this part of the economy are categorised as independent contractors, with implications for working conditions and tax revenue. This affects the nature of the employment relationship, as companies in the "gig" economy define their workers as independent sub-contractors, thereby excluding them from the protection of the labour code. They are not entitled to social security benefits or the minimum wage, and this business model might put pressure on the financial sustainability of social benefits at the macro level. Taxing the on-call economy can also be challenging, as some of these activities are performed without tax registration even in industrialised countries, where, for example, individuals renting out flats on Airbnb commonly omit to declare the income generated. At the same time, the on-demand economy may provide more flexibility for workers and their families, and create opportunities for environment-friendly solutions.

The reaction of policy makers to this trend has tended to focus on defining whether this new type of work belongs to the standard employment relationship, or whether it is self-employment, or a new grey area of work. Reaction has been mixed, and it is difficult to identify trends, even at the regional level. A review of decent work in the "gig" economy from a legal perspective in October 2015 showed that in India, Uber has faced legal problems in a few states. These include legislative review, court decisions and state investigations, as has also been the case in the Philippines (Martinsson 2016). Some states and cities have taken the step of banning Uber in particular places (e.g. Karnataka and New Delhi), similar to the response of a number of East and Southeast Asian countries: Indonesia, Malaysia, Thailand, the Philippines, China, Hong Kong (China), and Korea. (There has been no restriction on Uber activity in Singapore and Vietnam.) The development of the on-demand economy may add pressure to the developing casualisation of work in India, but anecdotal evidence suggests that it has given (some) workers higher earnings and more freedom in determining their working time.

Another perhaps more positive trend is the effort to "activate" the working age population, which places India on a par with many other developed and emerging countries. On the one hand, a combination of wage-related measures (MNREGA, and minimum wages for the unorganised sector) can have an impact on the supply side while increased access to basic social protection and education for the poor may also impact positively on productivity.

Conclusion

India has experienced significant disruptions of its economy and labour market since the mid-1990s. Globalisation can enable or disrupt job creation, depending on whether it leads to increased production within a country or the substitution of domestic production with imported goods and services. Other large-scale processes are also driving the future of work: the digitalisation of the economy, demographic change, migration, and the erosion of the standard employment relationship, even in the formal economy. The policy responses in India have been significant, as illustrated by the focus on employment creation, the extension of social protection and efforts to strengthen labour statistics to inform policy making. Yet the outcomes have been disappointing. The fact that challenges to employment creation have occurred simultaneously – and often complementarily – in addition to their scale, suggest the need for more radical solutions than those that have been attempted so far.

Notes

1 See ILO Convention 122 on employment policy. http://www.ilo.org/dyn/normlex/en/f?p=NORMLEXPUB:12100:0::NO::P12100_INSTRUMENT_ID:312267
2 See United Nations 2015 Declaration: Transforming our World: the 2030 Agenda for Sustainable Development. Full text available at https://sustainabledevelopment.un.org/post2015/transformingourworld
3 Observation of the Committee of Experts on the Application of Conventions and Recommendations (CEACR), adopted in 2011 and published at the 101st International Labour Conference session (2012) as *Employment Policy Convention, 1964 (No. 122) – India (Ratification: 1998).*
4 It is the mandate of the ICLS and the ILO to introduce and modify existing standards on employment statistics. The ICLS has been meeting roughly every five years since 1923.
5 The full text of the Convention is available at http://www.ilo.org/dyn/normlex/en/f?p=NORMLEXPUB:12100:0::NO::P12100_INSTRUMENT_ID:2551460
6 See ILO (2013) *The Regulatory Framework and the Informal Economy.* http://www.ilo.org/wcmsp5/groups/public/---ed_emp/---emp_policy/documents/publication/wcms_210450.pdf
7 Uber is an international transportation network company that offers a taxi, private car or rideshare via a mobile application.

References

ADB and ILO. 2016. *Bangladesh Employment Diagnostics: Looking Beyond Garments.* Mandaluyong City, Philippines ADB and ILO. https://www.adb.org/sites/default/files/publication/190589/ban-beyond-garments-eds.pdf

Belser, Patrick, and Uma Rani. 2011. "Extending the Coverage of Minimum Wages in India: Simulations from Household Data." *Economic and Political Weekly* 46 (22): 47–55.

Broecke, Stijn, Alessia Forti, and Marieke Vandeweyer. 2016. *The Effect of Minimum Wages on Employment in Emerging Economies: A Survey and Meta-Analysis.* Oxford. Oxford Development Studies. http://nationalminimumwage.co.za/wp-content/uploads/2015/09/0221-Effect-of-Minimum-Wages-on-Employment-in-Emerging-Economies-A-Literature-Review.pdf

Chaudhary, Ruchika, and Sher Verick. 2014. *Female Labour Force Participation in India and Beyond.* [ILO Asia-Pacific working paper series, International Labour Organization, ILO DWT for South Asia and Country Office for India]. New Delhi: ILO. http://www.ilo.org/wcmsp5/groups/public/---asia/---ro-bangkok/---sro-new_delhi/documents/publication/wcms_324621.pdf

Einat, Albin, and Virginia Mantouvalou. 2012. "The ILO Convention on Domestic Workers: From the Shadows to the Light." *Industrial Law Journal* 41 (1): 67–78.

Ghose, Ajit K. 1996. "Current Issues of Labour Policy Reform in India." *The Indian Journal of Labour Economics* 39 (3).

ITU (International Telecommunication Union). 2015. *Facts and Figures 2015*. Telecommunication Development Bureau, Geneva. http://www.itu.int/en/ITU-D/Statistics/Documents/facts/ICTFactsFigures2015.pdf

ITU (International Telecommunication Union). 2013. *Facts and Figures 2013*. Telecommunication Development Bureau, Geneva. https://www.itu.int/en/ITU-D/Statistics/Documents/facts/ICTFactsFigures2013-e.pdf

ICLS (International Conference of Labour Statisticians). 2003. *Guidelines Concerning a Statistical Definition of Informal Employment*. Geneva, ILO. http://www.ilo.org/global/statistics-and-databases/standards-and-guidelines/guidelines-adopted-by-international-conferences-of-labour-statisticians/WCMS_087622/lang—en/index.htm

International Labour Conference 2012. Geneva, ILO http://www.ilo.org/dyn/normlex/en/f?p=NORMLEXPUB:12100:0::NO::P12100_INSTRUMENT_ID:2551460

ICLS (International Conference of Labour Statisticians). 2013. *Resolution Concerning Statistics of Work, Employment and Labour Underutilization*. Geneva, ILO. http://www.ilo.org/global/statistics-and-databases/meetings-and-events/international-conference-of-labour-statisticians/19/WCMS_230304/lang—en/index.htm

ILO. *Social Protection Database*. Geneva, ILO http://www.ilo.org/secsoc/areas-of-work/statistical-knowledge-base/lang—en/index.htm

ILO. 1996. *Report to the International Labour Conference on Home Work*. Geneva: ILO.

ILO. 2008. *ILO Declaration for Social Justice for a Fair Globalisation*. Geneva: ILO.

ILO. 2010a. *World Social Security Report*. Geneva: ILO.

ILO. 2010b. *Decent Work for Domestic Workers, Report to the International Labour Conference*. Geneva: ILO.

ILO. 2013. *Statistics of Work, Employment and Labour Underutilization, Report to the International Conference of Labour Statisticians*. Geneva: ILO. http://www.ilo.org/wcmsp5/groups/public/---dgreports/---stat/documents/publication/wcms_220535.pdf

ILO. 2014a. *ILO Global Employment Trend: The Risk of a Jobless Recovery?* Geneva: ILO. http://www.ilo.org/wcmsp5/groups/public/---dgreports/---dcomm/---publ/documents/publication/wcms_233953.pdf

ILO. 2014b. *ILO Resolution Concerning the Second Recurrent Discussion on Employment*. Geneva: ILO. http://www.ilo.org/ilc/ILCSessions/103/reports/committee-reports/WCMS_249800/lang—en/index.htm

ILO. 2014c. *World Social Protection Report: Building Economic Recovery, Inclusive Development and Social Justice*. Geneva: ILO.

ILO. 2015. *Indispensable Yet Unprotected: Working Conditions of Indian Domestic Workers at Home and Abroad*. [International Labour Office, Fundamental Principles and Rights at Work Branch (FUNDAMENTALS)] Geneva: ILO. http://www.ilo.org/wcmsp5/groups/public/---ed_norm/---declaration/documents/publication/wcms_378058.pdf

ILO. 2016. *Word Employment and Social Outlook*. Geneva: ILO.

ILO and World Bank. 2012. *Inventory of Policy Responses to the Financial Crisis*. International Labour Office, Geneva, APRIL 2012. The World Bank, Washington, DC

APRIL 2012. http://www.ilo.org/wcmsp5/groups/public/---ed_emp/---emp_elm/documents/publication/wcms_186324.pdf

IMF. 2000. *World Economic Outlook: Focus on Transition Economies.* Washington: IMF. http://www.imf.org/external/pubs/ft/weo/2000/02/

Institute for Human Development. 2014. *India Labour and Employment Report.* New Delhi: Academic Foundation.

Martinsson, Sara. 2016. *Decent Work in the "Gig-Economy": A Global Review of Challenges and Opportunities.* Geneva: ILO.

OECD. 1994. *The OECD Jobs Study: Facts, Analysis, Strategies.* Paris. OECD. https://www.oecd.org/els/emp/1941679.pdf

OECD. 2006. *OECD Employment Outlook: Boosting Jobs and Incomes.* Paris: OECD. http://www.oecd.org/els/emp/oecdemploymentoutlook2006.htm#press

Papola, T. S. 2014. *An Assessment of the Labour Statistics System in India.* New Delhi: ILO Country Office for India.

Saget, Catherine. 2005. *Wage Fixing in the Informal Economy: Evidence from Brazil, India, Indonesia and South Africa.* [Conditions of Work and Employment Series No. 16] Geneva, International Labour Office.

Unni, Jeemol, and Uma Rani. 2005. *Impact of Recent Policy on Home-Based Work in India.* Human Development Resource Centre, UNDP, New Delhi India.

Rani, Uma, Patrick Belser, Martin Oelz, and Setareh Ranjbar. 2013. "Minimum Wage Coverage and Compliance in Developing Countries." *International Labour Review* 152 (3–4): 381–410.

WIEGO (Women in Informal Employment Globalizing and Organising). 2013. *Home-Based Workers in India: Statistics and Trends.* [WIEGO Statistical Brief No 10]. Manchester: WIEGO. http://wiego.org/sites/wiego.org/files/publications/files/Raveendran-HBW-India-WIEGO-SB10.pdf

World Bank. 2012. *World Development Report 2013.Jobs.* Washington, DC: World Bank. http://siteresources.worldbank.org/EXTNWDR2013/Resources/8258024-1320950747192/8260293-1322665883147/WDR_2013_Report.pdf

3 Judicial production of labour market flexibility

Contract labour employment in Indian organised manufacturing

Deb Kusum Das, Jaivir Singh and Homagni Choudhury

Existing empirical work on Indian organised manufacturing in the 2000s examines the effects of labour legislation, trade unions, and the wage setting system on manufacturing performance (Ahsan and Pagés 2009; Aghion et al 2008; Dutta 2007; Besley and Burgess 2004). The focus of most of these studies has been on the effects of trade liberalisation and industrial deregulation with the majority suggesting that the unimpressive performance of the manufacturing sector during this period could have been reversed through labour market reforms. Yet the little empirical evidence available on labour market rigidities is quite mixed and inconclusive, and focuses almost exclusively on the Industrial Disputes Act (IDA) of 1947, despite the existence of several other labour laws. Examining central and state level amendments to the IDA over time, the unanimous verdict of these studies is that pro-worker amendments to labour legislation have resulted in rigidities and inflexibilities in the labour market and impaired industrial performance and employment generation. As a result, these studies emphasise the need for *de jure* labour market reforms. Nevertheless, there is also contrasting evidence which suggests that *de facto* reforms over the last two decades have sometimes enabled the formal private sector to evade the legal requirements of protective labour legislation and to restructure their technological and managerial practices.[1] Given this disparity in the empirical evidence, there is need for a study on just how flexible the Indian labour market is in practice. The first step must be to assess the extent to which labour market flexibility exists, and what its character might be. This is important, as the creation of decent jobs is a key challenge facing Indian policy makers and employment generation clearly depends (at least in part) on the nature and flexibility of labour markets.[2]

In the light of this background, this chapter examines the overall legislative and regulatory framework that governs India's labour markets and outlines the current debate surrounding the impacts of restrictive labour market institutions and their implications for job creation. Drawing on our previous studies of aspects of Indian labour markets (see Das, Choudhury, and Singh 2015; Singh 2015; Choudhury 2012), the chapter focuses on the Contract Labour

(Regulation and Abolition) Act, 1970 (hereafter CLA), which has not received much attention in the labour literature.[3] Specifically, we examine the extent to which recent judicial interpretations of the CLA may have added to labour market flexibility in India and present empirical evidence for the increased employment of contract labour in Indian manufacturing as a result of these changes. In general, we see the expansion in contract labour as a mark of increased labour market flexibility.[4]

The following section outlines the overall legislative and regulatory framework that governs Indian labour markets, before moving to a consideration of its implications for employment and a review of the existing empirical literature. From here we proceed to examine the various nuances of the CLA and its implications for labour market flexibility and employment generation. This is followed by an empirical exercise designed to assess the overall trends in the employment of contract labour in formal manufacturing in India. A short conclusion summarises the chapter's main findings.

Labour regulations in India and the current debate on labour market reforms

Labour law in India essentially covers only workers in the formal sector. While on paper there are many laws regulating conditions of work in the informal sector as well, in practice the administration and enforcement of these laws is hampered by the sector's decentralised nature and geographic dispersion. Further, even where there is scope for the laws to come into play, enforcement is problematic and difficult, given that employment contracts are informal in nature and workers in this sector are largely illiterate and are unaware of their rights. As such the informal sector, which accounts for the bulk of employment in the country, has by and large remained outside the scope of laws and institutions that regulate the labour market. On the other hand the formal sector, which is governed by the labour laws and is under the purview of the labour market institutions, employs only a small proportion of the Indian workforce. In 2009–10 the formal sector constituted only about 15 per cent of the economy's total workforce (Mehrotra et al, 2012).

Legislative authority over labour issues in India is exercised by both the central government and individual state governments, which means that the latter have the power to amend central legislation or to introduce subsidiary legislation. In fact the state governments are responsible for the enforcement of most of the labour regulations, even those enacted by the central government. There is considerable variation in labour regulations and/or their enforcement across different states in India, a variation that led Besley and Burgess (2004) to identify 16 different states in India as "pro-worker", "pro-employer" or "neutral", based on their amendments to the Industrial Disputes Act over the period 1958–1992.

Collective institutions: legislation, trade unions and wage-setting systems

While there are as many as 165 pieces of labour legislation in India, including 47 central government Acts (Debroy 1997), the primary pieces of legislation are:

- the Factories Act, 1948
- the Industrial Employment (Standing Orders) Act, 1946
- the Industrial Disputes Act (IDA), 1947
- the Trade Union Act (TUA), 1926
- the Contract Labour (Regulation and Abolition) Act, 1970
- the Payment of Wages Act, 1937
- the Minimum Wages Act, 1948
- the Workmen's Compensation Act, 1923
- the Employees State Insurance Act, 1948
- the Employees Provident Funds Act, 1952

These Acts together represent the *de jure* legal framework governing industrial and labour management relations and regulating aspects of labour interests like job/employment/income security, trade union activity, working conditions of regular workers and contractual workers, social security and insurance, particularly in the organised sector.[5] It should be noted that the actual impact of such laws passed by the legislature is mediated both by the executive and the judiciary.

In addition to these pieces of labour legislation, there is a prevalent system of wage-setting in India, whereby the Wage Boards and Pay Commissions generally set wages in the public sector, and this in turn establishes a benchmark for private sector wages (Dutta 2007). Wages are often set at above market clearing levels despite the existence of surplus labour in the economy. The downward pressure on wages is mitigated by labour market imperfections such as the prevalence of trade unions and minimum wages guaranteed by law. This particularly applies to the public sector, where government employees are mostly unionised, assured of lifetime employment and face very little risk of being fired (Dutt 2003).

The formulation of such complex labour laws and legislation was obviously intended to protect labour by regulating working conditions, ensuring job security, managing industrial relations and encouraging collective bargaining. The fundamental idea behind social policy concerning labour and employment in India, particularly during the first three decades of planning, was to treat labour not just as a mere resource for development but rather as a significant partner in and beneficiary of social and economic development – an orientation with its roots in the independence movement prior to 1947. In fact, while several pieces of legislation designed to protect labour were enacted prior to independence, they were further strengthened in independent India through comprehensive and detailed legislation governing industrial relations.

The end result was a complex set of laws that create a complicated regulatory environment for both employers and workers.

In recent times, policy analysts, industry associations and the mainstream media, both within and outside India, have argued that India's archaic labour laws are responsible for rigidities and inflexibility in the labour market. This has led to calls for the deregulation of the labour market in order to improve employment generation and industrial performance.[6]

A review of the existing literature

There is a modest but growing literature that seeks to address labour market flexibility in India, which can be classified according to two distinct and contrasting schools of thought. The first approach is the "pro-employer-reforms school" which argues that collective institutions, along with labour redundancy, have created rigidities in the labour market that have resulted in the substitution of capital for labour, preference for casual over regular labour and a rise in the sub-contracting of work to smaller enterprises. Together, these outcomes have constrained the effective redeployment of labour during the process of adjustment to changes in demand and technology. This strand of literature therefore advocates strong *de jure* reforms in the labour market.[7] The empirical studies belonging to this strand of literature have focused almost exclusively on the Industrial Disputes Act (IDA), 1947 despite the existence of several other labour laws. Exploiting state level amendments of the IDA, these studies have investigated the effect of the IDA on employment generation and industrial performance. The unanimous verdict is that pro-worker legislation has caused rigidities and inflexibilities, thus impairing industrial performance and the creation of new jobs.[8]

The second approach to labour market flexibility constitutes a distinct "pro-worker-reforms school". This line of thought offers counter-arguments to the former approach by highlighting the fact that poor regulatory compliance and spotty or circumvented enforcement have rendered labour legislation ineffective. It points out that although *de facto* reforms have taken place in India in the last two decades, resulting in a lessening of the rigidities and inflexibilities in the labour market, the organised private sector has sometimes been successful in evading the legal requirements of protective labour legislation and restructuring their technological and managerial practices. This view suggests that the issue of labour market rigidity is not as serious as the pro-employer-reforms school would have it. Proponents of this line of thinking also suggest that these *de facto* reforms have in fact adversely affected workers, and emphasise that any further *de jure* reforms without the institution of adequate social protection mechanisms or retraining facilities are not likely to have any impact on the problem.[9]

Thus, the existing empirical evidence available on labour market rigidities in India is quite mixed and inconclusive. To better approach the issue there is a need for studies that aim to understand the various channels through which labour legislation and labour market institutions affect industrial performance.

Despite the extensive and radical trade and industrial policy reforms of the 1990s, legislative reforms in the labour market are yet to gain momentum. While the structural adjustment programme initiated in 1991 was designed to ensure greater flexibility in labour laws, a lack of political consensus prevented the implementation of the required changes. A handful of changes have been introduced since 1991, and it can be argued that there was some decline in rigidities and inflexibilities in the labour market, particularly towards the end of the 1990s. However, many would regard these changes as far too little.[10] The pro-employer reforms literature suggests that there is a need for further direct and bolder attempts at institutional reforms, particularly changes to the strict and protective labour laws, so that the labour market can adjust and reap the benefits of liberalisation.

Nevertheless, the literature discussed here largely fails to acknowledge that in addition to the weak measures taken by the executive government, the judicial interpretation of labour laws by the Supreme Court has played a significant role in producing a relatively more flexible labour market. These changes in the interpretation of law are quite extensive (Singh 2015; Bhattacharjea 2006), but particularly important has been the Supreme Court's interpretation of the CLA in favour of employers. Such judicial interpretation of legislative provisions on matters pertaining to contract workers in the 1990s and 2000s adds a hitherto unexplored dimension to India's emerging policy landscape and changing regulatory environment. Judicial intervention of this kind has direct implications for labour market outcomes, including flexibility and employment generation. It is thus important to look closely at the law covering "contract" labour and the interpretation of such law by the Indian Supreme Court.

The Contract Labour (Regulation and Abolition) Act 1970

As a first step in understanding the significance of the CLA, it is important to emphasise once again that from the viewpoint of the employer, Indian labour laws are deemed highly restrictive. It is very hard for employers to fire workers, particularly so in the case of larger employers who need government permission to retrench workers. In addition there is a wide range of diverse laws and regulations that have to be followed in relation to issues such as working conditions, minimum wages, provident funds and workers' safety. At the same time, however, it needs to be emphasised that for a worker to benefit from these measures she must be employed in an establishment that is covered by these laws, as well as fit the legal definition of a worker or, more precisely, "workman". These details are not discussed here,[11] but it is important to note that these legal definitions mean that only about ten to fifteen per cent of the Indian labour force is covered by standard labour legislation. For the typical employers of this ten per cent of the Indian workforce, the Supreme Court's decision to allow the use of "contract labour" – labour hired through a labour contractor – has eased some of the pressure to comply with the strict provisions of the law. In this context note needs to be taken of the judgment of the Supreme Court in the 2001 case of Steel Authority of India v. National Union Water Front Workers.[12] This judgment was critical in allowing the widespread employment of contract workers, one of the primary virtues of which, from the viewpoint of the employer, is that such workers can be fired far more easily than regular workers. As this was an important step towards flexibility of the labour market, it is important to look at the details of the legislation pertaining to this category of worker as well as the crucial judicial interpretation of the law.

The Contract Labour (Regulation and Abolition) Act, 1970 set out to both regulate and abolish contract labour. The Act is applicable to establishments employing a minimum of 20 contract workers and requires both the principal employer to register with the labour department and the contractor supplying labour to gain a licence from the labour department. It also governs aspects of the wages paid to contract workers. In general, wages paid to contract workers must not be lower than the prescribed minimum wage and, while responsibility for the payment of wages rests with the contractor, if the contractor falls short, the principal employer is liable to make up for the payment due. Central government regulations, as well as at least some state level rules, require parity of wages and conditions of work (hours, holidays etc.) for contract workers with that of directly employed workers, if they are both doing the same work. The Act makes provisions for labour inspectors to examine relevant records as well as to speak with contract workers and initiate prosecution for contravention of the provisions of the Act.

However, the CLA was legislated not to just "regulate" contract labour but also to prevent its use and to abolish it whenever it was found to be used for jobs that qualified as permanent work. Under Section 10 of the Act, central and state governments are empowered to prohibit the use of contract labour in cases where contract workers are being used for perennial jobs or where regular workers are doing the same jobs, and to assess whether the work is incidental or necessary for the industry concerned. Since the enactment of the law in the 1970s, both central and state governments have indeed issued notifications prohibiting the employment of contract workers, emboldened by the Indian Supreme Court, which has supported action of this kind.[13] However upon such abolition, the question of what would happen to such "rescued" workers was not very clear and a number of cases ended up in the courts. One prominent case was Air India Statutory Corporation v. United Labour Union,[14] where the Indian Supreme Court ruled that in the event of abolition of contract labour the principal employer was obliged to employ the former contract labourers as regular workers. This view was, however, overturned in the Steel Authority judgment, which stated that once the government had abolished contract labour, there was no obligation on the employer to employ former contract labourers in regular jobs.[15]

One of the arguments offered by the Court for this interpretation was that "the contract labour is not rendered unemployed as is generally assumed but continues in the employment of the contractor as the notification does not sever the relationship of master and servant between contractor and contract labour." This stance is out of tune with the fact that the notification made under Section 10 (2) of the Contract Labour (Regulation and Abolition) Act is ostensibly made because the appropriate government has information that the activity for which contract labour has been hired is either necessary for the industry, perennial in nature, is/can be performed by regular workmen or that the work is sufficient to justify the employment of full time workers. If this is the case, then logically speaking, there is a direct link between the employer and the contract workers. However the court strongly upheld the view that the question of whether the relationship between the employer and the abolished contract labour is real or sham is to be distinguished from the act of abolishing contract labour, and that this is an issue to be litigated independently as an industrial dispute under the Industrial Disputes Act. More recently there has been further clarification from the Supreme Court on whether the contract labour agreement is "sham, nominal and a mere camouflage". If the contract is for the supply of labour then the work will be performed under the "directions, supervision and control of the principal employer", but since the salary is paid by the contractor the "ultimate supervision and control lies with a contractor".[16]

As these judgments indicate, the Supreme Court has made it very easy for employers to use contract labour for a variety of jobs, with the government almost never taking any action against the use of such labour because even if they were to "abolish" it, employers are no longer obliged to absorb contract workers as permanent employees. Furthermore, as indicated by the Court's recent clarifications, it has become very difficult to show that contract labour has been employed under sham contracts.

The courts have also set the terms regarding wages paid to contract workers. As described above, while the Act requires wage parity between regular and contract workers, the Supreme Court has clarified that the assessment of wage parity requires consideration of a host of factors including, but not limited to, the nature, quality and reliability of work done and the difference in skills and experience of the workers involved. Similarly, in a case relating to the issue of the same kind of work being performed by regular and contract workers, the Court clarified that the principal employer is not liable to make up for a shortfall in wages paid to contract workers. In essence the courts have provided enough scope for employers to justify paying different wages to regular and contract workers.[17]

The timeline of major judicial cases that has led to changes in the way the legislative provisions of the CLA are interpreted is summarised in Table 3.1 below. The regime engendered by these judicial interpretations has made the task of employing contract labour easier and cheaper, in terms of both hiring and firing. Taking this one step further, one might suggest that it is not merely a matter of being able to hire labour more cheaply but that in the face of no overall change in the law, the use of contract labour by employers can be a device to circumvent some of the restrictions imposed by other restrictive labour legislation (such as the Industrial Disputes Act) and labour market institutions (like trade unions). It allows establishments access to a set of workers whose employment can be terminated at will, the effect of which has been to increase labour market flexibility – an assertion for which we next seek to provide empirical support.

Table 3.1 Timeline of judicial interpretation by the Supreme Court of India on the legislative provisions of the CLA

Year	*Case*	*Verdict*	*Stance*
1974	Gammon India Limited versus Union of India	Government has the power to prohibit the use of contract labour	Pro-worker
1996	Hindustan Steelworks Construction Limited versus Commissioner of Labour	Principal employer is not liable to make up for a shortfall in wages paid to contract workers performing same work as regular workers	Pro-employer
1997	Air India Statutory Corporation versus United Labour Union	Abolition of contract labour requires the erstwhile principal employer to employ the workers in regular jobs	Pro-worker
2001	Steel Authority of India versus National Union Water Front Workers	There is no obligation on the principal employer to employ contract labour in regular work if the government abolishes the employment of contract labour	Pro-employer
2009	International Airport Authority of India versus International Air Cargo Union	If a contract between the principal employer and the contractor is for supply of labour, then the contract workers will work under the direction of principal employer, but since the salary is paid by the contractor, the ultimate supervision, control and responsibility lies with the contractor	Pro-employer
2009	Uttar Pradesh Rajya Vidyut Utpadan Board versus Uttar Pradesh Vidyut Mazdoor Sangh	While the CLA requires wage parity between regular and contract workers for similar kind of work, the principal employer can take various factors in to consideration such as skill, reliability and responsibility of workers in deciding whether similar work done by the two categories of workers can be considered to be at par or otherwise for payment purposes	Pro-employer

Source: various Supreme Court cases, cited as cases under bibliography.

Contract labour employment in organised manufacturing: empirical patterns

In order to examine the implications of the changing judicial interpretations of the CLA on the employment of contract labour and to assess the flexibility of the labour market, this section explores the pattern of contract worker usage in Indian formal manufacturing. The data used in this empirical analysis is for the formal manufacturing sector and its various sub-groups and has been sourced from the Annual Survey of Industries (ASI) undertaken by the Central Statistical Organization (CSO), Government of India. ASI covers the entire factory sector, where "factories" are workplaces which are registered as such under the Factories Act, 1948 and refers to units which employ 10 or more workers with the aid of power and units which employ 20 or more workers without the aid of power. ASI carries out a complete enumeration of large factories on a census basis, and of the remainder on a sample basis. In this case, "large units" are defined as factories employing 50 or more workers with the aid of power or 100 or more workers without the aid of power. The period under consideration in the current study is from 2000–01 to 2011–12.

Total manufacturing perspective

We begin by looking at the growth in workers in formal manufacturing. As shown in Figure 3.1, growth in the number of workers has undergone several interruptions between 1985–86 and 2011–12.[18] The first half of the 1990s saw very low growth, while the second half of the decade, in contrast, saw a drastic fall in growth coinciding with the period of jobless growth. This was the period of economic growth following drastic trade liberalisation and industrial reforms; the inelastic employment at this time partly captures the restrictiveness of collective labour institutions. However, there was a turnaround in the 2000s, with worker numbers undergoing a steady increase until 2006–07. Overall growth remained positive throughout most of the 2000s.

These figures for the 2000s raise the question of the role of contract labour during this period. Between 2000–01 and 2009–10 the proportion of contract workers in total employment increased across factories of all sizes, as shown in Figure 3.1. This lends support to the conjecture that changes in the judicial interpretation of the CLA in favour of employers during the 2000s has enabled firms to employ contract workers more widely across all factory sizes. Figure 3.1 also shows that the proportion of contract workers in smaller factories (those with less than 100 workers) rapidly increases with the size of the factory, remains more or less constant for medium to big factories (those with over 100 but less than 2000 workers), and then increases rapidly again for very large factories (those with over 2000 workers). There are two potential explanations for this increase. First, very large factories (employing more than 5000 workers) are capital-intensive industries and as such, labour employed is relatively less important in the production process, where repetitive machine-based work

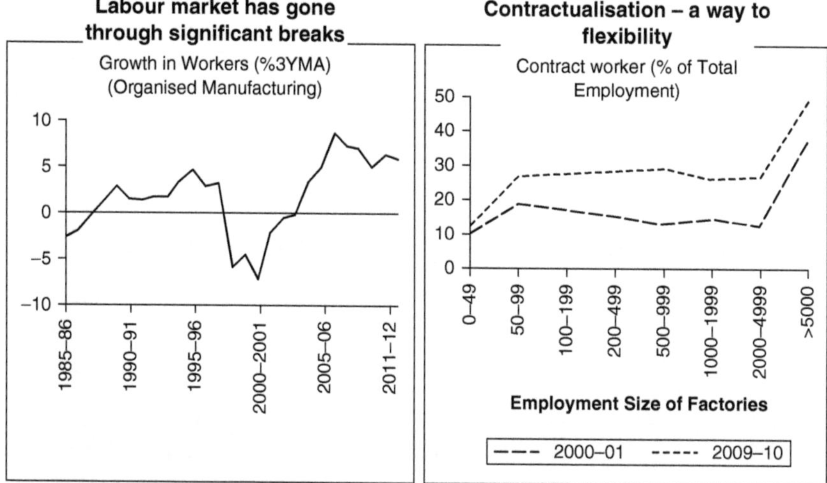

Figure 3.1 Contract workers in all manufacturing.

Source: Authors' computation based on ASI data.

or operation/repair/maintenance of relatively permanent machines can be easily achieved through the employment of non-permanent contract workers.[19] Second, it is relatively cheaper for larger factories to engage contract workers in their production processes. In fact, in 2009–10, factories with over 5000 workers employed nearly 50 per cent of their workers through contract.

In terms of the total employment scenario from 2000 to 2012, we find that there has been an increase in total employment (including managerial staff as well as production workers) from 8 million to around 13 million over a decade (see Figure 3.2). Of this number, the largest component is the "workers" category, in which the number of contract workers across all manufacturing increased from 1.3 million in 2000–01 to around 3.6 million by 2011–12. Interestingly, the share of the "workers" category in the total number of persons engaged has remained remarkably stable, at about 77 per cent, but the share of contract workers in the total workforce increased from 20.43 per cent in 2000–01 to 30.37 per cent in 2006–07 and then 34.61 per cent in 2011–12, as evident in Figure 3.3. This indicates that in the period of our study there has been a shift in the preference of employers for contract workers over regular workers, thus providing evidence for our hypothesis that the judicial interpretations of the CLA in the 2000s have made it easier to engage contract workers and increase flexibility in the labour market. In addition, we also find an increase in contract workers in all manufacturing during the 2000s when we consider the figures for factory-level employment. This is evident from Figure 3.3, which clearly shows that from 2000–01 until 2009–10, the number of directly employed employees per factory remained at around 50, after which it declined to

45 in 2011–12. In contrast, the number of contract workers per factory went up from just under 10 in 2000–01 to 19 in 2009–10, before declining slightly to 17 by 2011–12. This overall fall in the number of permanent employees per factory and the overall increase in contract workers per factory over the decade suggest that the bargaining power of labour has been continuously eroded during the period under consideration, once again providing evidence of an increase in labour market flexibility.

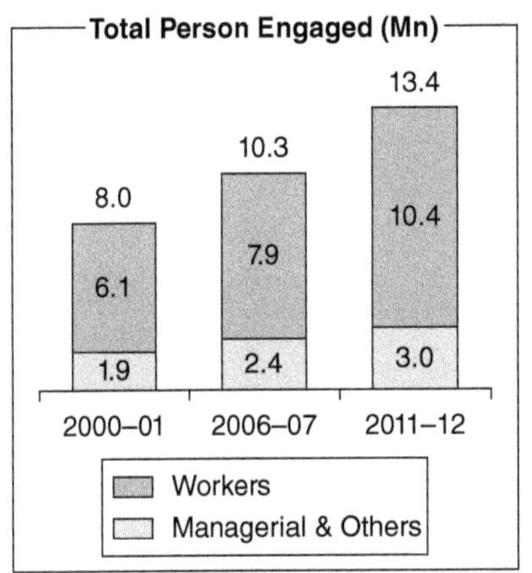

Figure 3.2 Total persons, permanent workers and contract workers, 2000–2012.

Source: Authors' computation based on ASI data.

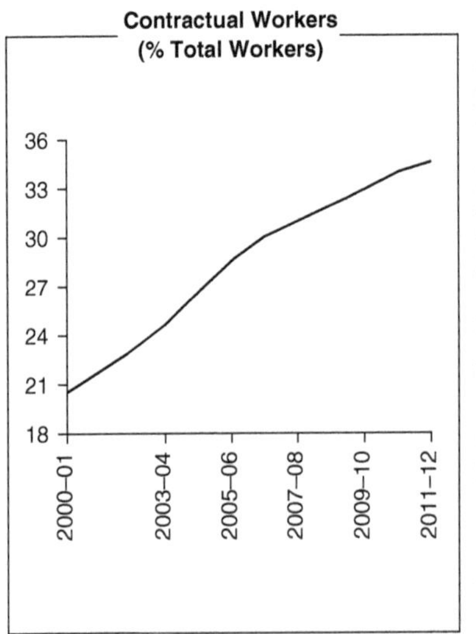

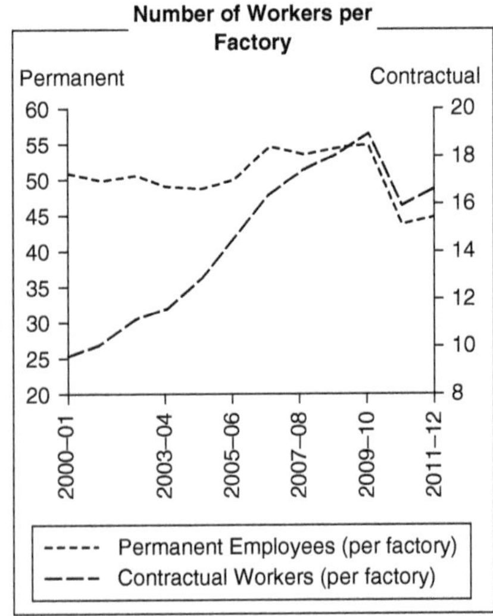

Figure 3.3 Contract workers in all manufacturing.

Source: Authors' computation based on ASI data.

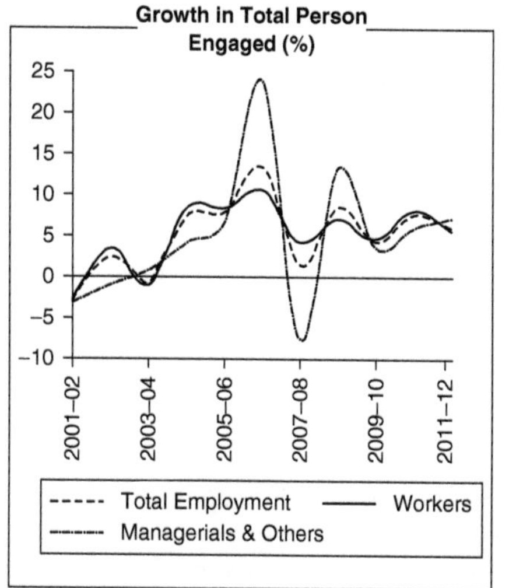

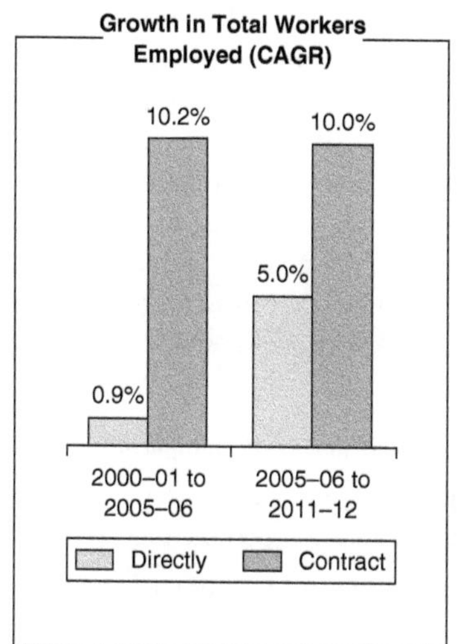

Figure 3.4 Growth in total persons, total workers and contract workers.
Source: Authors' computation based on ASI data.

Another way of observing the increase in contract worker employment in India's formal manufacturing sector is by comparing the growth rates between the two five-yearly periods 2000–01 to 2005–06 and 2005–06 to 2011–12. Figure 3.4 plots the yearly growth rates of total persons engaged (disaggregated into "workers" and "managerial and other staff"), and shows that there is clear break in 2005–06. It should be noted that annual growth rates in all categories of employment remained positive throughout most of the 2000s. Figure 3.4 also shows the compound annual growth rate (CAGR) for total workers engaged by two categories directly employed and contract workers, over the periods 2000–01 to 2005–06 and 2005–06 to 2011–12. Clearly, the growth in contract workers over the two periods remained high, at about 10 per cent, while growth in directly employed workers was a marginal 0.9 per cent during the first period and a moderate 5 per cent during the second.

A disaggregated view of the manufacturing sector

In this section, we undertake two forms of disaggregated analysis. First, we analyse the engagement of contract labour by factor intensity of manufacturing (labour versus capital intensive manufacturing[20]) and by the use-based classification of manufacturing into consumer, intermediate and capital goods. Second, we identify patterns in contract labour use at 2-digit level of disaggregation of manufacturing industries (using the National Industrial Classification 1998, NIC-98). The division of manufacturing along these lines has been guided by many considerations. First, existing evidence shows that labour intensity in India has undergone a sustained decline in the post reform period (Sen and Das 2015), not only in capital-intensive industries but also in labour-intensive industries. Given this backdrop, it is important to analyse the pattern of contract labour use in these industries. Second, there is evidence that trade reforms since the early 1990s have targeted capital and intermediate goods more than consumer goods (Das 2004), so an analysis of contract labour in industries classified by the use-based sectors[21] is also relevant to our concerns. Third, an analysis at the 2-digit level of classification allows us to identify which broad industry groups have seen higher growth in contract labour over the period of our study.

Contract labour in manufacturing by factor intensity and use-based sectors

Figure 3.5 highlights the patterns in employment of contract workers by factor intensity and use-based classification in two panels. The upper panel shows that across all manufacturing the absorption of contract workers is concentrated in capital-intensive segments of formal manufacturing. Between 2000–01 and 2011–12, the total number of workers (both directly employed as well as contract) employed in all manufacturing increased by 4.3 million, from 6.1 million in 2000–01 to 10.4 million in 2011–12. Of this increase, the growth in worker numbers in capital-intensive industries accounted for 81.4 per cent, 60 per cent of which was due to an increase in the use of contract workers. As for the growth in worker numbers by category of worker, capital-intensive sectors saw the highest growth in the number of contract workers – over 12 per cent in both sub-periods under study. While the number of directly employed workers in capital-intensive sectors saw no growth in the first sub-period and a moderate 5.8 per cent increase in the second sub-period, labour intensive sectors saw moderate growth of about 3.1 per cent in directly employed workers over both the sub-periods. At the same time, there was a fall in the growth of contract workers, from 5.3 per cent in the period 2000–01 to 2005–06 to 2.6 per cent in 2005–06 to 2011–12.

This pattern of contract labour usage across labour and capital intensive sectors suggests that labour employed in capital intensive sectors is relatively less important in production processes where repetitive machine-based work or operation/repair/maintenance of relatively permanent machines can be easily undertaken by non-permanent contract workers. As such, there was a faster growth in the number of contract workers in the capital intensive segment of manufacturing, as these workers were simply required to manage and operate production floors, work which could be undertaken by semi-skilled or unskilled workers sourced through contactors and trained on the job. On the other hand, the fact that in labour-intensive industries there was a consistent growth in the number of directly employed workers and a fall in the number of contract workers implies that these industries require non-transferable industry-specific skills which cannot be achieved with non-permanent contract workers but by on the job training of directly employed workers.

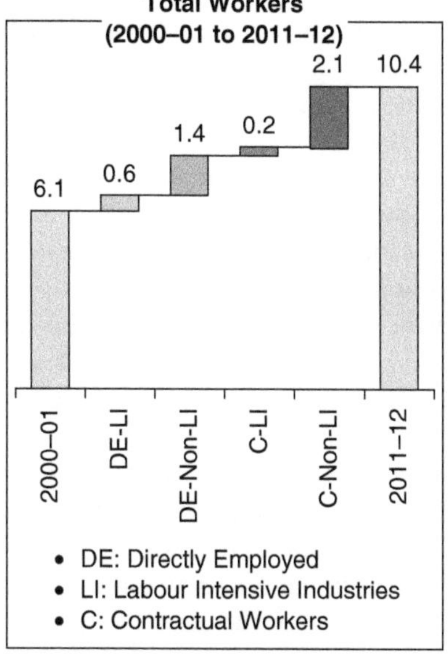

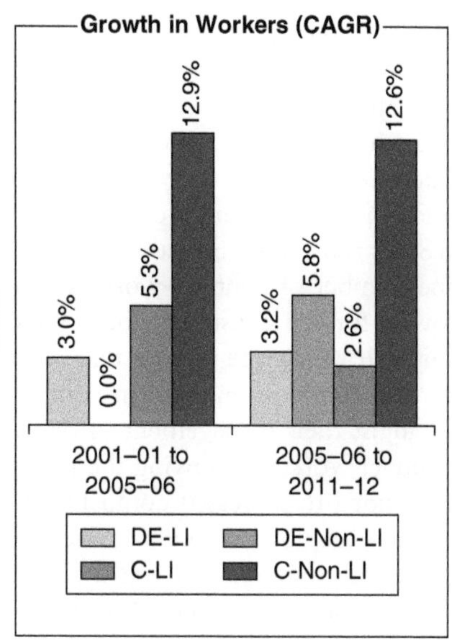

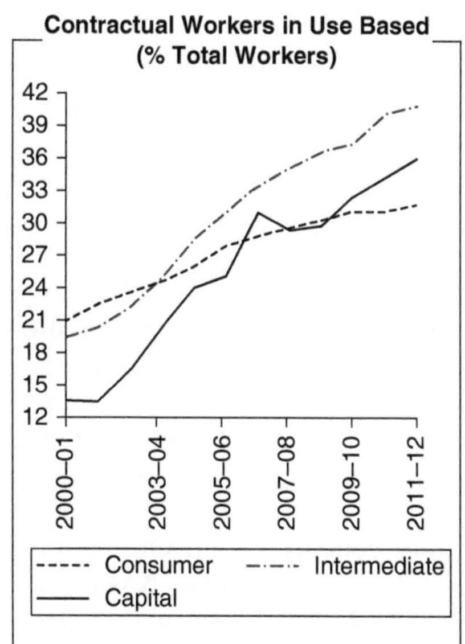

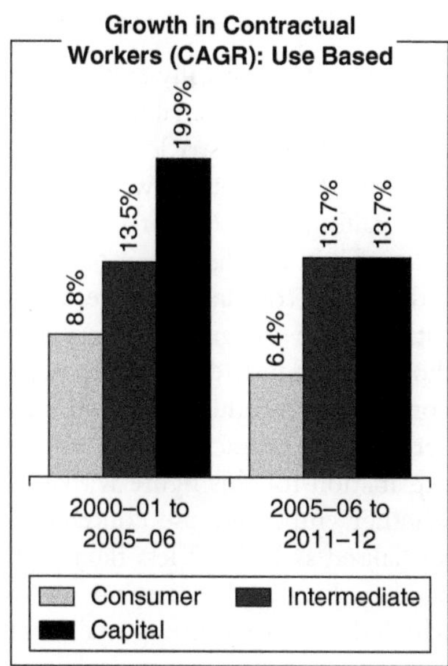

Figure 3.5 Contract workers in organised manufacturing: labour intensive, capital intensive and use based sectors.

Source: Authors' computation based on ASI data.

The lower panel in Figure 3.5 shows that the consumer goods segment of manufacturing had the highest share of contract workers as a proportion of total workers engaged in 2000–01. However, following the judicial pronouncement in 2001 making it easier to engage contract workers, and the trade reforms targeting capital and intermediate goods sectors in the preceding decade, we see faster growth in the use of contract workers for both the capital goods and intermediate goods sectors over the two sub-periods under study. At the same time, there is a fall in the number of contract workers for the consumer goods sector, from 8.8 per cent in the first sub-period to 6.4 per cent in the second. Consequently, the number of contract workers as a proportion of total workers engaged was lowest for the consumer goods sector in 2011–12. A possible explanation for this is that the trade reforms that targeted the capital and intermediate goods sector resulted in an increase in competition in these sectors, requiring employers to adjust their management of resources. As it became much easier to engage contract workers following the judicial interventions of the 2000s, these sectors responded to increased competition by engaging contract workers rather than directly employed workers. Since the consumer goods sectors were relatively protected, they did not feel the pressure for adjustment and hence they made relatively less use of contract workers than was the case for the other two sectors.

Contract labour in manufacturing: the 2-digit perspective

This section empirically explores the use of contract labour at the 2-digit level of NIC-98, which enables us to document contract worker employment at the individual industry level. In the sub-period 2000–01 to 2005–06, the average growth in contract workers across all 23 2-digit industries was 72.91 per cent, falling to 61.68 per cent in the sub-period 2005–06 to 2011–12, along with a fall in the dispersion of these workers.[22] Figure 3.6 presents the share of 2-digit industries in the usage of contract labour over time. A detailed examination of the sub-groups of formal manufacturing at the two-digit classification shows that industries such as food products (15–16), basic metals (27–28), other non-metallic products (26) and transport equipment (34–35) absorb almost 65 per cent of contract workers employed in formal manufacturing. A potential explanation for this figure is that the nature of industry-specific skills dictates whether employers use contract labour or not. Industries that require more specialised skills have less flexibility to engage contract labour. On the other hand, industries that depend on workers doing repetitive floor-based work, which does not require specialist skills or technical knowledge, can easily meet their needs with contract workers.

Figure 3.7 presents the proportion of permanent and contract workers per factory for each of the 2-digit industry groups in 2011–12. In order to assess the contract worker intensity by industry groups, we highlight the ratio of contract workers to directly employed workers. The right hand panel of Figure 3.7 compares the number of permanent and contract workers in millions; as might be expected, we find wide differences in contract worker employment. Further, when the line graph depicting the number of factories

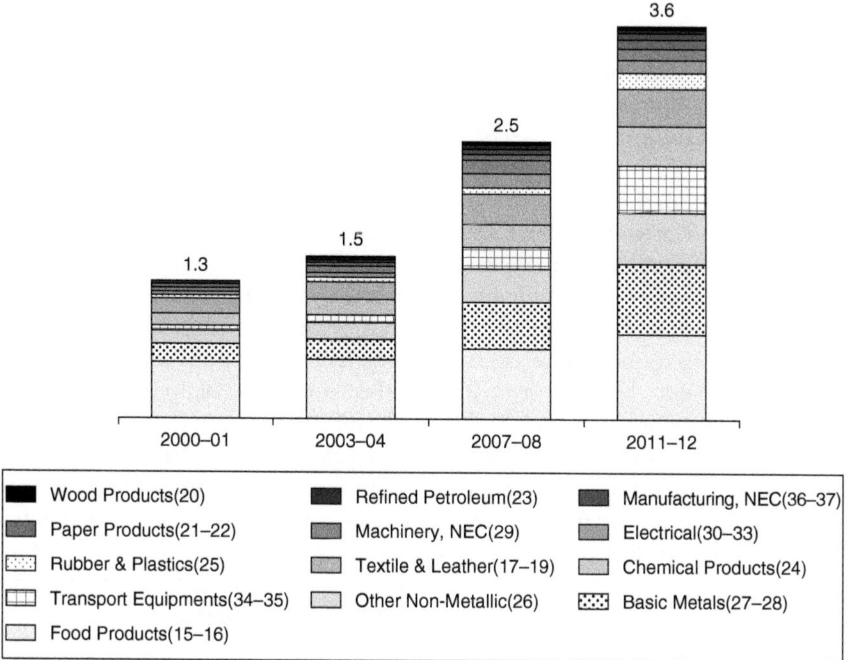

Figure 3.6 Contract workers in 2-digit NIC-98 sub-groups: 2000–2012.

Source: Authors' computation based on ASI data.

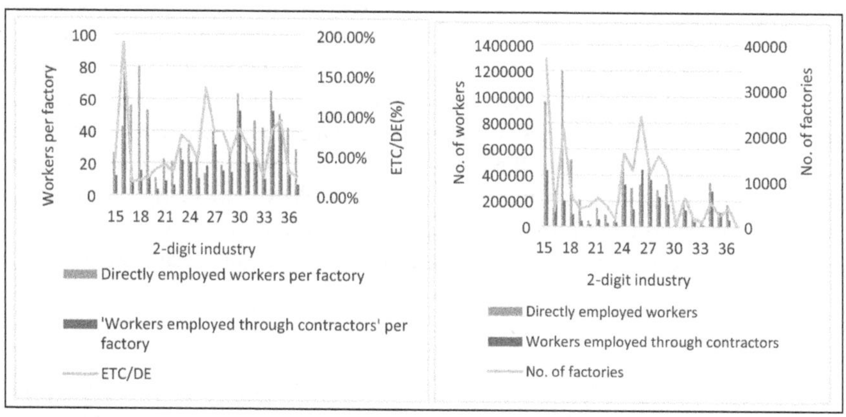

Figure 3.7 Permanent workers, contract labour and factories in 2-digit NIC sub-groups.

Source: Authors' computation based on ASI data.

for these industry groups is added, further wide variations appear. Our key observation is that the variation across industry groups implies variation in the bargaining power of labour. In industries with a higher ratio of contract workers to directly employed workers, it might be expected that the bargaining power of labour would be lower.

The preceding two sub-sections have documented the evidence for the employment of contract workers across the spectrum of formal manufacturing in India. At both the aggregate level and the various levels of disaggregation we find that contract workers have a significant presence. This becomes even more apparent when we compare contract workers with directly employed workers. The analysis thus provides supporting evidence for our hypothesis that the judicial interpretation of the legislative provisions of the CLA in the 2000s has paved the way for factories to hire contract labour with ease, thus increasing labour market flexibility. In contrast to the widely-held view that Indian labour law imposes institutional rigidities that inhibit employment expansion, our analysis presents new evidence of labour market flexibility in India. This has been achieved through increasing employment of contract labour, where the proportion of contract workers working alongside permanent workers has resulted in the 'contractualisation' of the workforce.[23] While we do find evidence of flexibility, our analysis also suggests that the increase in the employment of contract workers has mainly taken place in larger factories and in relatively more capital-intensive sectors. This indicates that the increase in contract worker employment is taking place in areas where specialised skills are not required and where work can be performed by relatively unskilled contract labourers. The changes in the interpretation of the CLA have not led to any significant creation of productive work opportunities. There is some evidence to suggest that employers are substituting regular workers with contract workers in order to circumvent the IDA and other restrictive legislation.[24] If this is the case, the increase in contract labour employment must be seen as an outcome of the rigidities caused by restrictive labour market institutions. We await a detailed empirical investigation of this issue, but the fact remains that India needs to roll our labour reforms in order to create decent and productive opportunities for an increasing workforce. These reforms should target both efficiency-enhancing changes that will allow more flexibility and lead to enhanced employment generation and industrial performance, as well as welfare-enhancing changes that will allow workers to improve their skills and productivity without the threat of losing their income, thus bringing about improvements in social justice.

Conclusion

This chapter has undertaken an exploratory and investigative exercise designed to assess the Contract Labour Act (CLA) and its implications for employment in the formal manufacturing sector in India. Our main finding is that the CLA has undergone drastic changes in its interpretation since its inception in 1970. Although originally intended to protect contract workers against exploitation and to enhance their overall welfare, the Act has seen judicial interventions in the 2000s that go against the rhetoric associated with its original intention. The judicial verdicts concerning the legislative provisions of the Act have been predominantly in favour of employers, which has paved the way for flexibility in the labour market and the wider and easier employment of contract workers in manufacturing. Although there is a modest but growing literature examining the use of contract labour in Indian manufacturing, the judicial interpretations of the CLA have largely been overlooked in existing empirical studies. To address this gap, this chapter has argued that the evolution of the CLA represents a critical labour issue, adding a new dimension to the emerging policy landscape and changing regulatory regime in India. Our empirical analysis of the patterns of contract labour employment provides evidence that Indian labour markets have become more flexible following pro-employer judicial interpretations of the CLA. But at the same time, the analysis shows that contract workers are increasingly replacing regular workers in low skills work and in larger establishments. This suggests that changes in the interpretation of the CLA have helped employers to circumvent restrictive labour market institutions, thus providing further evidence of the rigidities caused by existing labour legislation.

Notes

1 See, for example, Mathur (1991), Shyam Sundar (2005), Anant et al (2006), Deshpande et al (2004), Sharma (2006), Fagernäs (2010) among others.

2 This is also reflected in the Government of India's 2020 vision statement "India Vision 2020", which clearly states that India needs to generate around 200 million additional employment opportunities over the next 20 years. The current government under Narendra Modi has also put special emphasis on the need for creation of quality jobs for all through their recent "Make in India" and "Digital India" campaigns and their attempts to undertake labour reforms (Dhoot, 2015).

3 For some recent studies that address the issue of contractualisation of the workforce, see Saha et al (2013), Chaurey (2015), and Sakpal (2016). These studies conclude that increasing contractualisation is an outcome of restrictive labour legislation. Our study takes a different approach, and assesses the various nuances of the Contract Labour Act. It specifically examines how recent changes to judicial interpretations of the CLA may have added to labour market flexibility.

4 For existing studies of rigidities and inflexibility in the Indian labour market, see Besley and Burgess (2004), Gordon and Gupta (2004), Kochhar et al (2006), Panagariya (2006), and Gupta, Rana, and Kumar (2009).

5 For a detailed review of some of these Acts and other labour market institutions, their nature, scope and empirical implications, see Choudhury (2012) and Ahsan, Pagés, and Roy (2008).

6 The 1990s saw some reforms in the labour market although the scope and pace of such reforms have been quite slow. See Choudhury (2012) and Das, Choudhury, and Singh (2015) for a discussion of the various types of rigidities caused by restrictive labour legislation in India.

7 See Fallon and Lucas (1991), Ghose (1995, 1999), Datta Chaudhari (1996), Besley and Burgess (2004), Panagariya (2007), Aghion et al (2008), Saha, Sen and Maiti (2013), and Sakpal (2016), among others.

8 See Besley and Burgess (2004), Sanyal and Menon (2005), Ahsan and Pages (2006, 2007, 2009), Hasan, Mitra, and Ramaswamy (2007), Aghion et al (2008) and Bhattachajea (2006, 2009). Bhattachajea points out that the methodology which exploits variation in state level amendments to the IDA is flawed. This means that studies that have drawn upon this methodology are themselves automatically flawed. He also points out that the literature in this genre suffers from various other methodological shortcomings, particularly their inadequate tests for robustness.

9 See Nagaraj (2002, 2004), Datta (2003), Ramaswamy (2003), Anant et al (2006), Bhattacharjea (2006, 2009), and Das, Choudhury, and Singh (2015).

10 See Das, Choudhury, and Singh (2015). There have been some recent state-level changes in Rajasthan, Madhya Pradesh and Gujarat, largely aimed at removing more and more workers from the coverage of labour laws. However these changes have been largely piecemeal and they do not represent comprehensive reform. See http://sanhati.com/excerpted/12592/; http://www.business-standard.com/article/current-affairs/madhya-pradesh-assembly-passes-labour-law-amendments-115072200606_1.html; and http://timesofindia.indiatimes.com/india/Controversial-labour-law-amendments-to-come-into-force-in-a-week-in-Gujrat/articleshow/49053309.cms

11 See Singh (2015).

12 Steel Authority of India v. National Union Water Front Workers AIR 2001 SC 3527.

13 For instance see Gammon India Ltd. v. Union of India (1974) 1 SCC 596, 601.

14 (1997) (9) SCC 377

15 Steel Authority of India v. National Union Water Front Workers AIR 2001 SC 3527.

16 International Airport Authority of India v. International Air Cargo Workers Union and another (2009) 13 SCC 374.

17 See UP Rajya Vidyut Utpadan Board v. UP Vidyut Mazdoor Sangh (2009), and Hindustan Steelworks Construction Limited v. Commissioner of Labour and Others (1996), cited in Das, Choudhury, and Singh (2015).

18 "Workers" here refers to blue collar production workers, excluding managerial and other staff.

19 There is some evidence for this hypothesis when the analysis is extended to a disaggregated state and industry level. See Das, Choudhury, and Singh (2015) for details.

20 We follow Sen and Das (2015) in our classification of the manufacturing industries by factor intensity.

21 Use-based classification is an alternate classification of industrial production in India that was first used by the Reserve Bank of India in the early 1970s and was subsequently adopted by the Central Statistical Office in its reporting of data on industrial production. The conventional definition of use-based classification adopted by official agencies in India classifies industrial production as: (1) Basic Goods (bulk or raw material products used for further production of new items in agriculture, manufacturing or construction); (2) Intermediate Goods (products produced as incomplete products and that goes as input at production time for further finishing); (3) Capital Goods (Plants, machinery and goods used for physical capital or assets formation), and; (4) Consumer Goods (Products directly used by consumers, which is sometimes further split into Consumer Durables and Consumer Non-Durables). It is to be noted that Basic Goods and Intermediate Goods may appear to have similar uses, but the official agencies have retained the distinction as originally made by the Reserve Bank: Basic Goods are essentially bulk products, originate in primary sources, and they largely constitute finished products used for application elsewhere; on the other hand, intermediate products primarily constitute incomplete products

or are by and large intended as intermediate inputs for further production or processing. In our analysis, since our focus is on manufacturing industries, we have classified them as Intermediate Goods, Capital Goods and Consumer Goods.

22 See Table 2 in our earlier work, Das, Choudhury, and Singh (2015), for variations in the growth of contract workers across 23 individual industry groups as well as over the two sub-periods discussed in this chapter.

23 These findings are further reinforced when the analysis is undertaken at a disaggregated state and industry level. See our earlier work, Das, Choudhury, and Singh (2015).

24 See Saha, Sen, and Maiti (2013), Chaurey (2015) and Sakpal (2016).

References

Aghion, P., R. Burgess, S. J. Redding, and F. Zilibotti. 2008. "The Unequal Effects of Liberalization: Evidence from Dismantling the License Raj in India." *American Economic Review* 98 (4): 1397–1412.

Ahsan, A., and C. Pagés. 2006. "Helping or Hurting Workers? Assessing the Effects of De Jure and De Facto Labor Regulation in India." Paper presented at the "India: Meeting the Employment Challenge" conference, Institute for Human Development, New Delhi, July 28.

Ahsan, A., and C. Pagés. 2007. *Are all Labour Regulations Equal? Assessing the Effects of Job Security, Labour Dispute, and Contract Labour Laws in India*. Washington DC: The World Bank. [Policy Research Working Paper Series 4259].

Ahsan, A., and C. Pagés. 2009. "Are All Labour Regulations Equal? Evidence from Indian Manufacturing." *Journal of Comparative Economics*. 37 (1): 62–75.

Ahsan, A., C. Pagés, and T. Roy. 2008. "Legislation, Enforcement and Adjudication in Indian Labour Markets: Origins, Consequences and the Way Forward.", In *Globalization, Labour Markets and Inequality in India*, edited by D. Mazumdar and S. Sarkar, 247–280. Abingdon: Routledge.

Anant, T. C. A., R. Hasan, P. Mohapatra, R. Nagaraj, and S. K. Sasikumar. 2006. "Labor Markets in India: Issues and Perspectives." In *Labor Markets in Asia: Issues and Perspectives*, edited by J. Felipe and R. Hasan, 205–300. Basingstoke: Palgrave Macmillan.

Besley, T. and R. Burgess. 2004. "Can Labor Regulations Hinder Economic Performance? Evidence from India." *Quarterly Journal of Economics* 119 (1): 91–134.

Bhattacharjea, A. 2006. "Labour Market Regulation and Industrial Performance in India: A Critical Review of the Empirical Evidence." *Indian Journal of Labour Economics* 49 (2): 211–232.

Bhattacharjea, Aditya. 2009. "The Effects of Employment Protection Legislation on Indian Manufacturing." *Economic and Political Weekly* 44 (22): 55–62.

Chaurey, R. 2015. "Labor Regulations and Contract Labor Use: Evidence from Indian Firms." *Journal of Development Economics* 114: 224–232.

Choudhury, H. 2012. "Essays on the Changing Inter-Industry Wage Structure in India." PhD diss., University of Dundee.

Das, D. K., H. Choudhury, and J. Singh. 2015. *Contract Labour (Regulation and Abolition) Act 1970 and Labour Market Flexibility: An Exploratory Assessment of Contract Labour Use in India's Formal Manufacturing*. New Delhi: ICRIER. [ICRIER Working Paper 300].

Das, D. K. 2004. "Manufacturing Productivity Growth under Varying Trade Regimes, 1980–2000." *Economic and Political Weekly* 39 (05): 423-433.

Datta Chaudhari, M. 1996. *Labor Markets as Social Institutions in India*. College Park, MD: Centre for Institutional Reform and the Informal Sector, University of Maryland. [IRIS-India Working Paper 10].

Debroy, B. 1997. *Labour Market Reform*. New Delhi: UNDP. [Policy Paper 22, Project LARGE].

Deshpande, L., A. N. Sharma, A. Karan, and S. Sarkar. 2004. *Liberalisation and Labour: Labour Flexibility in Indian Manufacturing*. New Delhi: Institute for Human Development.

Dhoot, V. 2015. "Labour Law Reforms: Narendra Modi Government Moves Afresh for 'Makeover' of 1948 Factories Act."*Economics Times*, October 16.

Datta, R. 2003. "Labor Market, Social Institutions, Economic Reforms and Social Cost." In *Labour Market and Institution in India, 1990s and Beyond*, edited by Shuji Uchikawa, 9-30. New Delhi: Manohar Publications.

Dutt, P. 2003. "Labor Market Outcomes and Trade Reforms: The Case of India." In *The Impact of Trade on Labor: Issues, Perspectives, and Experiences from Developing Asia*, edited by R. Hasan and D. Mitra, 245–274. Amsterdam: Elsevier.

Dutta, P. V. 2007. "Trade Protection and Industry Wages in India." *Industrial and Labor Relations Review* 60 (2): 268–285.

Fallon, P. R., and R. E. B. Lucas. 1991. "The Impact of Changes in Job Security Regulations in India and Zimbabwe." *World Bank Economic Review* 5 (3): 395–413.

Fagernäs, Sonja. 2010. "Labor Law, Judicial Efficiency, and Informal Employment in India." *Journal of Empirical Legal Studies* 7 (2): 282–321.

Ghose, A. K. 1995. "Labour Market Flexibility and the Indian Economy." *Indian Journal of Labour Economics* 38 (1): 55–62.

Ghose, A. K. 1999. "Current Issues of Employment in India." *Economic and Political Weekly* 34 (36): 2592–2608.

Gordon, J. P. F., and P. Gupta. 2004. *Understanding India's Services Revolution*. Washington DC: International Monetary Fund. [IMF Working Papers 04/171].

Gupta, P., H. Rana, and U. Kumar. 2009. *Big Reforms but Small Payoffs: Explaining the Weak Record of Growth and Employment in Indian Manufacturing*. Munich: University Library of Munich. [MPRA Paper 13496].

Hasan, R., D. Mitra, and K. V. Ramaswamy. 2007. "Trade Reforms, Labour Regulations, and Labour-demand Elasticities: Empirical Evidence from India." *The Review of Economics and Statistics* 89 (3): 466–481.

Kochhar, K., U. Kumar, R. Rajan, A. Subramanian, and I. Tokatlidis. 2006. "India's Pattern of Development: What Happened, What Follows?" *Journal of Monetary Economics* 53 (5): 981–1019.

Mathur, A. 1991. *Industrial Restructuring and Union Power: Micro-Economic Dimensions of Economic Restructuring and Industrial Relations in India*. Geneva: ILO, Asian Regional Team for Employment Promotion (ARTEP).

Mehrotra, S., A. Gandhi, P. Saha, and B. K. Sahoo. 2012. *Joblessness and Informalisation: Challenges to Inclusive Growth in India*. New Delhi: Institute of Applied Manpower Research, Government of India. [IAMR Occasional Paper 9/2012].

Nagaraj, R. 2002. *Trade and Labour Market Linkages in India: Evidence and Issues*. Honolulu: East-West Center. [East West Centre Working Papers Economic Series 50].

Nagaraj, R. 2004. "Fall in Organised Manufacturing Employment: A Brief Note." *Economic and Political Weekly* 39 (30): 3387–3390.

Panagariya, A. 2006. "Transforming India" Paper presented at the "India: An Emerging Giant" conference, Columbia University, October 13–15.

Panagariya, A. 2007. "Why India Lags behind China and How It Can Bridge the Gap." *The World Economy* 30 (2): 229–248.

Ramaswamy, K. V. 2003. "Liberalization, Outsourcing and Industrial Labor Markets in India: Some Preliminary Results." In *Labour Market and Institution in India, 1990s and Beyond*, edited by Shuji Uchikawa, 127–146. New Delhi: Manohar Publications.

Saha, B., K. Sen, and D. Maiti. 2013."Trade Openness, Labour Institutions and Flexibilisation: Theory and Evidence from India." *Labour Economics* 24: 180–195.

Sakpal, R. S. 2016. "Labour Law, Enforcement and the Rise of Temporary Contract Workers: Empirical Evidence from India's Formal Manufacturing Sector." *European Journal of Law and Economics* 42: 157–146.

Sanyal, P., and N. Menon 2005. "Labor Disputes and the Economics of Firm Geography: A Study of Domestic Investment in India." *Economic Development and Cultural Change* 53 (4): 825–854.

Sen, K., and D. K. Das. 2015. "Where Have All the Workers Gone? The Puzzle of Declining Labour Intensity in Organised Indian Manufacturing." *Economic and Political Weekly* 50 (23): 108–115.

Sharma, A. N. 2006. "Flexibility, Employment and Labour Market Reforms in India." *Economic and Political Weekly* 41 (21): 2078–2085.

Shyam Sundar, K. R. 2005. "Labour Flexibility Debate in India: A Comprehensive Review and Some Suggestions." *Economic and Political Weekly* 40 (22–23): 2274–2285.

Singh, J. 2015. "Who is a Worker? Searching the Theory of the Firm for Answers." In *Labour, Employment and Economic Growth in India*, edited by K.V Ramamaswamy, 265–291. Delhi: Cambridge University Press.

Websites

http://sanhati.com/excerpted/12592/;

http://www.business-standard.com/article/current-affairs/madhya-pradesh-assembly-passes-labour-law-amendments-115072200606_1.html;

http://timesofindia.indiatimes.com/india/Controversial-labour-law-amendments-to-come-into-force-in-a-week-in-Gujrat/articleshow/49053309.cms

Cases Cited

Air India Statutory Corporation. United Labour Union (1997) (9) SCC 377

Gammon India Limited v. Union of India (1974) 1 SCC 596, 601

Hindustan Steelworks Construction Ltd. v. Commissioner of Labour and Others (1996) LLR, 865(SC)

International Airport Authority of India v. International Air Cargo Workers Union and another (2009) 13 SCC 374

Steel Authority of India v. National Union Water Front Workers (2001) AIR SC 3527

Uttar Pradesh Rajya Vidyut Utpadan Board v. Uttar Pradesh Vidyut Mazdoor Sangh (2009) 17 SCC 318.320

4 Employment and education

Policy challenges[1]

Ratna M. Sudarshan[2]

In India educational qualifications are seen as the key to attaining regular formal employment. But in an economy dominated by informal employment this expectation is fulfilled for very few people. Even so there has been little change since independence in the widespread belief that there is a linear and positive relationship between educational qualifications and employment outcomes. Contemporary concerns around unemployment and perceptions of low employability have translated into a focus on skill development initiatives and a new emphasis on strengthening the vocational education stream within the secondary school curriculum. However, work-centred pedagogy has remained confined to small islands of experimentation. This chapter argues that in the context of high rates of informal employment, a different relationship between education and work is needed. An alternative pedagogy would emphasise the ongoing and mutually reinforcing relationship between education, skill development, livelihood and well-being. Given the size of the problem and the diversity within India's economy and education system, the pursuit of a single uniform format across the country is likely to be self-defeating. This chapter argues that the most effective policy response to contemporary education and employment challenges would be to innovate through multiple strategies.

The current scenario

The current education system in India is oriented towards encouraging the aspiration for regular formal work and imparting the abilities needed to achieve formal employment. Rapid expansion in educational enrolments at all levels, alongside virtually stagnant opportunities for formal employment among school leavers is, however, creating a situation of imbalance. The government's policy response to this situation has been varied. While no formal employment policy exists, discussions around the policy challenges have prioritised the employment side of the equation, focusing on the need to enhance skill development opportunities, improve legal compliance with existing laws, provide better access to labour market information, and extend social security provisions for all workers.[3] There is also some emphasis on generating increased and better employment opportunities through the introduction of active labour market programmes. This chapter argues that it is equally necessary to examine the education system. Instead of focusing on how to better fit people to jobs, a different approach to the relationship between education and work is needed. Rather than the conscious creation of jobs within well-defined structures, it is the loosening of structures and opening up of diverse opportunities that offers the greatest hope of removing the currently high levels of segmentation and division within the work force. An educational paradigm that sees learning as a lifelong process and values different kinds of learning processes could alter the relationship between work and education in important and positive ways. The current view that school education opens up a pathway to regular and secure employment as a linear process could be replaced by a lifelong approach to learning that emphasises and supports the continuous application of skills to life and work, which generate livelihood and knowledge resources simultaneously. This chapter suggests that multiple strategies are needed to develop an education system that actively encourages these diverse livelihood trajectories.

The world of structured learning, through attendance at school and university, is possibly valued most for its instrumental worth, both by managers and planners and by the students themselves. This includes learning the sorts of capacities that are required by industry or government, and from the point of view of society in general, awareness regarding health, political participation, lower fertility, and so on. Learning is also about developing the power of critical thought, as well as problem solving skills, empowerment and agency. Yet all too often the single measure used to assess the value of education is the extent to which it translates into improved work opportunities.

Employment in the Indian economy is highly stratified, as the economy itself consists of a modern, organised sector and a large unorganised sector, with high levels of income inequality.[4] The organised sector is subject to regulation, whereas the unorganised sector is largely unregulated. In the organised sector, most employment generated is formal in nature, providing employees with a written employment contract, regular work and some benefits, although an increasing proportion is informal (such as piece rated work, outsourced work, or casual wage work). In the unorganised sector most work is informal, without legal protection, regularity or social security benefits. In the agricultural sector all work is informal, except on plantations. The unorganised sector and informal employment are substantial in both manufacturing and services, with the share of informal employment in non-agriculture being estimated at 85.6 per cent in 2009–10 (Mehrotra et al. 2012, 13). Over the past three decades the share of the unorganised sector/informal work has remained significant and even increased as a proportion of the economy. While there has been a reduction in the absolute number as well as the percentage of workers in agriculture, new work has largely been generated in the informal economy. Growth in the organised modern sector has been in terms of GDP rather than employment.[5] The processes of economic growth and globalisation have generated new forms of informality, with an increase in the share of contractual and piece rate workers within the formal sector. As Ela Bhatt argues, there are several economies existing simultaneously even within one product market: "the vendor with a basket of fruits on her head moving in the streets, selling from door to door; the vendor with a push cart; the small corner store or kiosk; and the large supermarket exist because they are part of several mini-economies" (Bhatt 2006:4).

Taking into account this complex economic context, this chapter begins with a discussion of three alternative approaches to the relationship between formal education (as provided in schools and universities), the realities of India's economic structure and associated labour market policies and employment programme interventions. The first of these approaches is what could be called the "conventional view" which is the basis of structured learning today. A second approach focuses on training and skills development. A third and more radical view seeks to alter the basic pedagogy of education. The final section concludes with some thoughts on how a more equitable structure for both education and employment in India might be pursued.

Education and work: the conventional view

Several decades ago, India's first Minister for Education and independence movement leader Maulana Abul Kalam Azad noted that "[u]nfortunately, the one goal of those who seek higher education in our country seems to be to secure Government service" (The Publications Division Ministry of Information and Broadcasting 1954, 5). Here Azad refers to the conventional view that education, or structured learning, "prepares" individuals, allocates them to various classifications of persons and knowledge, and defines who has access to valued positions in society. In broader terms, this view sees the role of education as the transformation of society through the creation of new classes of personnel with new types of authoritative knowledge (Meyer 1977). Such an understanding of the allocative/legitimating role of education motivates the search for the type of formal employment that is seen as the outcome of successful educational achievement. Implicit in this view is the assumption that there is a free market that allocates people to jobs. However the Indian reality is more complicated, and access to formal employment opportunities as a result of educational achievement is limited. Many jobs require fluency in English, and only some schools are capable of imparting this skill. Furthermore, caste-based labour market discrimination persists and gendered social norms continue to influence access to jobs. To the extent that "market clearing" occurs, solutions emerge through the sustained presence of an enormous diversity within the education system, corresponding to unequal outcomes in the work space that are marginally moderated through policies designed to reduce inequality through formal policies of reservation and affirmative action. Those from weaker economic backgrounds find themselves in poorer learning environments and thus screened out of a range of employment opportunities (Ramachandran 2014). Empirical data demonstrate stratification within the schooling system and that families who can afford better schooling access the higher quality schools. The poorest households find themselves effectively allocated the weakest schools. Inequality in schooling translates into employment opportunities and outcomes, even while reservation policies do modify this to some extent. Equality in educational quality across all schools might change the composition of those who qualify for regular jobs, but the lack of such jobs overall will continue to be a constraint.

The association of modern formal education with full-time regular employment in industry and services dates back to the colonial period, when educating Indians to run offices and factories was the main objective behind British investment in education. While there has been enormous expansion in the number of colleges and universities since independence – in 1950–51, there were just 30 universities and 695 colleges in India; In 2010–11 there were 564 universities and 31,324 colleges – there has been significant "degree devaluation" and erosion of the integrity of educational credentials (Singh 2006). Enrolments in higher education have been rising at an annual average rate of growth of five per cent, around two and a half times the rate of population growth. Alongside rapid expansion in the education sector the slow growth of employment, particularly of salaried employment, is striking and has led to an ever-increasing gap between job seekers and employment opportunities (Singh 2006). The proportion of formal wage employees as a percentage of all wage employees was 13.2 per cent in 2000 and 16.3 per cent in 2012. Over the same period, however, the share of formal employment in the organised sector fell from 63 per cent to just 49 per cent (Ghose 2014).

The belief that regular, formal employment for all adult citizens is a feasible policy goal is rooted in theories that argue that the process of economic development will necessarily lead to the transition of labour from traditional into modern sectors where the nature of work will tend to be regular and secure. The idea of a "standard employment relationship" remains attractive and the persistence of informality in the midst of rapid economic development is still viewed with some disbelief.[6] The International Labour Organisation (ILO) has started some projects seeking a way out of economic informality, a quest that leads to attempts to identify what factors would help to increase the employment-intensity of new job creation in the private sector.[7] Encouraging formalisation of micro and small enterprises is now a target under Goal 8 of the new Global Sustainable Development Goals: to promote employment and decent work for all. Cross country data fuels expectations that the worst forms of involuntary informal work will be replaced either by voluntary entrepreneurship or by the introduction of regular wage work. In their global study, Gindling and Newhouse (2014) found that while 70 per cent of workers in low income countries are own-account or unpaid employees, in high income countries only 10 per cent of workers fall into this group. The study showed that self-employed workers who are not suited to self-employment find work as regular wage employees as countries develop. On the basis of their data Gindling and Newhouse conclude that with economic development, the quality of work opportunities improves and that this historical experience in developed economies can be expected to be duplicated in developing economies.[8]

Limitations of the conventional approach

It is possible that when the educational curricula and socialisation processes continue to be directed towards a narrow range of known formal occupations, and less value is placed on the ways in which education can equip persons to alter, amend or improve their existing sources of livelihood, the result may be disempowerment. In India, the introduction of the Right to Education Act 2005 and the expansion of access to primary education has meant that there are now many more potential aspirants to formal work. When formal work is not available, people move into various forms of self-employment. As Ghose has pointed out, it is only the educated and the well-off who can afford to record their employment status as "unemployed and seeking work". This is demonstrated in the unemployment rate of persons with no schooling: 0.4 in 2000 and 0.5 in 2012. The unemployment rate of persons with tertiary education was 10.5 in 2000 and 8.0 in 2012 (Ghose 2014). For a small percentage of urban, well-educated persons, the availability of better jobs may have increased – urban areas accounted for 57.2 per cent of the growth of employment between 1999/2000 and 2011/12, although only 31 per cent of the population are urban dwellers (ILO 2013). As shown in a study by Amman Madan (2013), for those located elsewhere, education may lead to dissonance, even disempowerment. The schooled villager who is unable to obtain middle-class work in towns and returns to the village becomes a new structural player, a member of a new status group. This produces some dissonance within older social structures, as the process of socialisation through schooling seems to make people less amenable to traditional roles and more oriented towards commercial exchanges. The formal education process has long been understood to facilitate processes of socialisation, and qualification and role allocation that assign people to particular types of employment. When the schooling process distances people from their family environment but leaves them unable to access regular work in the formal sector, their return to the available sources of livelihood is often accompanied by a sense of disappointment and even disempowerment.

It should be noted here that there are also caste, community and gender differences that produce a highly nuanced relationship between education and employment in the Indian context. Gendered social norms mean that the work-related outcomes of education are likely to be different for men and women, sometimes in unexpected ways. The common assumption is that certain types of work are appropriate to women, and given parental pressures, social norms and workplace expectations, this acts to keep the occupational segregation sharp and relatively unchanged. However, there is some evidence that this may be changing in places where new work opportunities are being generated.

In a Mumbai-based study, Munshi and Rosenzweig (2006) showed that girls from working class castes who were previously not part of any labour market networks may be making full use of new employment opportunities, while boys from the same caste groups continued to be channeled into occupations similar to their fathers, due to the strength of male labour market networks. Similar observations have been made in regard to fishing communities, where boys are inducted into the traditional occupation at a young age, while girls acquire higher levels of educational qualifications making them well placed to take up new work opportunities. The emerging disparities between school and occupational choice of boys and girls could threaten the viability of arranged marriages within castes/sub castes. In this situation, wider social changes such as marriage outside one's caste, out-migration and increased exposure to the modern economy are likely to reduce the strength of old caste-based networks and hence, over time, the observed gendered outcomes. Thus there is one set of influences that tend to restrict or limit the ability of girls to use their educational qualifications to enter and be retained in the workforce and another that may be giving them greater freedom in this regard as compared to boys.

Achievement and merit are two concepts that are central to the view that education is a means of upward mobility in work and life more generally. However, they can also operate as "a gloss over less easily recognisable divisions which obstruct those same principles which merit claims to defend" (Madan 2007, 3048). The discourse of merit is particularly problematic, Madan argues, because it "legitimises striving and hope while at the same time existing in highly unequal realities of opportunity" (p. 3044).

While a proportion of the educated are able to access regular jobs with the much coveted standard employment relationship, the goals of an education-for-employment approach ought to be to facilitate access for all citizens, or at least the large majority, to decent work and the associated benefits of a minimum wage, safe working conditions and access to basic social security. However, the recent employment picture in India shows that an overwhelming majority of workers, 82.2 per cent in 2011–12, remained part of the unorganised sector (ILO 2013:3). And while employment in the organised sector increased between 2009–10 and 2011–12, 85 per cent of the increase was due to the expansion of informal work in the organised sector. Overall, in 2012–13, the share of total employment represented by regular wage and salaried workers was 15.6 per cent (17.7 for men and 10.1 for women), while the unemployment rate stood at 2.0 per cent (ILO 2013). The characteristics of workers in formal and informal employment are for the most part sharply differentiated, with the better educated, urban, middle class, and predominantly male workers being employed formally and the less well-educated, rural, working class and predominantly female workers employed informally.

The limitation of the conventional approach to education is that the linearity anticipated by the curriculum is only partially realised in practice. For those who do not go on to higher education, and even for many of those who do, the curriculum and its accompanying socialisation effects do not provide students with the required confidence to seek new pathways for livelihood.[9] Active social learning is essential to enhance the relevance of this approach to social realities. Within the mainstream education system there have been many efforts to improve and adapt the curriculum, for example the activity-based learning model pioneered in Tamil Nadu. However, in general it does appear that mainstream, well-established structures, through their emphasis on appropriate procedures and norms of engagement, tend to inhibit active social learning.[10] As we see in the information technology sector, there are many examples of people with low formal educational qualifications employed in new forms of work that apply technology to the creation of new products and services.

Training and skills development

Skill development has been accorded a high priority in Indian education over the last few years. The National Policy on Skill Development (2009) is premised on the understanding that "skills and knowledge are the driving forces of economic growth and social development for any country. Countries with higher and better levels of skills adjust more effectively to the challenges and opportunities in the world of work".[11] Most of the discourse on skills is oriented to the labour market, and the question of whether or not skills are an integral part of education. The school curriculum remains oriented to higher education, and not to the acquisition of skills. In contrast, the expectation in many other countries is that the educational process will impart the skills needed for work and there is little emphasis on on-the-job training or separate skills development training. The National Vocational Education Qualifications Framework (NVEQF), discussed below, is an attempt to strengthen skills development within schools.

In India, most of the effort directed towards skilling focuses on those who are out of school. According to the National Policy: "the target group for skill development comprises all those in the labour force". This excludes those who are positioned within the education system on a full time basis. Skills development can focus on linking training to the projected employment requirements of high growth sectors, the approach that lies at the core of the Skills Development Initiative in India. This initiative sets an ambitious skills development target of 500 million skilled persons (or approximately 37 per cent of the population) by 2022. It has been developed in response to the observed inability of many graduates to translate educational qualifications into work, leading to high unemployment rates among educated youth. For example, 40 per cent of graduate job seekers on the live register in 2009 were arts graduates, while at the same time industry reports a shortage of suitably skilled and qualified workers. Skills training attempts to bridge these gaps, enabling a matching of education and training with the jobs available.[12] The need for both generic and specific skills is recognised, including personal and problem solving skills (Khare 2012). This approach has led to many projections around future employment gaps in fast growing sectors, and the development of programmes that could fill these gaps. Historically, Technical and Vocational Education and Training (TVET) in India has been state driven and supply led. A major criticism has been its weak market responsiveness. To address this, the Vocational Training Improvement Project will upgrade 400 Industrial Training Institutes (ITI) into Centres of Excellence with World Bank assistance, and another 100 with domestic resources. The active co-operation of industry is essential to the success of the programme. However industry experts point out that there is very high attrition (estimated at 100 per cent in the business processing operations and retail sectors), which reduces the incentive for employers to invest in skills development programmes (Brookings India 2014).

The Skill Development Initiative Scheme of the Ministry of Labour and Employment (MOLE) that was begun in 2005–6 uses a Modular Employable Skills approach targeting early school leavers and existing workers with priority being given to those above the age of 14 years who have experienced child labour. The scheme develops the curriculum content in close consultation with industry, micro enterprises, state governments, experts and academia, and aims to provide employable skills to school leavers, existing workers and ITI graduates. Existing skills can also be tested and certified under this scheme. Over 650 courses have been approved.[13] Training can also be offered as a way of upgrading existing skills in current occupations. The STEP-UP programme, under the Ministry of Housing and Urban Poverty Alleviation, targets the urban population below the poverty line, and offers training in a variety of service, business and manufacturing activities as well as in local skills and crafts.[14] Services such as construction, carpentry, plumbing, electrical equipment and manufacturing low-cost building materials are included. The current annual target under STEP-UP is 200,000, of which about 150,000 are expected to secure wage/salaried employment and 50,000 to take up self-employment. The National Rural Livelihood Mission launched in 2009–10 seeks mainly to encourage micro-enterprises, with some placement-based skills training. There are also older schemes for upgrading skills (for example, the Support to Employment and Training (STEP) scheme of the Ministry for Women and Child Development, which was begun in 1986[15]). It can be noted that all these schemes target those who are not currently in education, and who come from economically weaker sections of the population.

The Ministry of Human Resource Development (MHRD) approaches the question of skills through vocational education. It is currently developing a National Vocational Education Qualifications Framework (NVEQF) starting from Class 9, which will set common principles and guidelines for a nationally recognised qualification system covering schools, vocational education institutes and institutes of higher education. It is intended that students will have the scope for vertical and horizontal mobility with multiple entry and exits. The NVEQF also seeks a close partnership with the industry/potential employers at all stages, starting from the identification of courses, content development, training and provision of resource persons, assessment, accreditation, certification and placement.[16] As such, the NVEQF is attempting to build an interface between education and the labour market (IAMR 2012).

As this survey indicates, there are at present a large number of skills development programmes spread across different ministries, with the biggest efforts stemming from MOLE and MHRD. Mostly, skills development is associated with poverty alleviation efforts, and not seen as a part of the education system. However MHRD is trying to address employability and work opportunities for current students through the NVEQF, a strategy that seeks to address the basic difficulty noted in the previous section, the current linearity of the education system. Ideally, a well-functioning NVEQF would break down the current sharp divide between education and training. Singh points out that "although it is commonplace to refer to 'education' in terms of activities aimed at acquiring general knowledge, attitudes and values, and the term 'training' to the acquisition of occupational or job-related skills, the division needs to be seen as a purely analytical one as the two are interrelated dimensions within the domain of learning" (Singh 2000, 607). However, equivalence between vocational and general education will only be achieved when the social status and economic potential of, say, a degree in plumbing is similar to that of a degree in economics.

Limitations of the skilling approach

The test of the skills approach lies primarily in its ability to translate acquired certification into jobs. Whether the focus is on learning new skills or on upgrading existing skills, skilling by itself is insufficient unless it is supported by the creation of employment through the development and expansion of enterprises (Brookings India 2014). Horizontal and vertical movements within and across the vocational and general educational streams also need to be enhanced.

Assessments of previous interventions have not been very favourable. For example, an Operational Research Group (ORG) evaluation of a scheme designed to enhance the development of vocational skills through secondary education in 1996 found several problems, including a lack of co-ordination between departments, a shortage of personnel (as there was uncertainty about the longevity of the scheme, full-time staff were not being appointed and part time teachers were inexperienced and lacking in industry knowledge), no in-service training, and, most significantly, only 28 per cent of the Vocational Education pass-out students were employed/self-employed (NCERT 2007, 100). The NVEQF and the MES approaches are yet to be tested in this regard. Programmes such as STEP, or the encouragement of micro enterprise through micro credit given to women's self-help groups, are focused on self-employment. A large proportion of those with skills certification are likely to end up self-employed and not in wage or salaried employment. This is significant, because while a percentage of small-scale self-employed persons may develop into successful entrepreneurs, most are likely to remain at subsistence levels. According to the transnational study by Gindling and

Newhouse (2014), the proportion of workers who are, or have the potential to be, successful entrepreneurs is around 10 per cent, irrespective of income levels and country.

The skills approach complements, rather than substitutes for, the conventional education approach, offering alternative pathways to those who drop out, or select out, of the mainstream. But the large majority of those who acquire a skills certification are likely to remain in the informal economy as self-employed workers. The question, then, is whether the informal economy environment into which they graduate is a supportive one that encourages and enables small enterprise.[17] Advocacy for the rights of informal workers, recognising the reality that the large majority is likely to remain in the unorganised sector of work for the foreseeable future, leads to a focus on improving the conditions for workers in unorganised enterprises. This mainly involves expanding entitlements to social security benefits and/or minimum wage legislation and greater public investment in public infrastructure used by the poor and informal workers.

There are also non-economic barriers that can constrain employment outcomes for people with acquired skills. Gowda (2011) points out that the hair and beauty industry, which was worth Rs 6,900 crores in 2008 (approximately USD$1.4 billion), is estimated to attract Rs 98,500 crores in 2020 (USD$20.5 billion). Notwithstanding this rapid expansion, barbers with many years of experience continue to lack access to economic capital or the fluency in English that would support enterprise development. Class and caste barriers also remain pervasive obstacles. The Self-Employed Women's Association (SEWA) in Ahmedabad found that women who had been trained as masons were still unable to negotiate with male builders, engineers, supervisors and clients on their own. What was required was the formation of a co-operative of trained and organised women construction workers capable of building linkages with the market.[18]

The skills training programmes being offered under the Skill Development Initiative largely focus on low-end occupations. With services being the most rapidly growing sector, much of the work created so far has been in organised retail. While the salary levels are marginally higher than in traditional informal work, organised retail also delivers higher, white collar status for workers. However it is a moot point whether or not it meets the expectations of youth for either educational or occupational mobility.[19] Just as the developed world casts its shadow on the formal economy, the formal economy continues to hover over the informal economy and to represent the aspirations of those who are outside it.

Building a work-centred pedagogy

Informality is a dominant feature of the Indian economy and it is unlikely to disappear in the foreseeable future. It must, therefore, be allowed to influence and shape the education system. Policies that encourage formalisation of the economy are desirable and every effort to improve the quality of jobs needs to be made. Yet many small enterprises and groups of workers will continue to remain informal.[20] With the expansion of the education system more and more young educated people are entering the labour market. However, as noted earlier, the nature of this education may be at odds with the economic structure and the opportunities that are available or are likely to emerge in the future. One important aspect of this dissonance is the low value given to manual labour.

Mahatma Gandhi argued that "[t]he brain must be educated through the hand" (NCERT 2007, 1) and proposed a work-centred pedagogy. Under the Gandhian proposal of *Nai Talim* active participation in work becomes the medium of knowledge acquisition, the development of values, and skills formation. Considerable thought has gone into the question of how the worlds of work and education could be better integrated and change the current situation where the pedagogic role of productive work is not integrated into the school curriculum. Educationists have discussed this approach since independence, with K.M. Munshi, freedom fighter and educationist, arguing that education in urban areas, both at the primary and the secondary level, should include technical and vocational training, so that every student spends part of his or her educational time in practical training with registered artisans. In this way vocational education would be woven into the educational pattern of India (The Publications Division Ministry of Information and Broadcasting 1954, 26). The Position Paper of the National Focus Group on Work and Education outlined what might be the main features of this approach in a contemporary context (NCERT 2007). These include the understanding that the knowledge base, social insights and skills of all children (including those excluded from formal education) in relation to their habitat, natural resources and livelihoods can be deployed as a source of strength and dignity within schools. Centrally prescribed textbooks could be replaced by a library of resource materials, so that the path to knowledge becomes "entirely open-ended, non-linear and contextual". Under this approach, individual schools or clusters of schools would have operational autonomy within a defined national framework. Skills development would therefore be correlated with knowledge acquisition and the building of values, rather than being viewed as an isolated objective.

The enabling conditions required to realise a work-based pedagogy, as stated by the position paper, include a common school system with non-negotiable minimum infrastructural, curricular and pedagogic norms for all schools, including private schools. The paper points out that there is considerable knowledge of how a work-based pedagogy works in practice, derived from innovative efforts throughout the country. Among the examples mentioned are the experiences and methods used by Digantar, Jaipur; four Nai Talim institutions in Gujarat; Uttarakhand Seva Nidhi's environmental education programme; artisans and farmers as "'honorable teachers" as part of the Lokshala process of Bharat Jan Vigyan Jatha; Sumavanam in Andhra Pradesh; Jeevanshalas of the Narmada Bachao Andolan; Kishore Bharati in Madhya Pradesh; Adharshila School in District Badwani, and Vigyan Ashram in District

Pune, among others. The paper argues that incremental implementation does not work, and that one of the reasons why *Nai Talim* did not gain formal status was because the leaders of that movement did not engage with or attempt to transform the mainstream education system. Moreover, curricular reforms cannot be de-linked from structural changes in the school system. The paper also noted that there was likely to be strong opposition to the proposed changes, both by marginalised groups who see education as a pathway to formal work, and by the elite who sees this type of reform as a backward step that would constrain student educational achievement.

In this approach, education plays an important role in bringing about a more equal and more open work environment. However, making a work-centred education a reality calls for several major shifts, including an educational perspective that sees learning as a lifelong process open to all types of educative influences, and school learning that places ever-stronger emphasis on enhancing the value of, and of learning from, the immediate environment. Such "localisation" of knowledge would hopefully forestall the kind of disempowerment noted in Madan's study (2013), enabling each locality to develop its own active learning processes, underpinned by the required financial support and intellectual space implicit in this type of approach. While there are good pedagogical reasons for a single curriculum, the ability of the teacher to develop and modify basic concepts according to each locale is essential. Teaching also needs to seek to impart the power of critical thought applied to the immediate environment and to build the capacity to negotiate with, rather than simply reject, traditional practices and norms. Only in this way will there be sustainable change in inequitable norms, opening education up to multiple pathways and valuing different life situations and choices, rather than generating the single aspiration of a regular job at the end of the tunnel.

Limitations of the work-centred approach

Despite its path-breaking analysis of the problem itself, the NCERT position paper has so far produced little in the way of change. Upscaling from the small experiments this approach has generated remains a problem. But perhaps the major limitation in the current situation is the absence of any sustained thinking about how these ideas could be effectively translated into a different pre-existing educational practice. A large part of the difficulty in changing or re-orienting the education system is precisely that it consists of a large bureaucracy and many specialised agencies, making transformation in the attitudes and orientations of all its stakeholders extraordinarily difficult. The fact that the ordinary people who are the users of these services are likely to resist such changes makes it all the more so.

Looking ahead

From a policy perspective, the biggest challenge facing educational reform is that of addressing the current rigidities in both the education and work environments so as to reduce inequality and enhance mobility. The three approaches to education policy discussed above are distinct and yet could also complement one other, if, for instance, a work-centred pedagogy was adopted for primary schools and the NVEQF offered multiple pathways beyond the one laid out in the conventional system. One commonality in all three approaches discussed above is that each visualises a single uniform system across the country. Whether it is the NVEQF, or the NCERT paper on work-centred pedagogy, the emphasis is on integrating reformist ideas into the government system so that they apply to all schools and students and across all parts of India. The possibility of a patchwork of many different strategies, developed in different contexts but sharing the same goals of equity, inclusiveness, and quality within and through education, remains unexplored.

Similarly, the existing employment policy does not adequately emphasise the need for a context-specific response. It is generally felt that policy goals set at a national or even international level cannot be achieved without large scale action. A uniform approach appears to make implementation and monitoring easier, but, as I have outlined above, it is unlikely to meet the challenges posed by a highly heterogeneous economy dominated by informality and social stratification.

To date, the approach known as "best practice-replication and upscaling" or transferring best practices across or within countries has had only limited success. The template that is upscaled or replicated may be technically accurate but lacking the human motivation and innovating capacity of the original best practice. There is a need for bottom-up and evolutionary change processes to shift social norms and established ways of working, and these are less amenable to codification and replication. This means that the effort to bring about nation-wide change from the top may need to be re-considered. Instead of seeking uniformity and total transformation (whether through the NVEQF framework or the work-centred pedagogy approach) a more promising way forward would be to encourage, not suppress, multiple experiments in educational reform, both within and outside the formal education sector. Similarly, existing work patterns and enterprises need to be recognised as the basis for sustained economic growth, with education and innovation strengthening and not rejecting the prevalent informality of the Indian economy.

The challenge, then, is for India to develop a different approach to upscaling, one which emphasises the sharing of knowledge and experience but which leads to innovation rather than replication. Evaluation of these new interventions will be crucial and must be designed to assess how effectively a worker's social status and geographical location interact with the economic and political context to promote education and employment. Inspiring examples of educational curriculum and learning processes that successfully bridge the worlds of education and work must be publicised and used to promote further innovation in different contexts. The challenge is to encourage creativity and continuous innovation, not only to seek to replicate models that have been successful in other contexts. This is one way we can challenge our outdated and inflexible educational architecture.

Notes

1 An earlier version of this chapter was published by the *Journal of Educational Planning and Administration*, Vol.XXIX, No. 2, April 2015, pp. 121–135. We thank the editor for permission to develop the chapter in this volume.

2 I would like to thank an anonymous reviewer and Prof N.V. Verghese for very helpful comments on earlier drafts of this chapter. I am also grateful to Mike Jackson, Lalit Pande and Bhoomika Joshi for reading and commenting. Needless to say none of the above bears any responsibility for the product itself. I also thank participants at the Research Roundtable on The Indian Employment Challenge: Determinants, Dimensions and Dynamics, organised by the Institute of South Asian Studies (ISAS), the National University of Singapore and the Department of Political Economy, University of Sydney, at ISAS on February 25–26, 2014, for comments on an earlier version presented there.

3 See http://www.labour.gov.in/upload/uploadfiles/files/BackgroundNoteOn_NEP_16June2014%20FINAL.pdf

4 The organised sector consists of enterprises with 10 or more workers using power, or 20 or more without power; the unorganised sector consists of those enterprises falling below this cut-off. The organised–unorganised definitions refer to type of enterprise. Formal–informal refers to type of employment. The NCEUS (2008) defines informal workers as follows: "Unorganised/informal workers consist of those working in the unorganised sector or households, excluding regular workers with social security benefits, and the workers in the formal sector without any employment and social security benefits provided by the employers" (GOI 2008).

5 Mehrotra et al. (2012) point out that employment elasticity has declined from 0.44 to 0.01 since the early 2000s. This, they argue, is evidence of "jobless growth".

6 The "standard employment relationship" can be defined as full-time, continuous employment in which the employee works at the employer's premises or under the employer's supervision. An employment contract specifying a fixed duration, standardised working hours/weeks and minimal social security is also part of a regular job.

7 For "Way Out of Informality" projects in South Asia, see http://www.ilo.org/newdelhi/whatwedo/projects/WCMS_211687/lang---en/index.htm and http://www.ilo.org/wcmsp5/groups/public/---asia/---ro-bangkok/---sro-new_delhi/documents/meetingdocument/wcms_216487.pdf

8 It is of course true that informality persists in developed countries and that it has been increasing. However the scale and nature is still very different from the situation in developing countries.

9 Maxine Berntsen notes that "[t]he basic problem with the Standard 10 examination is that despite the fact that only a small percentage of students go on to higher secondary school and college, the curriculum is designed exclusively for that small number. According to my estimates [in Maharashtra], of the cohort of children who enter (or should enter) school in the first standard, only 14 per cent pass the public examination at the end of Standard 10. Thus 86 per cent of the students are lost along the way. Of the 14 per cent remaining, the number of those who actually go on to college is, of course, much smaller." (NCERT 2007, 52)

10 For example, in the area of policy research, there is greater experimentation and more grounded social science research taking place within smaller, non-mainstream NGOs than many mainstream organisations. This is partly because of the freedom from disciplinary constraints enjoyed by NGOs, and partly because of their commitment to social relevance (see Sudarshan 2009).

11 http://labour.nic.in/upload/uploadfiles/files/Policies/NationalSkillDevelopment PolicyMar09.pdf
12 See, for example, Planning Commission (2011).
13 http://www.dget.nic.in/mes/index.htm
14 http://mhupa.gov.in/w_new/STEP-UP-OperationalGuidelines-2009-2010.pdf
15 http://wcd.nic.in/stepnew.pdf
16 http://mhrd.gov.in/voc_eduu
17 For a discussion of Ghana's skills development policies and the lack of investment in supporting its informal economy, see Palmer (2007).
18 *Rachaita – Synergizing the Strength of Women Construction Workers* (Brochure). See also www.sewarachaita.org
19 This issue needs to be researched more carefully. See Sudarshan (2012).
20 See the discussion on comprehensive but context-specific approaches to formalisation at http://wiego.org/informal-economy/rethinking-formalization-wiego-perspective

References

Bhatt, Ela. 2006. "Cities are People." Paper presented at the WIEGO colloquium "World Class Cities and the Urban Informal Economy: Inclusive Planning for the Working Poor", Durban, South Africa, April. http://wiego.org/sites/wiego.org/files/resources/files/Bhatt_Cities_are_People_2006.pdf

Brookings India. 2014. *India's Skilling Challenges: Moving Ahead*

Brookings India: New Delhi. http://brookings.in/indias-skilling-challenges-moving-ahead/

Ghose, Ajit K. 2014. "Employment in a Time of High Growth: Clearing up a Few Basic Misconceptions about the Nature of Unemployment and Underemployment in India." *Business Standard*, February 15. http://www.business-standard.com/article/opinion/ajit-k-ghose-employment-in-a-time-of-high-growth-114021501132_1.html

Gindling, T. H., and David Newhouse. 2014. "Self-Employment in the Developing World." *World Development* 56: 313–331.

Gowda, Chandan. 2011. "Barbers and Hairstylists." *Hindu Magazine*, August 21.

IAMR. 2012. *A Proposed National Qualifications Framework for Vocational Education for India.* [IAMR Occasional Paper No.4/2012] New Delhi: Institute of Applied Manpower Research, Government of India. http://www.iamrindia.gov.in/proposed.pdf

ILO. 2013. *India Labour Market Update.* Geneva: ILO Country Office for India. http://www.ilo.org/wcmsp5/groups/public/---asia/---ro-bangkok/---sro-new_delhi/documents/genericdocument/wcms_232565.pdf

Khare, Mona. 2012. *Aligning India's Higher Education to the Employability Needs of a Global Economy.* New Delhi: National University of Educational Planning and Administration.

Madan, Amman. 2007. "Sociologising Merit." *Economic and Political Weekly*, July 21, pp. 3044–3050.

Madan, Amman. 2013. "Does Education Really Change Society?" In *Sociology of Education in India: Changing Contours and Emerging Concerns,* edited by Geetha B. Nambissan and Srinivasa Rao, 136–153. New Delhi: Oxford University Press.

Mehrotra, Santosh, Ankita Gandhi, Partha Saha, and Bimal Kishore Sahoo. 2012. *Joblessness and Informalisation: Challenges to Inclusive Growth in India.* [IAMR Occasional Paper No. 9] New Delhi, IAMR.

Meyer, John W. 1977. "The Effects of Education as an Institution." *American Journal of Sociology* 83 (1): 55–77.

Ministry of Information and Broadcasting, 1954. *The Future of Education in India (A Symposium).* The Publications Division, Cottonpet, Bangalore: Government of India and B.B.D. Power Press.

Munshi, Kaivan, and Mark Rosenzweig. 2006. "Traditional Institutions Meet the Modern World: Caste, Gender and Schooling Choice in a Globalizing Economy. *The American Economic Review* 96 (4): 1225–1252.

National Skill Development Policy. 2009. http://skilldevelopment.gov.in/assets/images/NationalSkillDevelopmentPolicyMar09.pdf

NCERT. 2007. *Position Paper of National Focus Group on Work and Education.* New Delhi: National Council of Educational Research and Training.

NCEUS. 2008. *Report on Definitional and Statistical Issues Relating to the Informal Economy.* New Delhi: National Commission on Enterprises in the Unorganised Sector, Government of India.

Palmer, Robert. 2007. "Skills for Work? From Skills Development to Decent Livelihoods in Ghana's Rural Informal Economy." *International Journal of Educational Development* 27 (4): 397–420.

Planning Commission. 2011. *Report of the Working Group on Employment, Planning and Policy for the Twelfth Plan (2012–17).* New Delhi: Government of India.

Ramachandran, Vimala. 2014. *Equity and Quality are Two Sides of the Same Coin in India's School Education.* [NMML Occasional Papers, Perspectives in Indian Development, New Series 23] New Delhi: Nehru Memorial Museum and Library.

Singh, Avinash Kumar. 2006. "Degree Devaluation in Higher Education: Unemployment and Unemployability among the Graduates in India." *Journal of Educational Planning and Administration* 20 (4): 411–428.

Singh, Madhu. 2000. "Combining Work and Learning in the Informal Economy: Implications for Education, Training, and Skills Development." *International Review of Education*, Vol.46, no. 6: 599–620.

Sudarshan, Ratna M. 2009. "Policy Research and Practice in India." http://www.rcuk.ac.uk/RCUK-prod/assets/documents/india/policyresearchandpracticeinindiasundarshan.pdf

Sudarshan, Ratna M. 2012. "National Skills Development Strategies and the Urban Informal Sector: the Case of India." Background paper prepared for the Education for All Global Monitoring Report 2012, UNESCO, Paris http://unesdoc.unesco.org/images/0021/002178/217887e.pdf

Part II

Employment policy in practice

5 Economic growth without employment

The story of Indian manufacturing

Jayan Jose Thomas

In the early 1950s, India launched an ambitious programme of state-led industrialisation. For a newly independent country that had suffered almost two centuries of colonial domination, this was an audacious move. At this time, India's efforts to build scientific and technological capabilities despite the poverty of its population generated much hope, not only within India itself but also among other newly independent countries of the mid-twentieth century. Today, almost seven decades later, India's record with respect to economic growth and development is mixed. Its gross domestic product (GDP), when measured at purchasing power parity (PPP), is the third largest in the world. Also, according to the latest statistics, the Indian economy is the fastest growing of the world's large economies. Yet, it might appear paradoxical that the *Human Development Report 2014* ranks India only 135 out of 187 countries with respect to achievements in human development. Why has India failed to convert its relatively good performance in economic growth into even modest improvements in conditions of living for millions of its poor citizens? Part of the reason lies in the nature of India's economic growth, which has largely been driven by the services sector. At the same time, the performance of the manufacturing and agricultural sectors has been far from impressive. In 2010, manufacturing accounted for only 15 per cent of India's GDP, compared to 30 per cent in China.[1] In 2009–12, the manufacturing sector employed only 53.3 million – less than 12 per cent of India's total workforce of 462 million (Thomas 2012).

At the root of India's developmental challenges is the slow pace of employment generation. Thomas (2014) found that, given the rate of increase in India's working-age population, the workforce employed in industry and services could *potentially* have grown at the rate of 15 million a year between 2004–05 and 2011–12. But the *actual* growth during this period was far slower, around 7 million jobs annually. Almost half of the net increase in non-agricultural employment occurred in construction, a relatively low-wage sector. The contribution of the manufacturing sector to the employment growth during these years was particularly slow, less than a million jobs a year (Thomas 2014; Thomas 2015a).[2]

India's inability to build a manufacturing sector large enough to absorb a substantial part of the country's labour reserves is striking. The problem has its origins in the heady days of Indian planning, when manufacturing was the sector accorded the highest priority in economic development. As is well known, Indian development shifted decisively from a state-led to a market-led path from 1991 onwards. One of the early promises of the market-led economic reforms was that they would stimulate manufacturing employment, as it was thought that India's labour intensive industries stood to gain from exposure to global markets. But the creation of employment opportunities, promised first by India's planners and then in later years by its market-led reformers, failed to eventuate. Given this context, this chapter aims to examine the challenges faced by Indian manufacturing over the years, especially in regard to employment creation.

Indian manufacturing is made up of organised and unorganised (or registered and unregistered) sectors. The organised sector comprises factories that employ more than 10 workers and operate with the aid of electric power, as well as factories that employ more than 20 workers without the aid of electric power. In 2009–10, manufacturing workers belonging to the factory sector numbered 11.3 million and made up 21 per cent of all manufacturing workers. The rest of the manufacturing workforce, 42.2 million, were engaged in small, informal enterprises in the unorganised sector. It is notable that despite its low share of employment, the organised sector contributed 67.6 per cent of India's total manufacturing GDP in 2010–11 (GOI, 2016).

This chapter begins with an examination of the early phase of state-led industrialisation in India. Discussion then moves to an evaluation of "jobless growth" in Indian manufacturing during the 1980s and the impact of the 1991 economic reforms on Indian industry. This is followed by an examination of the major constraints currently facing Indian manufacturing.

Indian planning and capital-intensive industrialisation

When India became independent in 1947, there were steep challenges facing the new nation on the economic front. During the first half of the eighteenth century, before the country was colonised by the European powers, India had been a major manufacturer of handicrafts. However, as the country came under the dominance of British imperialism over the century that followed, Indian handicrafts, unable to compete with factory-produced cloth from Britain, faced annihilation in both the export and domestic markets. Bagchi (1976) points to the steep decline in the share of the workforce engaged in industry in Gangetic Bihar during the nineteenth century as a result of this massive process of deindustrialisation.

Factory-based manufacturing had begun in India in the 1850s, with the setting up of cotton- and jute-textile factories in Bombay and Calcutta respectively. Despite this early start, India's modern industries stagnated under the discriminatory trade, tariff and industrial policies of the British colonial regime.

The growth of agriculture, and especially food grain production, was extremely sluggish during the first half of the twentieth century. One of the driving factors behind the nationalist struggle for Indian independence was the setback faced by the country's economy during the colonial period. It was these economic circumstances that led India to inaugurate state-directed efforts to promote modern industrialisation immediately after independence. Planning for industrialisation was carried out under the leadership of Jawaharlal Nehru, India's first Prime Minister. The Second Five-Year Plan, which, according to Chakravarty, "reflected a major watershed in India's economic thinking" (1987, 8), provided the blueprint for the industrialisation strategy. It emphasised the building of "heavy" or capital-intensive industries that were capable of substituting imports with domestically produced machinery.

Given its relative abundance of labour reserves and relative deficiency of capital, India's choice of capital-intensive techniques for its industrialisation strategy went against the theory of comparative advantage. The economic justification for this strategy had its roots in the development debates of the 1950s, which identified low rates of savings as the biggest constraint facing post-colonial countries in their early stages of development. Low rates of savings translate into shortage of capital stock in relation to the availability of employable persons, which prevents the introduction of new technologies in the economy (Chakravarty 1987, 9–10). As a result, India's Second Five-Year Plan envisaged the allocation of larger shares of investment to capital-goods-producing industries or to the building of machines that produce other machines. According to the model, this would result in a higher savings rate on the margin and a higher rate of growth in output.

India's industrial policies during the early years of planning (1950s and 1960s) accorded primary importance to the public sector in many areas, especially in infrastructure building. Trade and tariff barriers were introduced to protect domestic industries from foreign competition. Investments by the private sector were subject to a wide range of regulations, such as controls on the creation of production capacities, on prices, and on the import of machinery. At the same time, private entrepreneurs received financial assistance through public-sector financial institutions (Chandrasekhar 1988). But even as India's policy makers envisaged revolutionary changes in the sphere of industry, the country's agrarian base and social settings remained largely untouched by the planning process. For example, attempts at land reform met with little success in most parts of India, making rural inequality a persistent feature of the Indian political economy. The unfinished agrarian transformation was in many respects responsible for the slow growth of Indian agriculture during the post-independence period.[3] In this context, India's planned industrialisation was only partially successful. Drawing on Keynesian, Kaleckian and Marxian theories, a number of scholars at this time attributed India's industrial stagnation from the mid-1960s mainly to the slow expansion of domestic demand arguing that the slow growth of demand was a consequence of the unequal distribution of incomes and the sluggish growth of agricultural incomes in the country (Patnaik 1972; Mitra 1977; Chakravarty 1979).

There are many ways in which a slow growing agricultural sector can become a barrier to industrial growth. To begin with, as agriculture employs the bulk of India's working population, slow agricultural growth depresses the incomes of the majority. Slow progress in agricultural production, especially of food-grains, leads to a rise in inflation, which affects urban workers and landless agricultural workers in particular (Patnaik 1972; Mitra 1977). Furthermore, a slowdown in agriculture reduces the production of raw materials for industries such as textiles and food-processing. Skewed distribution of incomes also adversely affects industrial growth, mainly by preventing firms from exploiting economies of scale. In a situation of high inequality, the demand for consumer durables and luxury goods consumed by a few may grow fast, while the demand for mass-consumption goods, such as textiles, may not (Chakravarty 1979). Patnaik and Chandrasekhar (2007) argue that the inability of the Indian state to impose some measure of "discipline" on capital weakened the state's intervention in industrial development.

At the same time, an equally important alternative explanation for India's industrial growth stagnation, which is based on neoclassical theories, focused on the supply constraints in the economy (Bhagwati and Desai 1970; Ahluwalia 1985). Bhagwati and Desai advanced several criticisms of the country's industrial policy framework. In their view, the licensing regime in particular was ill-designed and concerned itself with excessive detail, slowing down industrial growth (1970).

Growth during the 1980s

After a long phase of stagnation between the mid-1960s and late 1970s, India's industrial growth revived during the 1980s. This revival has been attributed to several factors, including the improvement in public sector investment from the mid-1970s on. Public investment in infrastructure had a positive impact on general productivity and reflected a more pro-business attitude in government (Sen 2007; Kohli 2006; Rodrik and Subramanian 2004). Even so, India's industrial growth during the 1980s has been described as "jobless" growth. That is, despite the acceleration in the growth of factory sector output, factory sector employment during this decade remained stagnant (see Table 5.1 and Figure 5.1). This was because the output-growth acceleration during the 1980s was accompanied by important changes in the structure of the factory sector. On the one hand, capital-intensive industries such as chemicals, petroleum and plastics underwent significant growth. On the other, the factory-based production of cotton and jute textiles suffered a steep decline and thousands of mill workers lost their jobs in Mumbai, Kolkata, Ahmedabad, and other industrial centres. Total organised manufacturing employment in India increased only marginally, by 0.4 million, between 1980–81 and 1991–92. In comparison, an additional 2.6 million factory jobs were created in the country between 1969–70 and 1979–80 (Thomas 2013).

Table 5.1 Net increase in manufacturing employment in India (thousands)

Period	*Organised Sector*	*Unorganised Sector*	*Total Manufacturing*
1982–83 to 1993–94	569	7021	7590
1993–94 to 2004–05	629	12553	13182
2004–05 to 2011–12	4005*	1090	5095

Notes and Sources: *Refers to the period 2004–05 to 2010–11. Data on organised-sector manufacturing is obtained from Annual Survey of Industries. Data on total manufacturing employment is obtained from the National Sample Survey Organisation's Employment and Unemployment Surveys, held in 1983 (38th round), 1993–94 (50th round), 2004–05 (61st round) and 2011–12 (68th round). For more details on data sources and methodology, see Thomas (2012) and Thomas (2014). Net increase in unorganised manufacturing employment is estimated as the net increase in total manufacturing employment minus the net increase in 'organised-sector manufacturing employment.

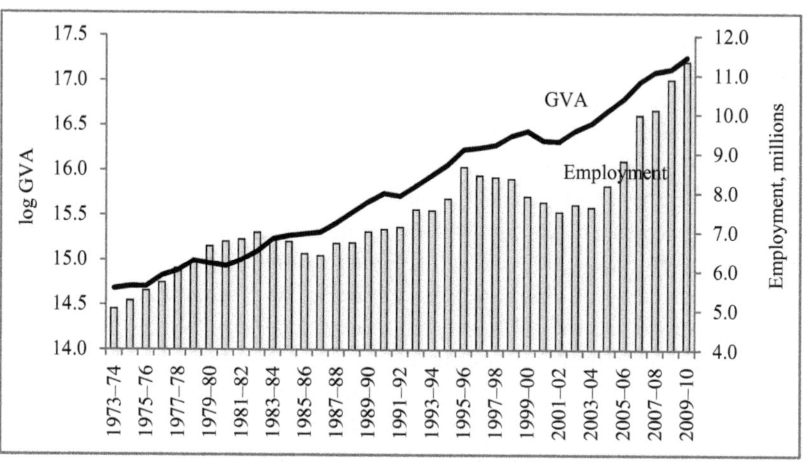

Figure 5.1 Gross value added (in log values) and employment (in millions) in India's factory sector manufacturing[1], 1973–74 to 2009–10.

Source: Annual Survey of Industries, various years.

1 Factory sector manufacturing refers to the sum total for two-digit industry groups from 15 to 36.

In spite of the slow growth of factory or organised manufacturing employment, overall manufacturing employment in India increased by a substantial 7.6 million during the 1980s (Table 5.1). This was largely the result of job creation in the unorganised sector. The major generators of employment during this period were food products, tobacco, wood products, furniture, and also chemical products (Thomas 2012; Thomas 2013). Overall, the growth of non-agricultural employment during the 1980s was relatively fast, especially in the rural areas. This, along with government financed poverty-reduction programmes such as the Integrated Rural Development Programme (IRDP) contributed to a substantial reduction in poverty during this decade (Sen 1996).

Studies of labour rigidity: A critical review

A widespread view in academic and policy circles is that the slow growth of factory employment in India during the 1980s and in later decades was due to rigidity in the country's labour market (Fallon and Lucas 1993; Besley and Burgess 2004; GOI 2013, 42–49). Most academic studies attribute labour market rigidity in India to the Industrial Disputes Act (IDA) of 1947 and its amendments in 1972, 1976 and 1982. With the 1976 amendment, industrial establishments in India employing 300 workers or more were required to obtain government permission to retrench workers or close factories. The 1982 amendment made this requirement applicable to establishments employing 100 or more workers. However, there are grounds to contest this assessment. To begin with, academic studies of labour rigidity have been based almost entirely on the IDA, which is only one of many labour regulations in India. Moreover, the IDA is applicable to only a small segment of India's workforce: 5.5 per cent of all workers and 12 per cent of all hired workers in 1999–2000, according to Pais (2008). It is also well known that more than 90 per cent of India's working population who are in the unorganised sector are not protected by any labour regulations nor covered by social security benefits.

Scholars have also questioned the methodologies used in studies that see labour regulations as responsible for jobless growth (Bhattacharjea 2009). As an example, it is worth examining some of the methodological issues in the study by Besley and Burgess (2004), which is widely quoted and has influenced later academic and policy thinking in this area. Besley and Burgess focused on the amendments made to the IDA – which is a central (or national) piece of legislation – in various Indian states. Besley and Burgess categorised Indian states as "pro-worker", "pro-employer" or "neutral", using an index based on their reading of the various state-level amendments to the IDA. Their econometric investigations revealed that during the 1958–92 period, the "pro-worker" states experienced a relative slowdown in output and employment growth in the organised manufacturing sector. A number of later studies, which were greatly influenced by this methodology, also argued that the IDA was the main factor responsible for the slowdown in industrial growth across the country. However, according to Bhattacharjea,

> Besley and Burgess misinterpreted several of the state-level IDA amendments; assigned identical scores to minor procedural amendments and major changes in job security rules; aggregated incommensurable pro-worker and pro-employer amendments occurring in the same year to give a summary score of +1 or −1 to a state for that year; used a misleading summation of these scores over time (so that a state that passed amendments in different years was assigned a higher score than one that passed the same amendments simultaneously); and ignored hundreds of other labour laws, including some whose provisions overlap with the IDA
>
> (2009, 55).

Besley and Burgess (2004), Fallon and Lucas (1993) and other studies that attributed jobless growth to labour rigidity conveniently overlooked the slow pace of employment growth during the 1980s; in fact, joblessness was restricted to few industries and regions. In absolute numbers, factory employment declined sharply during this decade, in the jute textile industry in West Bengal, and in the cotton textile industries in the states of Maharashtra and Gujarat. However, rather than labour regulations, it was actually a number of structural factors affecting the industry (some of which will be discussed below) that were responsible for the decline of the organised textile-mill industry in India. At the same time, new jobs were added in fairly large numbers during the 1980s in industries such as chemicals and machinery, and in several states, notably Tamil Nadu and Punjab (172,000 and 142,000 respectively) (Thomas 2002). The argument that the IDA discouraged employers from hiring more factory workers flies in the face of such evidence.

Analyses of industrial relations in Maharashtra and Gujarat indicate that the governments in these states were largely unsympathetic to the concerns of workers. It is well documented that in the 18-month long strike in the Mumbai cotton textile industry during 1982–83, mill workers ended up losing their jobs and livelihoods (Chandavarkar 2004; Breman 2004). Nevertheless, in their 2004 study, Besley and Burgess questionably classified Maharashtra and Gujarat along with West Bengal and Orissa as "pro-worker" states, based on the criteria they evolved in their study. In fact, Besley and Burgess' eventual conclusion, that employment growth slowed in the pro-worker states, hinges crucially on the "pro-worker" labels attached to Maharashtra and Gujarat (as they are two of the three states that suffered significant job losses in the factory sector during the period covered by the study). Several later studies analysed industrial growth in India during the post-1990 period using the Besley and Burgess index or following most aspects of the methodology.[4] Bhattacharjea argues that these later studies suffer from the same methodological issues that affect the Besley and Burgess study. In particular, they were "analysing [industrial] performance in the 1990s with reference to a classification of States based on their labour laws as they evolved before 1990" (Bhattacharjea 2007, 23). It is perplexing that despite its many problems, the argument that labour rigidity and tough labour laws constrain India's industrial growth continues to be heard even today.

Industrial growth after the 1990s

India introduced far-reaching economic reform measures from 1991–92 onwards. These reforms virtually eliminated licensing, reduced other regulatory barriers, and deepened the country's trade and financial relations with the rest of the world. External reforms have accelerated during the 2000s, especially since the middle of the present decade. The impact of these reforms on the growth of manufacturing output and employment has been mixed.

India's organised manufacturing sector experienced a sharp acceleration in output and employment growth during the early years of economic reform, from 1991–92 to 1995–96. Nevertheless, the country's organised manufacturing sector, as well as its overall GDP, decelerated between 1996–97 and 2001–02 (see Figure 5.1 and Thomas 2013). The fast growth recorded by manufacturing during the first half of the 1990s was led by a sharp revival in private-sector investment (see Figure 5.2). At the same time, however, as part of the structural adjustment programme, India tried to decrease its public expenditure and fiscal deficit. As a result, public investment as a share of GDP remained at a relatively low level during the whole of the 1990s. Private investment also began to decline from the middle of the 1990s, leading to an overall slowdown in the country's industrial growth (see Figure 5.2).

India's overall GDP growth, and the growth of the organised manufacturing sector in particular, recovered impressively during the early 2000s (see Figure 5.1). And as Figure 5.2 indicates, this growth was led by private corporate investment and exports. Capital- and skill-intensive industries, such as metals, machinery, automobiles and chemicals, recorded extremely fast rates of growth. During this period, segments of Indian manufacturing, such as the pharmaceuticals industry and the design and manufacture of low-cost vehicles, began to make a mark internationally for their specialised skills and capabilities.

With the onset of worldwide economic crisis in 2008, India's manufacturing sector was hit by a slowdown in demand from export markets. In response to the crisis, the authorities launched expansionary monetary and fiscal policies. Banks were encouraged to lend more, especially in the form of housing and automobile loans. These measures had some success in reducing the impact of

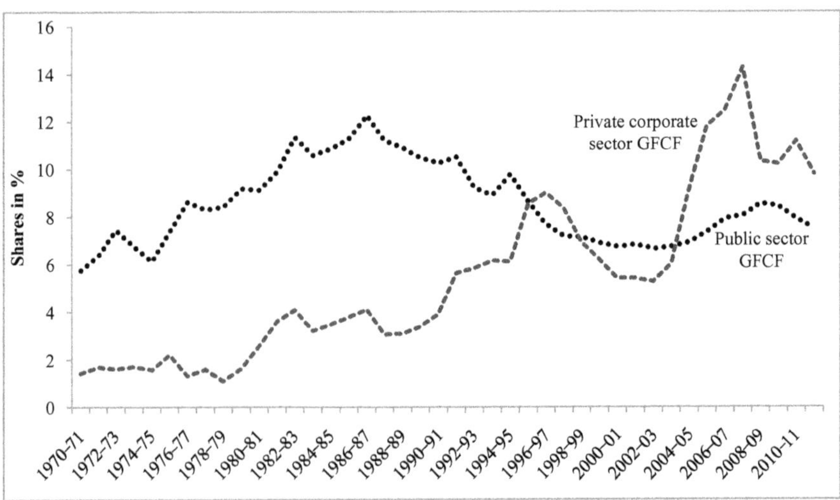

Figure 5.2 Gross fixed capital formation by public and private corporate sectors as % GDP in India, 1970–71 to 2011–12.

Source: National Accounts Statistics, various years.

the global slowdown. However, from 2011–12 onwards, private investment in India slowed, and with this downturn, the country's manufacturing sector entered yet another phase of stagnation from which it is yet to recover (see Figure 5.2). The impact of this industrial growth slowdown has been more adverse in the unorganised sector. As will be discussed below, the growth of employment in India's unorganised manufacturing has been particularly slow since the mid-2000s.

The growth of organised manufacturing employment in India remained stagnant until the middle of the 2000s: only 1.2 million jobs were generated in this sector between 1982–83 and 2004–05. However, since the mid-2000s, there has been a notable turnaround in the growth of employment in India's organised manufacturing, with a rise of 4 million between 2004–05 and 2010–11 (see Table 5.1). At the same time contract workers comprised an overwhelming proportion of the incremental employment in the country's organised manufacturing sector during the 2000s. In other words, employment in India's formal sector manufacturing has increased substantially since the mid-2000s, but this has occurred along with growing informalisation of the manufacturing sector.

The employment growth record of the unorganised sector has been particularly noteworthy. During the first half of the 2000s (1999–2000 to 2004–05), total manufacturing employment in India increased by 9.8 million, the bulk of it in the unorganised sector. Labour-intensive and export-oriented industries such as textiles, garments, leather, footwear, furniture, jewellery and gem cutting accounted for 7.2 million, or more than 70 per cent of the manufacturing employment growth during the first half of the 2000s (Thomas 2012). However, it was these very industries that suffered significant job losses during the late 2000s, particularly in the wake of a slowdown in export demand. Between 2004–05 and 2011–12, overall manufacturing employment in India rose by only 5.1 million, or just 10.6 per cent of the 48 million net addition to non-agricultural employment during the same period. Of the total increase in manufacturing jobs of 5.1 million, an increase of 4 million occurred in the organised sector. This implies that the increase in unorganised sector manufacturing employment in India since the mid-2000s was only 1.1 million, a sharp decline from the growth recorded by this sector during the previous decade (see Table 5.1). In the following paragraphs, I examine the reasons for the particularly poor growth record of India's unregistered manufacturing in recent years.

Not constrained by labour laws

The argument that labour laws have hindered India's industrial growth has become almost irrelevant in the light of recent evidence. As shown above, there has been a recent spurt in employment growth in organised manufacturing, the sector in which labour laws could have potentially discouraged employers from investing. In fact, contract workers or other employees (including employees designated as supervisory staff) who are outside the purview of the labour laws have accounted for 69 per cent of the employment growth in India's organised manufacturing during the 2000s. Contract workers as a proportion of all workers in India's factory sector rose from 19.8 per cent in 1999–2000 to 32.8 per cent in 2009–10. Annavajhula and Pratap (2012) found that contract workers were employed in almost every aspect of production operations and formed 70–80 per cent of all workers in Maruti Suzuki's plants in Gurgaon and Manesar.

The rising share of informal employment, even within the formal organised sector, makes the argument that India's labour markets lack flexibility seem quite unconvincing. In fact, trade union activism has been declining in India since the early 1990s, and labour's bargaining strengths relative to capital have been substantially reduced. With the central and the various state governments in India trying to attract investment, there has also been a growing laxity in the implementation of labour regulations.[5] The number of days lost due to industrial disputes have declined markedly since the mid-1980s. In recent years, lockouts – which are enforced on workers by their employers – have become a far more important source of industrial disputes than strikes, which are work stoppages by employees. It is also worth noting that since the beginning of the 2000s, growth in the real wages of India's factory workers has increasingly been falling behind the growth of labour productivity (Thomas 2013).

It is also notable that between 1999–2000 and 2004–05 women workers accounted for a substantial part of the net increase in manufacturing employment in India (3.9 million out of 9.8 million). The share of women in incremental employment was particularly high in textiles, garments, and gem cutting. On the other hand, 2.9 million out of the 3 million who lost jobs in Indian manufacturing during the second half of the 2000s were also women (Thomas 2012). The sharp rise and the subsequent fall in the number of women manufacturing workers indicates that women form an increasingly substantial proportion of the flexible component of India's manufacturing labour force.

Many of the regulations concerning industry and labour that exist in India today have their origins in laws that were first enacted during the British colonial period (Pais 2008). As such, it is undeniable that these regulations are in urgent need of updating. At the same time, however, there is little evidence to support the argument that labour regulations represent the main constraint on the growth of manufacturing employment in India.

Constraints on Indian manufacturing

In India, the growth of the infrastructure sectors such as electricity, roads, and ports has failed to catch up with the overall pace of economic growth. This has resulted in severe supply-side bottlenecks adversely affecting the growth of the country's manufacturing sector.

Supply-side constraints on Indian manufacturing and the role of public investment

Estimates by the Ministry of Power, for example, show that the energy availability in India during 2011–12 was 857.9 billion units (or kilowatt hours), which was 8.5 per cent less than the energy requirement for the year. Power demand and supply shortages have been reported from every region of India and from a majority of Indian states. In 2011–12, this deficit was 10.5 per cent in Tamil Nadu, 16.7 per cent in Maharashtra, 3.1 per cent in Punjab, and 21.3 per cent in Bihar (CEA, 2012, Annex II). Field research in Coimbatore in Tamil Nadu between 2008 and 2014 also revealed that power shortages have been the most serious constraint on growth in this industrial town since October 2007 (Thomas 2009). As a result of severe restrictions on the use of electricity imposed by the Tamil Nadu state government, several textile and engineering firms in Coimbatore and in other regions of Tamil Nadu were operating at 50 per cent or even less of their production capacities. Supply constraints such as power shortages affect micro and small industries much more than large industries. In Coimbatore, micro and small entrepreneurs were paying Rs. 4.30 or more per unit (or per kilowatt hour) of electricity, but were still experiencing production losses due to power interruptions. At the same time, multinational companies such as Hyundai in Chennai were being offered uninterrupted power supply at cheaper rates as part of agreements signed with the state government (Thomas 2009).

The huge deficit that India faces today in the infrastructure areas is, to a large extent, a result of the sharp fall in public investment in the Indian economy since the 1990s (Rao and Dutt 2006). Gross fixed capital formation (GFCF) in the public sector as a proportion of India's GDP actually declined from 12.3 per cent in 1986–87 to 6.6 per cent in 2002–03. It subsequently increased to 8.5 per cent in 2008–09, before falling again in recent years (see Figure 5.2).

Industrial policies

India's industrial policies in recent years – with respect to bank credit, prices and tariffs, to name just the three important ones – have not been helpful to the growth of the country's manufacturing sector.

Availability and cost of credit

During the pre-1990 years, the targeting of bank credit at agriculture and small-scale industry was an important aspect of India's banking policies. The availability of subsidised credit made sizeable contributions to the growth of small-scale industries, such as, for instance, the garment industry in Tiruppur (Chari 2000). However, the share of agriculture and industry in the total allocation of credit by scheduled commercial banks in India declined during the 1990s. As a proportion of non-food gross bank credit, advances to small-scale industries (SSIs) fell from 15.1 per cent in 1990 to just 6.5 per cent in 2005. The number of SSI sector loan accounts in commercial banks declined from 219 million in 1992 to 93 million in 2005. On the other hand, the share of personal loans and professional services as a proportion of total outstanding bank credit increased from 9.4 per cent in 1990 to 27 per cent in 2005 (RBI 2006, 132–139). Since the mid-2000s, there has been a boom in the allocation of bank credit to large-scale industries, especially in sectors such as power and telecommunications (Nagaraj 2013, 44). Nevertheless, during the second half of the 2000s, the share of small and micro industries as a proportion of total credit disbursed in India remained unchanged, at around 6 per cent (RBI 2012, 76).

Small and micro enterprises have been hit hard by inadequate access to bank credit. According to an NSSO survey of unorganised manufacturing enterprises in 2005–06, 42 per cent of all enterprises identified shortage of capital as a major constraint on growth; 92.2 per cent did not receive any financial assistance, and only 3.6 per cent received loans from institutional sources (NSSO 2007, 30–32). In Coimbatore, access to cheap, institutional credit was extremely difficult for micro enterprises, which had to depend on private banks and private finance companies. The interest rates charged by these private banks were often high; interest rates between 28 per cent and 36 per cent were common (Thomas 2009).

Exchange rates, price fluctuations and their links to capital flows

The gradual liberalisation of India's capital account during the 2000s and the accompanying increase in the inflow of foreign portfolio investments (FPI) have created problems for the country's manufacturing sector. The volatility in FPI flows since the 2000s has led to wide fluctuations in exchange rates, as well as in the prices of several commodities.

The Rupee–Dollar exchange rate appreciated sharply between May 2007 and April 2008. This resulted in a steep decline in the revenues and profits of export-oriented industries such as textiles, garments, leather, and engineering. At the same time, there have also been equally sharp depreciations of the Indian Rupee, such as those that occurred during the second half of 2008 and again during the period from May 2011 to August 2013. During these periods of currency depreciation, imports of machinery and raw materials became costlier. More importantly, many Indian firms, which had availed themselves of foreign-currency loans, incurred heavy losses when they were required to repay their loans in the depreciated rupee. It may also be noted that the volatility in availability and generally high prices of key raw materials such as cotton and steel were major obstacles to the growth prospects of Indian industry during the late 2000s.

Trade liberalisation and rising import intensity of manufacturing

During the 2000s, India reduced the tariffs on the import of several manufactured goods. These reductions mostly came about as a result of the country's commitments to international trade agreements, but they have adversely affected the prospects of India's manufacturing firms, which are already disadvantaged by many supply-side constraints, as noted above. Industrial growth in India since the 2000s has been accompanied by a marked rise in the level of imports, notably of capital goods.

It is significant that the industries that recorded fast rates of growth in imports during the 2000s were machine tools, electrical and non-electrical machinery, electronic and computer goods, and transport equipment. Imports as a share of domestic production have been rising rapidly in these industries, most likely as a result of the reduction in import tariffs. The weighted average of import tariffs in India on capital goods declined from 94.8 per cent in 1991–92 to 28.7 per cent in 1995–96, 23.1 per cent in 2001–02, 9.5 per cent in 2005–06, and just 5.6 per cent in 2009–10.[6]

Industrial growth that is increasingly based on imported components reduces the growth opportunities for domestic industry and depresses the possibility of linkages between the large and the small-scale sectors. Typically, a substantial part of the production of ancillaries and components for the machinery and transport-equipment industries in India has occurred in the small-scale or unorganised sector. With the rise in the import of components, such opportunities for production in the small scale sector are reduced. Indeed, studies have pointed to the growing technological distance separating the organised and unorganised sectors, and to the absence of a complementary relationship between the two (Kathuria, Raj and Sen 2010; Uchikawa 2011).

Demand-side constraints on industrial growth

The slow growth of effective demand, which was the result of low per capita incomes and high inequality in income distribution, has been identified as a key factor behind the deceleration in India's industrial growth since the mid-1960s (Chakravarty 1979). Amsden (1977) attributed the slow growth of the machine tool industry in Taiwan during its formative years to the nature of the demand, which originated from a "large number of low-income machine tool users", in other words, the type of market rather than the market size (218).

Is the Indian industry still constrained by the type, if not the overall size, of the domestic market? The 2009–10 NSSO survey on consumption expenditures revealed extreme disparities in per-capita consumption expenditures between the richest 10 per cent of households and their poor counterparts. For instance, the monthly per capita expenditure on consumer durables in urban areas was Rs. 969 for the 10th decile of households, falling drastically to just Rs. 74 for the 9th decile, and to even smaller amounts for households belonging to the lower deciles.

It is likely that the demand for consumer durables (e.g. furniture) in India is segmented, with the demand from the richest decile of households being fulfilled mainly by the organised sector industries, and to some extent imports. On the other hand, the small scale and unorganised sector enterprises largely cater to the demand from the vast majority of poor households. The market for the unorganised sector industries appears to be constrained by the low purchasing power of individual consumers. As a consequence, unorganised sector industries are likely to be trapped in a cycle of poor quality of production, outdated technologies, and low levels of profitability.

What happened To labour-intensive industries?

It is indeed perplexing that despite being a labour-surplus country, India's labour-intensive industries have not fared well, even after the introduction of market-oriented economic reforms (Kochhar et al. 2006). India's failure to emerge as a major player in textiles is noteworthy, especially given its relatively early start in this industry. In an attempt to understand the reasons behind this failure, this final section examines India's policies towards labour-intensive industries.

According to India's Second Five-Year Plan, the production of consumer goods such as textiles should ideally be carried out in the small scale sector. This, it was expected, would help to alleviate the problem of unemployment. The consumer goods sector was also expected to generate the savings required to sustain capital goods production (Mazumdar 1991). As a result, the government banned the creation of new textile-production capacity in mills from 1950 onwards, favouring instead small scale production in handlooms. There were restrictions on the use of synthetic fibres by mills, and excise duties were imposed on mill-made cloth. The government even discouraged the production of cloth in power looms. According to Mazumdar (1991), government regulations were the main reason for the stagnation in the growth of India's textile industry during the planning era. Technological progress was particularly sluggish, as the expansion of the industry occurred largely through the growth of unlicensed power loom units. At the same time, the slow growth of India's textile industry was mainly due to the low per capita domestic demand for textiles and the specific strategies adopted by the large business houses (Chandrasekhar 1984). As noted earlier, there were widespread closures of composite mills (engaged in both weaving and spinning) in India's cotton textile industry during the 1980s. In subsequent years, while the weaving industry shifted largely to power looms in the decentralised or unorganised sector, the spinning industry producing cotton yarn remained part of the organised sector. The share of the decentralised sector in total cloth production in India rose from 62 per cent in 1980–81 to 97 per cent by 2010–11 (GOI 2013, A-32).

Since the 1990s, there has been a degree of revival in the growth of India's textile and garment industries as a result of the removal of many of the earlier restrictions on the industry and the greater opportunities for export growth. In 2011, India was second only to China in the export of textile yarn. However, with respect to the export of cotton fabrics, India was ranked in fifth position, behind countries such as Pakistan and Hong Kong.[7] Some other labour-intensive industries in India, such as food products, beverages and tobacco, experienced a slowdown in the growth of both output and employment during most of the 1990s and the 2000s. In fact, this amounted to a reversal of the fast growth experienced by these industries during the 1970s and 1980s (Thomas 2012). Most of India's labour-intensive industries operate as small and micro enterprises. The supply, demand and policy-related factors discussed above, which constrain small firms in particular, are further major hurdles to the expansion of labour-intensive industries in India.

Conclusion

This chapter has attempted to explain why the manufacturing sector in India has had only a limited impact on the country's development, especially in regard to employment creation. Indian manufacturing provided employment for 53.3 million people in 2009–10, which was less than 12 per cent of the country's total workforce. Of all manufacturing workers in India, only around 21 per cent were engaged in the organised sector, while the rest of the workforce was attached to small, informal enterprises in the unregistered sector.

The growth of employment in India's unorganised manufacturing has decelerated sharply since the middle of the 2000s. The generation of jobs within organised manufacturing revived during the same period, but most of the incremental employment was informal in nature. A number of factors have constrained the growth of Indian manufacturing during the 2000s, and their effect has been more intense in micro enterprises and small scale industries in the unorganised sector. Foremost among these factors is the slowdown in the growth of investment, especially public investment. This has led to supply-side bottlenecks, mainly in infrastructure and power generation. Insufficient availability of bank credit and fluctuations in exchange rates and the price of raw materials have also been important constraints. There has been an unhealthy rise in import intensity in several areas of Indian manufacturing, particularly in machinery industries. Another issue is the low levels of demand for industrial goods from a vast majority of the country's population. In addition, the fast growth of high-paying sectors such as information technology and finance has increased the shortage of skilled workers facing Indian manufacturing.

India's labour laws have often been singled out as being the cause of most of the problems affecting the country's manufacturing sector. However, the argument that labour laws have hindered manufacturing growth is increasingly becoming irrelevant, as an overwhelming proportion of new employment in the country's organised sector falls outside the purview of those laws. As this chapter has argued, the slow growth of India's manufacturing sector has been largely due to a combination of external factors and inadequate policy responses on the part of the Indian government. For example, foreign direct investment (FDI) as a proportion of gross fixed capital formation (GFCF) was on average only 5.9 per cent during the period from 2001 to 2011 (Jadhav and Reddy 2013). Estimates by Rao and Dhar (2011) show that of the total FDI equity inflows into India during 2005–08, only 20.6 per cent went to manufacturing. Also large shares of FDI flows – 40.3 per cent in 2006–07 – have gone into the acquisition of shares in domestic enterprises and do not therefore represent the building of new facilities (Rao and Dhar 2011, 25–27).

In recent times, the Indian government has unveiled new programmes for the promotion of domestic manufacturing. The previous government, led by the United Progressive Alliance (UPA), launched a National Manufacturing Policy in 2011. The current government, led by the National Democratic Alliance (NDA), has launched a "Make in India" initiative. The thrust of both these initiatives has been to attract private investment, especially foreign investment. In both these initiatives, the government's role is confined to the creation of a facilitating environment for private investors. Foreign markets and foreign investors are themselves going through a tumultuous phase, with the global economy moving from one crisis to another. For this reason, it would be a mistake at this stage to rely too much on foreign investment or exports as drivers of growth in the Indian economy. Since 2011–12, India's domestic private firms have been reducing their levels of investment, partly because of the slowdown in demand at home and abroad, and the unutilised capacities they had built during the previous years. Many of them are also heavily indebted.

Given the current circumstances, there is a critical need for a rise in public expenditure as part of efforts to promote economic growth in India. The country has huge investment needs in irrigation, electricity, rural and urban infrastructure, as well as in many areas of basic research. Furthermore, the revival of traditional, labour-intensive and agro-based industries as a way of generating decent jobs in the rural areas requires funding for new areas of knowledge and technology. The long lead time associated with these projects has made private investors wary about investing in them, making these areas suitable for public investment. Only in this way will it be possible to remove some of the long-standing barriers to Indian development.

Notes

1 Data obtained from the World Bank's World Development Indicators. Available at http://data.worldbank.org/indicator.
2 See also Thomas (2015b) for regional aspects of employment growth in India.
3 See the set of articles in Byres (ed.) (1998) and Nayyar (ed) (1994), which engage with various aspects of this argument.
4 It should be noted here that the Besley and Burgess index was based on amendments to the IDA up to 1989.
5 See, for instance, Hiraway and Shah (2011), which notes that in Gujarat the State Labour Department's ability to enforce labour regulations has been substantially reduced over the last two decades.
6 Data obtained from http://planningcommission.nic.in/data/datatable/1705/final_76.pdf.
7 Data obtained from UN Comtrade. Available at http://comtrade.un.org/pb/.

References

Ahluwalia, I.J. 1985. *Industrial Growth in India: Stagnation since the Mid-sixties.*Delhi: Oxford University Press.

Amsden, Alice H. 1977. "The Division of Labour is Limited by the Type of Market: The Case of the Taiwanese Machine Tool Industry." *World Development* 5 (3): 217–233.

Annavajhula, J.C.B., and Surendra Pratap. 2012. "Worker Voices in an Auto Production Chain: Notes from the Pits of a Low Road – I." *Economic and Political Weekly* 47 (33): 46–59.

Bagchi, Amiya Kumar. 1976. "Deindustrialization in India in the Nineteenth Century: Some Theoretical Implications." *The Journal of Development Studies* 12 (2): 135–164.

Besley, Timothy, and Robin Burgess. 2004. "Can Labour Regulation Hinder Economic Performance? Evidence from India." *Quarterly Journal of Economics* 119 (1): 91–134.

Bhagwati, Jagdish, and Padma Desai. 1970. *India: Planning for Industrialization.* London: Oxford University Press.

Bhattacharjea, Aditya.2007. *Labour Market Regulation and Industrial Performance in India: A Critical Review of the Empirical Literature.* [Working Paper No. 141] Delhi: Delhi School of Economics. Available at http://www.cdedse.org/pdf/work141.pdf

Bhattacharjea, Aditya. 2009. "The Effects of Employment Protection Legislation on Indian Manufacturing." *Economic and Political Weekly* 44 (22): 55–62.

Breman, Jan. 2004. *The Making and Unmaking of an Industrial Working Class: Sliding Down the Labour Hierarchy in Ahmedabad, India.* Amsterdam: Amsterdam University Press.

Byres, T.J. (ed.), 1998. *The Indian Economy: Major Debates since Independence*. New Delhi: Oxford University Press

Central Electricity Authority (CEA). 2012. *Load Generation Balance Report 2012–13.* New Delhi: Ministry of Power, Government of India.

Chakravarty, Sukhamoy. 1979. "On the Question of Home Market and Prospects for Indian Growth." *Economic and Political Weekly* 14 (30/32): 1229–1242.

Chakravarty, Sukhamoy. 1987. *Development Planning: The Indian Experience.* New Delhi: Oxford University Press.

Chandavarkar, Rajnarayan. 2004. "From Neighbourhood to Nation." In *One Hundred Years, One Hundred Voices: The Mill Workers of Girangaon: An Oral History*, Meena Menon and Neera Adarkar (eds), 7–80. Calcutta: Seagull Books.

Chandrasekhar, C P. 1984. "Growth and Technical Change in Indian Cotton Mill Industry." *Economic and Political Weekly* 19 (4): PE22–PE39.

Chandrasekhar, C. P. 1988. "Aspects of Growth and Structural Change in Indian Industry." *Economic and Political Weekly* 23 (45–47): 2359–2370.

Chari, Sharad. 2000. "The Agrarian Origins of the Knitwear Industrial Cluster in Tiruppur, India." *World Development* 28 (3): 579–599.

Fallon, P., and R. E. B. Lucas. 1993. "Job Security Regulations and the Dynamic Demand for Industrial Labour in India and Zimbabwe." *Journal of Development Economics* 40 (2): 241–275.

Government of India. 2013. *Economic Survey 2012–13.* Ministry of Finance, New Delhi: Oxford University Press. Available at: http://indiabudget.nic.in/survey.asp.

Government of India. 2016. *Annual Survey of Industries 2011–12* Volume I. Kolkata: Central Statistics Office, Government of India.

Hiraway, Indira, and Neha Shah. 2011. "Labour and Employment under Globalization: The Case of Gujarat." *Economic and Political Weekly* 46 (22): 57–65.

Jadhav, Aditya Mohan, and V. Nagi Reddy. 2013. "Does FDI Contribute to Growth: Evidence from the Capital Goods Sector in India." *Economic and Political Weekly* 48 (12): 59-68.

Kathuria, Vinish, S. N. Rajesh Raj and Kunal Sen. 2010. "Organised versus Unorganised Manufacturing Performance in the Post-Reform Period." *Economic and Political Weekly* 45 (24): 55–64.

Kochhar, Kalpana, Utsav Kumar, Raghuram Rajan, Arvind Subramanian, and Ioannis Tokatlidis. 2006. *India's Pattern of Development: What Happened, What Follows.* [Working Paper 12023] Cambridge, MA: National Bureau of Economic Growth.

Kohli, Atul. 2006. "Politics of Economic Growth in India, 1980–2005." *Economic and Political Weekly* 41 (14): 1251–1259.

Mazumdar, Dipak. 1991. "Import-Substituting Industrialization and Protection of the Small-scale: The Indian Experience in the Textile Industry." *World Development* 19 (9): 1197–1213.

Mitra, Ashok. 1977. *Terms of Trade and Class Relations.* London: Frank Cass.

Nagaraj, R. 2013. "India's Dream Run, 2003–08: Understanding the Boom and Its Aftermath." *Economic and Political Weekly,* 48 (20): 39–51.

Nayyar Deepak, ed. 1994. *Industrial Growth and Stagnation- The Debate in India.* New Delhi: Oxford University Press.

NSSO. 2007. *Operational Characteristics of Unorganised Manufacturing Enterprises in India.* [62nd Round (July 2005–June 2006), Report No. 524] New Delhi: National Sample Survey Organization, Ministry of Statistics and Programme Implementation.

Pais, Jesim. 2008. *Effectiveness of Labour Regulations in Indian Industry.* New Delhi: Bookwell.

Patnaik, Prabhat. 1972. "Disproportionality Crisis and Cyclical Growth." *Economic and Political Weekly* 7 (5/7): 329–336.

Patnaik, Prabhat, and C. P. Chandrasekhar. 2007. "The Indian Economy under 'Structural Adjustment." In *India's Economic Transition: The Politics of Reforms,* Rahul Mukherji (ed.), 52–86. New Delhi: Oxford University Press.

Rao, Chalapati K. S. and Biswajit Dhar. 2011. *India's FDI Inflows: Trends and Concepts.* New Delhi: Research and Information Systems for Developing Countries and Institute for Studies in Industrial Development.

Rao, J. Mohan, and Amitava K. Dutt. 2006. "A Decade of Reforms: The Indian Economy in the 1990s." In *External Liberalization in Asia, Post-Socialist Europe, and Brazil,* Lance Taylor (ed.), 139–179. Oxford and New York: Oxford University Press.

RBI. 2006. *Report on Currency and Finance 2005–06.* Mumbai: Reserve Bank of India.

RBI. 2012. *Report on Trends and Progress of Banking in India 2011–12.* Mumbai: Reserve Bank of India.

Rodrik, Dani and Arvind Subramanian. 2004. *From "Hindu Growth" to Productivity Surge: The Mystery of the Indian Growth Transition.* [Working Paper WP/04/77] International Monetary Fund. Available at https://www.imf.org/external/pubs/ft/wp/2004/wp0477.pdf

Sen, Abhijit. 1996. "Economic Reforms, Employment and Poverty: Trends and Options." *Economic and Political Weekly* 31 (35/37): 2459–2477.

Sen, Kunal. 2007. "Why Did the Elephant Start to Trot? India's Growth Acceleration Re-examined." *Economic and Political Weekly* 42 (43): 37–47.

Thomas, Jayan Jose. 2002. "A Review of Indian Manufacturing." In *India Development Report 2002,* edited by Kirit Parikh and R. Radhakrishna, 84–101. New Delhi: Oxford University Press.

Thomas, Jayan Jose. 2009. "Hurdles to Growth." *Frontline,* October 10.

Thomas, Jayan Jose. 2012. "India's Labour Market during the 2000s: Surveying the Changes." *Economic and Political Weekly* 47 (51): 39–51.

Thomas, Jayan Jose. 2013. "Explaining the 'Jobless' Growth in Indian Manufacturing." *Journal of the Asia Pacific Economy* 18 (4): 673–692.

Thomas, Jayan Jose. 2014. "The Demographic Challenge and Employment Growth in India." *Economic and Political Weekly* 49 (6): 15–17.

Thomas, Jayan Jose. 2015a. "India's Labour Market during the 2000s: An Overview." In *Labour, Employment and Economic Growth in India,* K. V. Ramaswamy (ed.), 21–56. New Delhi: Cambridge University Press.

Thomas, Jayan Jose. 2015b. "Regional Aspects of Indian Industrialization." In *Indian Industrialization,* C. P. Chandrasekhar (ed.), 48–93. New Delhi: Oxford University Press.

Uchikawa, Shuji. 2011. "Linkage between Organised and Unorganised Sectors in Indian Machinery Industry." *Economic and Political Weekly* 46 (1): 45–54.

6 Self-employment

Dimensions, diversity and policy settings

Supriya RoyChowdhury and B. P. Vani

The persistence of self-employment in India defies the classical liberal understanding of development. While the Lewisian framework recognised a dualistic labour market in developing countries, the assumption was that as modernisation proceeded, enough jobs would be created in the modern sector to absorb those displaced from the traditional sectors. According to this paradigm, development should lead to a marked reduction in the share of individual entrepreneurs and own account workers in the labour force. As industrial capitalism advances, the size and scale of production occurs within ever-larger units, in pursuit of the economies of scale made possible by advanced technologies and large scale investment. As part of this process, the small producer and the self-employed are expected to have only a peripheral presence in the economy. This understanding, modelled on the experience of advanced industrialised economies, suggests the inevitability of the transition from petty self-employment to industrial wage work.

Nevertheless, far from disappearing, self-employment continues to provide a large number of people in developing countries with a source of livelihood and it is now acknowledged as an integral part of rural and urban economies. Yet there is a certain underlying ambiguity in the way in which scholars have come to consider the intransigence of self-employment. The links between self-employment and poverty are well acknowledged in the academic literature. However policy makers, civil society, and some scholars argue that through the provision of microcredit, it may be possible to create an economic domain which provides a meaningful livelihood for many of the urban and rural poor. For this reason, self-employment and microcredit remain important aspects of economic and development policy in India. This approach to policy pays little attention to the evidence showing that many people resort to self-employment because they cannot find wage employment in the organised sector, or even in the unorganised sector. Scholars have also shown that self-employment is a domain of low investment, productivity and profitability. Many empirical studies show that even when credit is made available to the self-employed it often does not reach the poorest, and that the poor lack the skills, resources and motivation to access profitable activities. Furthermore, ascriptive identities of caste, class, gender and religion continue to determine and limit the entrepreneurial initiatives of many self-employed people (Guerin 2015; Sridhar 2011). At a more theoretical level, scholars have argued that self-employment is a domain of exclusion in which unskilled labour, excluded from work in an increasingly knowledge and capital intensive economy, finds itself forced to resort to various forms of self-employment outside the more dynamic growth channels of modern capitalism (Sanyal 2007).

In this chapter, we problematise the understanding of self-employment in the context of these contesting positions. First we outline the diversities that exist within the category of the self-employed and provide a broad definition of informal work, within which self-employment is typically included. This incorporates the structure of self-employment across rural and urban sectors. Second, we provide a profile of the self-employed in terms of incidence of poverty, educational status, nature and scale of enterprises. This section draws on data from National Sample Survey (NSS) Employment and Unemployment Surveys, and surveys on Unorganised Enterprises. In this discussion self-employment is contextualised within the broad features of India's political economy, particularly the decline of manufacturing, the ascendance of services, and the critical perspectives that have emerged around the issue of whether the services sector can lead development in a context where large numbers of job seekers are unskilled or semi-skilled. Finally, we provide an outline of the ways in which government policy, civil society initiatives and academic discourse have positioned the issue of self-employment, juxtaposing contrasting perspectives.

Self-employment: diversity, definition and scope

Self-employment is an employment category that falls within the broad framework of the informal sector or informal work. The term "self-employment" encompasses a wide range of economic activities that vary in terms of their scale and sector. A thriving fruit shop owner in a busy market is a self-employed person. But so is the elderly woman who sits on the pavement with a few fruits laid out in front of her which she hopes to sell by the end of the day. The fruit shop owner sources his products from the wholesale market and makes a capital investment in the rent he pays for his space in the market and the vehicle he uses to cart his goods from the wholesale market to his shop each day. He employs a relative who takes care of the shop during certain hours, possibly has a bank account and access to institutional credit, and may even rent an additional shop in the same market that he uses to establish his son in business. In contrast, the woman who sits on the pavement might also source her material from the local wholesale market, but because she lacks capital, she buys fruit which is one or two days old at a lower price. She may also need to buy this fruit on credit from the wholesaler. Her daily earnings are meagre – just enough for two meals a day and the rent of a room in a slum. She has no access to institutional credit, but she often borrows from her neighbours when she fails to earn enough from selling fruit.

A large number of the so-called self-employed seek a daily livelihood in small exchanges of the kind described. These examples could be multiplied: the tea seller who sells tea and biscuits from a small, stationary cart located at the street corner; the familiar *pani puri* seller behind his roadside stand; the person who collects old newspapers from homes in a given neighbourhood; the woman who picks plastic out of trash at street corners; the child who sells newspapers at traffic signals. Each of these enterprises is characterised by minimal capital investment, use of self- and family labour, and a low, subsistence-level income.

While there is little qualitative similarity between the two fruit sellers described above, both these forms of income-generating work come under the umbrella term of "self-employment". Official policies such as credit and subsidies are geared to support small enterprises of the self-employed who are "poor" and below the poverty line. The *Swarna Jayanti Shahari Rozgar Yojana* (SJSRY), for example, is one of the largest national schemes, implemented by almost all states and designed to provide credit to the self-employed. Studies of the SJSRY and similar credit schemes have shown that programmes specifically designed for those who are poor, are most successful amongst those who have some experience in running a small enterprise and have ready access to information about the availability of government- and non-government-supported credit schemes (Sridhar 2011). The main beneficiaries are not so much the poor but those who already have some access to productive resources and who are already networked into the market in terms of access to products, distribution and credit. The point, then, is that while the self-employed are a highly diverse category, there have been few attempts to take account of these significant differences in the design and implementation of policy for the self-employed.

With this caveat, we can now move on to the more formal definitions of self-employment that have emerged over time. Self-employment falls within the broad category of informal work. The definition of informality itself has been broadened in recent decades, from the informal sector to informal work. Originally, "the informal sector" broadly referred to employment and production practices in small, unincorporated and unregistered enterprises. From the late 1990s, the concept was broadened to include certain types of informal employment which had earlier not been included in the enterprise-based definition (Narayana 2007). This new definition made the term applicable to informal work arrangements in industrialised as well as developing economies and informal labour practices in both informal and formal enterprises. Thus the focus was broadened from informal enterprises which are not regulated, to workers whose work is not regulated. With the broadening of the meaning of informal work from the size of enterprises to types of work, the term "informal" can now be used for a range of work categories, including contract work in public sector enterprises and in large private organisations.

Under the broad umbrella of informal work, the first distinction to be made is between self-employment and wage employment. Table 6.1 locates self-employment within the overall framework of employment in India.

Table 6.1 Percentage distribution of workers by working status

	Rural		*Urban*	
	Male	*Female*	*Male*	*Female*
Self-employed				
1987–88	58.6	60.8	41.7	47.1
1993–94	57.9	58.5	41.7	45.4
1999–2000	55.0	57.3	41.5	45.3
2004–05	58.1	63.7	44.8	47.7
2009–10	53.5	55.7	41.1	41.1
2011–12	54.5	59.3	41.7	42.8
Regular Salaried				
1987–88	10.0	3.7	43.7	27.5
1993–94	8.3	2.8	42.1	28.6
1999–2000	8.8	3.1	41.7	33.3
2004–05	9.0	3.7	40.6	35.6
2009–10	8.5	4.4	41.9	39.3
2011–12	10.04	5.6	43.4	42.8
Casual Labour				
1987–88	31.4	35.5	14.6	25.4
1993–94	33.8	38.7	16.2	26.2
1999–2000	36.2	39.6	16.8	21.4
2004–05	32.9	32.6	14.6	16.7
2009–10	38.0	39.9	17.0	19.6
2011–12	35.5	35.1	14.9	14.3

Source: NSS Employment and Unemployment Survey (various rounds).

Here we see a gradual decline in the share of self-employment – except for the year 2004–05, when there was an increase in both rural and urban areas. The years 2004–05 marked the culmination of three previous years of agricultural decline (growth in agriculture averaged just 1.5 per cent during this period) when there was a marked decline in the employment of casual wage labour in rural areas (1999–2000 to 2004–05), a possible explanation for the turn towards self-employment in the countryside (Papola 2012). In urban areas, the rise in self-employment between 1999–2000 and 2004–05 must be seen alongside the decline of regular salaried employment for males and of casual wage employment for both males and females. In the subsequent periods, 2009–10 and 2011–12, there was a marked increase in regular salaried employment for both men and women in rural and urban areas. Two recent studies have highlighted the decline in labour force participation due to rising enrolment in education in the age group 15–24 for both men and women (Rangarajan, Iyer and Seema 2011; Kannan and Raveendran 2012). These parallel trends need to be seen alongside the decline in self-employment during 2009–10 and 2011–12.

Self-employed workers: a profile

In this section we present a profile of self-employed workers based on education, economic status and activities, scale of enterprises and capital investment. As discussed earlier, the term "self-employed" covers a diversity of economic activities and labour arrangements that includes both the fairly prosperous merchant to the hand-to-mouth street vendor. However, the data below indicates that a significant percentage of the self-employed are marginal and vulnerable workers earning subsistence incomes at best. One quarter of the rural self-employed and 16 per cent of the urban self-employed are deemed poor (See Table 6.2).

Educational levels of the self-employed are also very low. In urban areas, 20 per cent of all self-employed have no more than primary school level education and 15 per cent are illiterate (See Table 6.3). A further 35 per cent have completed secondary school, reaching the 8th or 9th grade. This means a total of 70 per cent of the urban self-employed have very little education, making employment in the formal sector difficult. In rural areas, the educational profile of the self-employed is even worse, with 35 per cent illiterate and a total of only 10 per cent having completed higher secondary education, college or above. The profile of the self-employed is a person with little or no education/skills, and low employability.

The profile of poverty and low levels of human capital among the self-employed is compounded when we consider the industry sectors where most self-employment occurs (see Table 6.4). In urban areas, more than 55 per cent

Table 6.2 Incidence of poverty across different status of workers (2011–12)

	Rural	*Urban*
Self-employed	26.3	16.4
Regular salaried	15.2	7.4
Casual Labour	39.2	33.4

Source: NSS Employment and Unemployment Survey, 68th Round.

Table 6.3 Educational status of self-employed (2011–12)

	Rural	*Urban*
Illiterate	35.1	14.7
Primary	25.0	20.2
Secondary	29.6	35.2
Higher Secondary	6.1	11.5
College & Above	4.2	18.4
Total	100.0	100.0

Source: NSS Employment and Unemployment Survey, 68th Round.

of the self-employed work in trade and services, (37 per cent in trade, 5.2 per cent in hospitality, 8.8 per cent in transport and 4.1 per cent in real estate) and 22 per cent in manufacturing. Trade and services sectors are characterised by a highly varied structure in which small and tiny units coexist with larger operations. However income levels remain very low, particularly in retail, where the development of large supermarkets in the metropolitan centres has created new forms of competition. Small scale manufacturing of the type normally undertaken by the self-employed has also come under challenge, as the manufacturing sector in general has moved away from small scale production units to large scale, capital intensive processes driven by large, often multi-national, companies.

Although data with regard to capital investment is not available, the structure of self-employment (Table 6.5) reveals that most units are extremely small, involving low capital investment and the use of self and family labour. In urban areas, among those who are self-employed in manufacturing, 67.6 per cent are own account workers who own and operate their units without hired labour, and 26.7 per cent are working as unpaid family labour. In urban areas, employers constitute a very small percentage in the self-employed category – only 5.3 per cent in wholesale and retail trade, 5.7 per cent in manufacturing and 4.2 per cent in transport – a clear indication that only a small fraction of enterprises run by the self-employed can afford to hire additional labour. The predominance of own account workers and the use of unpaid family labour highlights the low levels of capital investment and productivity that can be achieved by small self-employed operators, most of whom are engaged in survival-based livelihood operations.

Table 6.4 Industry group structure of self-employed (2011–12)

	Rural %	*Urban %*
Agriculture, Hunting & Fishing	73.3	9.5
Mining & Quarrying	0.0	0.1
Manufacturing	8.1	22.4
Electricity, Gas & Water Supply	0.0	0.1
Construction	1.9	4.3
Wholesale & Retail Trade	9.8	37.0
Hotels & Restaurants	1.2	5.2
Transport, Storage & Communication	2.6	8.8
Financial Intermediation	0.2	1.2
Real Estate, Renting & Business Activity	0.4	4.1
Education	0.3	1.3
Health & Social Work	0.3	1.4
Other Services	2.0	4.5
Total	100.0	100.0

Source: NSS Employment and Unemployment Survey, 68th Round.

In rural areas, most self-employed are engaged in agriculture (73.3 per cent – see Table 6.4). The next largest category of work in rural self-employment is wholesale and retail trade – 10 per cent. This group of self-employed mainly operate small roadside shops in villages and towns. This can be deduced from data showing that of those who are self-employed in wholesale and retail trade in rural areas, 79 per cent are own account workers and 18.6 per cent work as unpaid family labour (see Table 6.5). Only 2.3 per cent are employers, possibly representing the upper crust of rural traders who are mostly wholesale traders of agricultural commodities.

When we analyse the available data we find that self-employment is predominantly undertaken by those with low levels of capital and skills. This is the defining feature of self-employment in both rural and urban areas. In the urban sector competition can be very high, with large numbers of people selling identical goods or services at similar low rates. This supply of cheap and bargainable goods and services draws on poor communities in marginalised neighbourhoods such as slums, and other peripheral settlements such as those housing migrant labourers. What emerges from this analysis is that self-employment is a residual category of employment in which the profile of the self-employed worker is defined by low levels of education and skills formation. Self-employment is possibly the only livelihood option available to these people. Given the profile of the self-employed and their activities, it is clear that the majority of the self-employed are poor.

Using a classification of the poor beyond the standard Below Poverty Line (BPL) and Above Poverty Line (APL) categories that are typically deployed to measure poverty in India, Arjun Sengupta and his team at the Committee on Unorganised Sector Enterprises developed a detailed analysis of the relationship between employment profile and economic vulnerability (Sengupta, Raveendran, and Kannan 2008). Drawing on consumption expenditure data

Table 6.5 Status of self-employed in industry (2011–12)

Rural	*Own Account Worker %*	*Unpaid Family Member %*	*Employer %*
Agriculture, Hunting & Fishing	58.2	39.4	2.4
Manufacturing	72.3	25.9	1.8
Wholesale & Retail Trade	79.1	18.6	2.3
Hotels & Restaurants	69.4	27.3	3.3
Transport, Storage & Communication	90.4	7.1	2.5
Urban			
Agriculture, Hunting & Fishing	63.6	31.3	5.1
Manufacturing	67.6	26.7	5.7
Wholesale & Retail Trade	75.1	19.6	5.3
Hotels & Restaurants	64.0	26.0	10.0
Transport, Storage & Communication	92.1	3.8	4.2

Source: NSS Employment and Unemployment Survey, 68th Round.

Table 6.6 Employment status across different income class (2011–12)

Rural	*Self-employed %*	*Regular Salaried %*	*Casual Labour %*
Vulnerable or ultra-poor	22.6	11.1	32.3
Poor	33.9	22.7	37.4
Not so poor	43.5	66.2	30.2
Urban			
Vulnerable or ultra-poor	23.2	10.9	44.2
Poor	26.2	20.0	31.7
Not so poor	50.6	69.1	24.1

Source: based on NSS Employment and Unemployment Survey, 68th Round.

as reported in the Employment–Unemployment Survey (EUS) schedules, Sengupta developed three categories: the vulnerable or ultra-poor – defined as those who had daily per capita consumption expenditure of less than Rs. 26 in rural areas and Rs. 38 in urban areas; the poor – those whose daily per capita expenditure was between Rs. 26 and Rs. 39 in rural areas and between Rs. 38 and Rs. 56 in urban areas; and the not poor – those whose daily per capita expenditure was more than Rs. 39 in rural areas and Rs. 56 in urban areas. Using this methodology, 23 per cent of the self-employed in both rural and urban areas are deemed vulnerable or ultra-poor. When the two poor categories are combined, 56 per cent of the rural self-employed are poor and almost half of the urban self-employed are poor (See Table 6.6).[1] Clearly there is a strong correlation between self-employment and poverty.

Self-employment in the Indian political economy

The data presented above portrays a profile of the self-employed as an economic category prone to significant socio-economic vulnerability: low earnings, low levels of education, and small size of enterprises. In spite of this empirical evidence, self-employment has been seen, particularly in policy circles, as a domain of the economy capable of generating income and employment. At the same time, others have seen self-employment/small enterprises as a sphere of exclusion. The framing of self-employment within this contradictory binary of economic inclusion and exclusion has created considerable confusion. In this section we contextualise self-employment within some of the broader dimensions and debates on India's political economy.

One of the most widely discussed themes in contemporary Indian political economy is the lack of economic transformation in agriculture. While the contribution of agricultural output to GDP has steadily fallen (see Table 6.7), the proportion of the population dependent on agriculture as a means of livelihood continues to be unusually high (Table 6.8). Thus the structural transformation of the economy, typically represented by the movement of large numbers of people from agriculture to industry, has not taken place in India on the scale that orthodox development theory predicts. The slow pace of job creation in rural areas makes the slow pace of urbanisation even more remarkable.[2] According to the India Urban Poverty Report 2009, there are complex reasons why agriculture continues to harbour workers beyond its capacity, but the problem is clearly related to the nature of industrial and urban growth. The lack of opportunities for relatively low skilled workers in urban areas is an important contributing factor. Several scholars have argued that the low share of manufacturing employment in India during a period of economic growth stands in sharp contrast to the rapid rise in manufacturing employment that was seen in South Korea, Thailand and China during comparable periods of growth (Ahsan and Narain 2007; Hashim 2009; Aggarwal 2015). In India, manufacturing sector employment remained virtually stagnant during the decade 1999–2000 to 2009–10 (Table 6.8), and between 2004–05 and 2009–10 there was an absolute decline of more than 5 million jobs (Table 6.9) (Sen and Das 2012).

Table 6.7 Sectoral share in GDP (2004–05 prices) as a percentage

Sector	*1999–2000*	*2004–05*	*2009–10*	*2011–12*
Agriculture & Allied Services	23.20	19.03	14.64	14.37
Industry	26.77	27.93	28.27	28.22
Services	50.03	53.04	57.09	57.41

Source: Economic Survey of India (relevant years).

Table 6.8 Sectoral share in employment as a percentage

Sector	*1999–2000*	*2004–05*	*2009–10*	*2011–12*
Agriculture	59.9	56.6	53.2	48.9
Manufacturing	11.1	12.2	11.0	12.6
Non-manufacturing	5.3	6.5	10.5	11.7
Services	23.7	24.7	25.3	26.8
Total	100.0	100.0	100.0	100.0

Source: NSSO Employment and Unemployment Survey (various rounds).

Table 6.9 Estimated number of work force (in millions)

Sector	*1999–2000*	*2004–05*	*2009–10*	*2011–12*
Agriculture	238.3	259.2	244.8	231.2
Manufacturing	44.2	55.9	50.6	59.6
Non-manufacturing	21.1	29.8	48.3	55.1
Services	94.3	113.1	116.4	126.9
Total	397.9	457.9	460.2	472.9

Source: NSSO Employment and Unemployment Survey (various rounds).

A more detailed exploration of this widely discussed feature of the Indian economy is not warranted for the present purposes.[3] However, a related and important issue is the question of what kind of employment is available to the unskilled workforce. As Table 6.8 shows, the share of the non-manufacturing sector more than doubled between 1999–2000 and 2009–10. Within the non-manufacturing sector, the most dramatic growth was recorded in employment in the labour-intensive construction sector. While its share of employment more than doubled, the rise in absolute numbers was even more dramatic (Table 6.9): between 2004–05 and 2009–10 an additional 18 million construction workers joined the labour force (Table 6.10). During these years, a general buoyancy in the economy led to the expansion of infrastructure and housing-related building works, as a result of which there was a huge increase in the number of construction workers. This increase, however, has to be seen within the framework of the broader economic environment, in which manufacturing sector employment had been steadily declining. In this context, the construction sector is frequently the inevitable destination of large numbers of unskilled workers, but it is also a domain where minimum wages are often not paid, work availability is irregular, and social insurance unavailable.[4]

Self-employment in petty trade and services, and in tiny manufacturing units, thus provides an alternative source of livelihood to those unable to find a foothold in an increasingly technology- and capital-intensive manufacturing sector or the harsh life of construction work. In a rapidly globalising economy, with industrial firms moving towards increasingly competitive global arenas, the old concepts of public sector, labour-intensive and employment/welfare-oriented industrialisation are becoming less relevant. And yet scholars tend to agree that there is a critical need to expand employment opportunities in the manufacturing sector. For example, Arvind Panagariya, otherwise known for his strong support for India's economic globalisation policies, has argued that an important reason for poverty and unemployment in India is that the manufacturing sector has remained stagnant, while in most poor, heavily populated countries experiencing rapid growth, manufacturing has typically led the way (for example, South Korea in the period 1965–75). Similarly, even as the World Bank remains a strong advocate of the need for India to open up to global markets and a private sector-led industrialisation model, a recent

Table 6.10 Increase in work force (in millions)

	1999–2000 to 2004–05	*2004–05 to 2009–10*	*2009–10 to 2011–12*	*2004–05 to 2011–12*
Agriculture	20.8	−14.3	−13.6	−27.9
Manufacturing	11.7	−5.2	9.0	3.7
Non-manufacturing	8.7	18.6	6.8	25.4
Services	18.8	3.3	10.5	13.8
Total	60.0	2.3	12.7	15.0

Source: NSSO Employment and Unemployment Survey (various rounds).

World Bank report sounded a cautionary note. Acknowledging the importance of the tertiary sector in economic development, the report states "it is unclear that India's human capital and infrastructure are adequately developed to allow India to leapfrog the labour intensive manufacturing stage and follow the growth path of an upper middle income or even an OECD-type economy" (Ahsan and Narain 2007). The report stresses the importance of policy emphasis on manufacturing employment and, particularly, the formal sector of manufacturing employment.

Much of this critical discussion is based on the developmental histories of countries like China, Thailand and the East Asian giants. In each of these contexts, a period of labour-intensive industrialisation made it possible to expand the domain of manufacturing sector jobs for the first generation of industrial workers, who were mostly unskilled or semi-skilled. This period of growth was followed by the shift to globally competitive, capital-intensive and export-oriented industrial development. It was accompanied by the necessary changes in the labour market, which saw the emergence of more skilled labour as well as the expansion of service sector work. For scholars who have consistently pointed to these developmental histories and maintained a sustained criticism of India's low levels of employment in manufacturing, the position seems to be that the impact of globalisation and privatisation can be moderated by more thoughtful policies directed towards job creation, universal education and skills development during this particular phase of development. Nevertheless, the policy establishment, while recognising the need to boost employment, has stressed the importance of self-employment, rather than the need to generate employment in the industrial/manufacturing sector. The issue of whether low income self-employment can actually address the problem of lack of employment in the manufacturing sector has not been seriously addressed by the policy establishment in successive governments.

Policy approaches to self-employment

While the links between self-employment, poverty and low income are clear there are competing policy and scholarly understandings of the sector as a whole. The overall thrust of government policy has been in the direction of providing the self-employed with necessary forms of support. There have been two kinds of policy initiatives: first, social security, broadly for the unorganised sector, and second, credit related schemes for the self-employed. In this chapter we do not directly engage with social security schemes, as these apply broadly to the self-employed as well as to wage workers. The framing and implementation of social policies also vary greatly, determined by political regimes and governance systems at state levels. Here the focus is on policies designed to facilitate the creation of small enterprises, that is, to encourage self-employment as a livelihood option. We also touch briefly on the policy philosophy that appears to frame such policies.

For several decades now, schemes designed to encourage self-employment have been enacted by both central and state governments. Among the policy initiatives of the central government, the Prime Minister's Rozgar Yojana (PMRY) and the Rural Employment Generation Scheme (REGS) have been running since the mid-1990s. When the Congress-led UPA government came to power at the Centre in 2004, there was a push to provide more focussed policy attention to the problem of employment generation. This led to the merging of the PMRY and the REGS and the creation of a new scheme, the Prime Minister's Employment Generation Program (2008). The main objective of this scheme is to generate employment by encouraging and facilitating small enterprises both in rural and urban areas. The implementing agencies are the Ministry of Micro, Small and Medium Enterprises, the Khadi and Village Enterprises Boards and the District Industries Centres at the local level. In this scheme, potential beneficiaries contribute 10 per cent of the project cost (5 per cent in the case of scheduled caste, women and minorities) and the balance is contributed by banks as term loans. The maximum project costs, up to 25 lakhs in the case of manufacturing and 10 lakhs in the case of services, indicate that support remains limited to extremely small enterprises. The nomenclature of schemes, such as "Self-Employment Scheme for Educated Unemployed Youth" (SEEUE) (1985) and "Motivation of Unemployed Persons to Start Self-employed Enterprises Scheme" (MUPSAS) (2006), suggests that over several decades, self-employment has been approached as a possible option for those who fail to find a foothold in the mainstream economy. There appears to be relatively little policy thinking on the impact of many small and micro enterprises on potential competitiveness, particularly in an economic environment which is increasingly being integrated into the global economy and therefore subject to vastly increased scales of competition.

In this context, there have been specific policy interventions to provide microcredit, organise self-help groups, credit groups and so on. In terms of state initiatives in providing credit, the Swarna Jayanti Shahari Rozgar Yojana (SJSRY) was a nationally enacted policy framework (introduced in 1997, revised in 2009, and implemented by most states) designed to provide loans to below poverty line individuals for setting up small enterprises in manufacturing or retail services. Under the SJSRY, the Urban Self-Employment Programme provides assistance to individual urban poor beneficiaries for setting up gainful self-employment enterprises, with particular emphasis on assisting poor women through the provision of skill training, as well as an emphasis on community development. The implementation and impact of the SJSRY have been varied across states. The overall impact has not been studied in depth, but some evaluations of the scheme have noted that the benefits frequently flowed to those who were not eligible for the credits available through the SJSRY. For example, a recent study of the implementation of the SJSRY in four cities in Karnataka concludes: "[T]his remains the single biggest stumbling block for all poverty alleviation programs in India – improper identification of the poor". The study also found that SJSRY expenditures are often much less than the maximum allowed, and that there is no real emphasis on crafts and skills formation (Sridhar 2011, 126).

Going beyond faulty implementation, other studies have highlighted the limitations of self-employment/microcredit as a policy framework for addressing poverty. These studies have pointed to the poor's lack of access to skills, resources and motivation to initiate entrepreneurial activities, as well as the limited capacity of markets to accommodate an ever-expanding number of micro businesses. A paper on self-employment and microcredit that drew on field work from small enterprises in rural Tamil Nadu argued that caste and gender significantly influence access to and use of microcredit, as well as the type of self-employment activities that are undertaken (Guerin, D'Espallier, and Venkatasubramanian 2015). The findings indicate that Dalits and women are confined to smaller and less profitable activities, and have significantly lower initial amounts of investment than other groups. Caste can also limit entrepreneurial activities. For example, Dalits have restricted entry into the food retail industry. The study's findings also show that microcredit services have not promoted income generating activities for women, with a large proportion of the microcredit given to women being used for immediate consumption purposes. These findings, understood within the broader social and political economy context, demonstrate that self-employment lacks the dynamism required to generate economic mobility, or even sustainable livelihoods, for a large percentage of the unskilled workforce, whether rural or urban.

Despite these drawbacks, ideas around microcredit and Self Help Groups continue to feature in the imaginations of both state and civil society, as well as academic researchers, as a preferred paradigm for addressing the economic exclusion of self-employed persons. A large number of non-government organisations and civil society organisations, including women's unions such as the Self-Employed Women's Association (SEWA), promote microcredit and self-help groups. SEWA was founded in Gujarat in 1972 by the trade unionist Ela Bhat, and it now has a presence in other states as well. Described as being not only a union but also a movement, SEWA has motivated and organised low income women to gain control of their lives and livelihoods. Its more specific and most iconic role, however, has been to enable poor women to organise themselves into credit and savings groups in order to start and sustain small businesses, and to improve their access to markets. The potentially transformative role of SEWA's banking and credit services saw these ideas pushed to the forefront of the developmental discourse about self-employed persons and households. The World Bank has highlighted SEWA as a model to be replicated (World Bank 2004).

An important intervention in this positive discourse has emerged from an international group of scholars, the Cornell–SEWA–WIEGO group, whose ethnographic study of self-employed/ informal workers, mostly women, spans India, Mexico and South Africa. The concluding view of this group of scholars was that governments can play an important role in addressing some of the critical drivers of the poverty and deprivation of informal workers especially through access to education and skills that enables those displaced from their traditional occupations to find alternative employment (Basu 2009). But they also argued there was an important role for non-government organisations and civil society. According to Ravi Kanbur, the study "highlights the importance of non-party-political, people-based organisations like SEWA [. . .] there is no shortage of government schemes [. . .] what is needed, however, is intermediaries like SEWA to help access these schemes [. . .] The central policy question, then, is – why are there not more organisations like SEWA?" (Kanbur 2009). Thus, within the SEWA paradigm, which is broadly endorsed by governments and multi-lateral institutions, as well as academics, a combination of state-sponsored social security, easily accessible credit and NGO activism holds out the promise of the future incorporation of self-employed workers into the larger growth story of capitalism. From this point of view, faulty implementation of self-employment and microcredit related policies can be potentially addressed through more civil society interventions.

A more disquieting analysis of, and insight into, self-employment and informal work more broadly as a structure of exclusion emerges from the work of Kalyan Sanyal. In his now widely cited book (2007), Sanyal departs from other work on the informal sector in his contention that while informalisation of work within capitalist production provides an important clue to the nature of exploitation therein, informal production *outside* the framework of capitalism characterises what he calls *exclusion* within the capitalist system. It is the latter category which speaks directly to the issue of self-employment. Large numbers of people from both rural and urban under-classes continue to be displaced from their traditional means of livelihood and separated from the means of production and survival, while at the same time they cannot be incorporated into the capitalist structures of production, whether in agriculture or in industry. Thus it is that huge numbers become *self-employed*. Given the nature of their operations, minimum capital investment, use of self and/or family labour, meagre earnings at subsistence levels, their singular characteristic feature is that they are, for the most part, isolated from the dynamic growth structures of the economy, although they may not be disconnected from them. For example, the home-based garment worker who supplies the garment factory owner, who in turn sells to local agents of global retailers, typically earns a subsistence living, although she is inserted into a global supply chain.

Sanyal's theorisation draws particular attention to the fact that given the declining rate of growth of jobs in the manufacturing sector, even informal wage employment in industrial manufacturing has declined. Thus there is a clear trend towards self-employment as the main source of livelihood for the informal labour force. While this labour force has no direct linkages to the formal economy, it nevertheless performs a vital function for capital in providing a peripheral basin which can absorb the ever-growing numbers who cannot be accommodated within the mainstream economy. From this perspective it is the structural exclusion of self-employed workers that matters. This exclusion can be seen from two related viewpoints: first, in terms of numbers, an ever larger space in the economy is occupied by those pursuing livelihoods which are disconnected from the mainstream capitalist economy. Second, what emerges is a new understanding of capitalism as a system that can survive only by the systematic and continuing dislocation and exclusion of self-employed workers. Thus, under the model Sanyal has outlined, even if self-employed workers increase their access to credit and income, they continue to exist within a broader exclusionary framework and on the vulnerable fringes of capitalist growth strageties.

Conclusion

This chapter has outlined a profile of the self-employed in India that draws on data showing that a significant percentage of the self-employed are poor and, with minimal levels of education, often resort to self-employment as their only livelihood option. In terms of state policy, the success or otherwise of schemes that encourage self-employment has varied across states and across sectors. However, much of the empirical research indicates that self-employment as a policy may be self-limiting because of its potentially infinite multiplication of units: large numbers of small and tiny units competing to provide the same goods and services, but with low capital and technology, have very little scope for expansion in terms of production and access to larger markets. Similarly, microcredit as a strategy of facilitating self-employment is subject to numerous flaws in governance and implementation, such that credits and subsidies often end up not with the most poor and needy, but those who are most resourceful.

The enduring feature of self-employment as a domain of poverty has thus given rise to two important political economy debates in contemporary India. As outlined above, in the first debate, on the issues of employment and industrial policy, several scholars agree that the declining rate of growth in manufacturing sector employment is a major cause of the persistence of poverty and unemployment, even as economic growth has made rapid advances. A central question that has emerged is whether the knowledge and skills-intensive services sector can indeed lead development in a context like India, where large numbers of the workforce are unskilled and otherwise asset-less. There appears to be a convergence of opinion that the manufacturing sector should possibly be revisited as a potential generator of employment. These views implicitly or otherwise question the efficacy of self-employment. The second major theoretical intervention in this context has located self-employment in an ambiguous space as a residual domain accommodating the large numbers of people who have been failed or bypassed by the more dynamic channels of a rapidly growing economy. Seen in this light, petty self-employment represents almost a parallel economy, called the need economy, which provides people with subsistence and contains them within its scope of operations. In this way, it allows the more affluent and wealth-generating economy to thrive.

Even as these critical perspectives have emerged, much public policy, academic research, and a large section of the NGO community engaged with livelihood issues of the poor, have at the same time remained committed to the idea of self-employment and microcredit. These opposing binaries of exclusion and inclusion create a confusing framework for analysis of the problems confronting the self-employed. The reality is that 56 per cent of rural workers and 41 per cent of urban workers are self-employed. And many of these are poor. The figures on poverty of the self-employed may be at least partially deceptive, since given the debates and controversies that have emerged around the notion of the poverty line, it is possible that those just above the poverty line may also be economically vulnerable. In this context one could say that theorisations of the self-employed as trapped in survival-based livelihood strategies deepens our understanding of the economic structure and the policy environment which generate this domain of exclusion. However, policy alternatives remain elusive within this critical paradigm. In the given framework of an increasingly globally integrated economy, we can only assume that labour-intensive technologies of manufacturing may not be an option, except in selected pockets of the economy. This approach means that self-employment will remain a compulsion rather than a choice. One possible response could be more focussed state attention on policies that promote education and skills development. These interventions would at least have the potential to address issues of productivity and profits in this domain.

Notes

1 Sengupta and others used the official estimate of Rs.11.6 per capita per day (2004–05 prices) as Poverty Line in their paper. The usual classification is Below Poverty Line (BPL) and Above Poverty Line (APL). Subsequently a revision to the poverty line by Prof S. Tendulkar was accepted by the Planning Commission. According to the Tendulkar Committee estimates, the Rural Poverty Line is Rs 27. 2 per capita per day in rural areas, and the Urban Poverty Line is Rs 33.3 in urban areas, at 2011–12 prices.

2 Between 1993–94 and 1999–2000, overall only about 9.4 million jobs were created in rural areas, while the rural labour force increased by 17.7 million workers (Sundaram and Tendulkar 2005 [as quoted in Ahsan and Narain 2007]) Aggregate employment in rural areas grew at a rate of 2.1 per cent during 1972–73/83, but declined to 1.7 and 1.4 per cent in the two subsequent decades. Between 2004–05 and 2009–10 it declined in absolute terms at a rate of 1.65 per cent per annum (Papola and Sahu 2012).

3 For recent lively discussions, see Sen and Das (2015) and Chowdhury (2011).

4 See RoyChowdhury (2016). For a critical and comparative discussion on this theme, see for example, Bannerjee, A.V., and E. Duflo (2011); Bateman (2010); Guerin, D'Espallier, and Venkatasubramanian (2015).

References

Ahsan, A., and Ashish Narain. 2007. "Labor Markets in India: Developments and Challenges." In *Job Creation and Poverty Reduction in India: Towards Rapid and Sustained Growth*, edited by Sadiq Ahmed, 293–338. New Delhi: Sage.

Aggarwal, A. 2015. "India's Services Sector, Gateway to Development?" In *Economic Growth and its Distribution in India*, edited by Pulapre Balakrishnan, 244–254. New Delhi: Orient Blackswan Pvt. Ltd.

Bannerjee, A.V., and E Duflo. 2011. *Poor Economics: A Radical Rethinking of the Way to Fight Global Poverty*. New York: Public Affairs.

Basu, K. 2009. "Among the Zapotecs." *Informal Sector and Social Policy: Compendium of Personal and Technical Reflections*. Cornell–SEWA–WIEGO Exposure and Dialogue Program, 63–66, WIEGO. http://wiego.org/sites/wiego.org/files/publications/files/Mexico2009Compendium.pdf

Bateman, M, 2010. *Why Doesn't Micro Finance Work? The Destructive Rise of Local Neoliberalism*. London and New York: Zed Books.

Chowdhury, S. 2011. "Employment in India: What Does the Latest Data Show?" *Economic and Political Weekly* 46 (32): 23–26.

Guerin, Isabelle, Bert D'Espallier, and G Venkatasubramanian. 2015. "The Social Regulation of Markets: Why Microcredit Fails to Promote Jobs in Rural South India." *Development and Change* 46 (6): 1277–1301.

Hashim, S R. 2009. "Economic Development and Urban Poverty." *India: Urban Poverty Report*. Ministry of Housing and Urban Poverty Alleviation: Government of India.

Kanbur, R. 2009. "Middlemen and Price Margins." *Informal Sector and Social Policy: Compendium of Personal and Technical Reflections*, Cornell–SEWA–WIEGO Exposure and Dialogue Program, 29–30, WIEGO. http://wiego.org/sites/wiego.org/files/publications/files/Mexico2009Compendium.pdf

Kannan, K. P., and G. Raveendran. 2012. "Counting and Profiling the Missing Labour Force." *Economic & Political Weekly* 47 (6): 43–59.

Narayana, M. R. 2007 "Formal and Informal Enterprises: Concept, Definition and Measurement Issues in India", in *Linking the Formal and Informal Economy: Concepts and Policies*, edited by B. Guha Khasnabis, R. Kanbur and E. Ostrom. New Delhi: Oxford University Press.

Papola, T. S. 2012. "Employment Growth in the Post-Reform Period." ISID Working paper No. 2012/07. Institute for Studies in Industrial Development, New Delhi.

Papola, T. S., and P. P. Sahu. 2012. *Growth and Structure of Employment in India: Long Term and Post Reform Performance and Emerging Challenge*. Institute for Studies in Industrial Development, New Delhi.

Rangarajan, C., Padma Iyer, and Kaul Seema. 2011. "Where is the Missing Labour Force?" *Economic and Political Weekly* 46 (39): 68–72.

RoyChowdhury, S. 2017. "New Paradigms in Labour Studies: How Much Do They Explain?" In *Political Economy of India*, edited by R. Nagraj and Sripad Motiram. London: Cambridge University Press.

Sanyal, K. 2007. *Rethinking Capitalist Development: Primitive Accumulation, Governmentality and Post-Colonial Capitalism*. New Delhi: Routledge.

Sen, K., and D. K. Das. 2015. "Where Have All the Workers Gone? Puzzle of Declining Labour Intensity in Organised Indian Manufacturing." *Economic and Political Weekly* 50 (23):108–115.

Sengupta, Arjun, G. Raveendran, and K. P. Kannan. 2008. "India's Common People: Who Are They, How Many Are They, and How Do They Live?" *Economic and Political Weekly* 43 (11): 49–63.

Sridhar, K. S, A.Venugopal Reddy, and Pavan Srinath. 2011. *Changing the Urban Face of Karnataka: Evidence from Three Urban Development Programs* Bangalore: Public Affairs Centre.

World Bank. 2004. "India's Self-Employed Women's Association (SEWA): Empowerment through Mobilization of Poor Women on a Large Scale." Paper presented at Scaling Up Poverty Reduction: A Global Learning Process and Conference, Sanghai, May 2004.

7 Employment policy to promote the participation of women in the Indian labour force

Sher Singh Verick

One of the most discussed and puzzling employment issues in India in recent years is the low and declining rate of female labour force participation (aged 15+) from 42.7 per cent in 2004–05 to 31.2 per cent in 2011–12 (Dasgupta and Verick 2016). This fall occurred during a period of rapid economic growth, averaging around 8 per cent per annum, along with increasing levels of female educational attainment and declining fertility rates. The decline in women's employment during this period points to the complex employment patterns that underpin the "jobless growth" thesis. Figures from the National Sample Survey Office's Employment and Unemployment Survey reveal that employment grew strongly in urban areas, and for men during this period. For example, from 2004–05 to 2009–10, total employment grew by just 1.1 million in net terms (from 457.9 to 459 million) but urban employment rose by 7.6 million (from 115 to 122.6 million). At the same time, employment in rural areas declined by 6.5 million (from 342.9 to 336.4 million). The same netting out of trends is evident when employment is analysed from a gender perspective: the number of working men increased from 309.3 million in 2004–05 to 331.7 million in 2009–10, while the number of working women fell from 148.6 million to 127.3 million over the same five-year period. Consequently, the unemployment rate did not increase; rather, women, particularly in rural areas, were withdrawing from the labour force altogether.

The unexpected decline in women's labour force participation has led to much research and discussion at the policy level, most of it focused on a number of key explanations for the downward trend.[1] This literature has considered four main hypotheses for women's declining participation in paid work: increased levels of educational attainment; mis-measurement; rising household incomes; and, a lack of job opportunities outside the home. Recent research has placed a particular focus on the lack of local job opportunities as a critical dimension of the trend.[2] Improving levels of educational attainment, declining fertility rates and changing social norms are not enough, if jobs are not being created in locations and sectors that women can access.

Overall, the factors behind the decline in female labour force participation relate to both the demand and supply-side of the labour market in a complex and interrelated manner. Social norms have played an historical role in defining how and whether women can engage in paid work or as entrepreneurs outside the home. These norms not only vary across the country but have also evolved over time, in line with increased levels of educational attainment and other changes in society. However, it is still common for women to cease working once they marry. At the same time, a disaggregated view reveals that economic growth has generated a considerable number of jobs, as noted above. But the distribution of these jobs across space and sectors is uneven: most of the growth in employment has occurred in urban areas and in sectors such as construction and services. The literature also includes evidence of a continuing occupational segregation, which reflects the fact that women are traditionally employed in occupations that are growing more slowly.[3] Linked to the distribution of jobs is the issue of access: the challenge is to provide women who can work outside the home with affordable transport and safety while commuting.

A key supply-side constraint is child care: most women in India are required to look after their children, elderly parents and other family members (Hill and Palriwala 2017). With spouses increasingly migrating for employment, the demands on women's time mean that many are unable to work outside the home even if they would like to. However, according to the National Sample Survey data for 2011–12, approximately 30 per cent of women classified as out of the labour force and primarily engaged in domestic duties would take up employment outside the home if paid work was available. Another much-discussed factor behind poor outcomes in the labour market is lack of appropriate skill. It is widely argued that many young Indians leave school without the skills demanded by employers. Though this situation is often portrayed as one of a skills mismatch, job seekers across the country struggle because they lack the foundation of a good quality education. At the same time, the proportion of the population with vocational education and training is low by international standards.

Given the broad economic and social dimensions of these issues, there is no simple policy solution to the problem of female labour force participation in a country like India. On the one hand, the low level of female labour force participation should be seen as a critical issue for economic policies. If India (and other countries with low levels of female labour force participation) are to sustain high levels of growth, women will need to participate in greater numbers. A key issue here is the need for investment that will lead to jobs in locations and occupations which women can access. On the other hand, efforts are needed to address supply-side constraints through the availability of child care, along with access to quality education and training linked to the needs of the labour market. Ultimately, policies should seek to provide more choice for women in accessing decent employment and opportunities for entrepreneurship, beyond the narrow options they currently have.

This chapter argues for an integrated and comprehensive approach to employment policy as a means of increasing opportunities for women in the labour market. Broad directions for such an approach are outlined in the ILO's Convention 122 on Employment Policy and the resolution on employment adopted by the International Labour Conference in 2014. In this regard, the Government of India, along with state governments and other partners, has made considerable efforts to promote skilling, entrepreneurship and access to social security. However, the challenge is implementation: practical and realistic programmatic responses are also needed, particularly at the state level. Moreover, it is critical that different initiatives are piloted and evaluated, in order to identify which interventions have the biggest impact in promoting women's participation and choice.The following discussion first reviews the trends in key labour market outcomes for women and identifies the main challenges and drivers of these outcomes. From here the chapter moves to an exploration of how various employment policies, along with an integrated approach, can make a difference in promoting more opportunities for women in the Indian labour market. A short conclusion summarises the chapter's main findings.

Trends in the Indian labour market and their implications for women

While the situation facing women in the Indian labour market, particularly the declining rate of female labour force participation, appears inconsistent with India's experience of rapid economic growth, it is by no means unique. In fact, apart from Nepal, countries in South Asia have some of the lowest female labour force participation rates in the world. In 2015, the average female labour force participation in South Asia stood at just 28.3 per cent, down from 34.8 per cent in 1995.[4] Participation rates in 2015 were only lower in the Arab States (21.1 per cent) and Northern Africa (22.6 per cent).

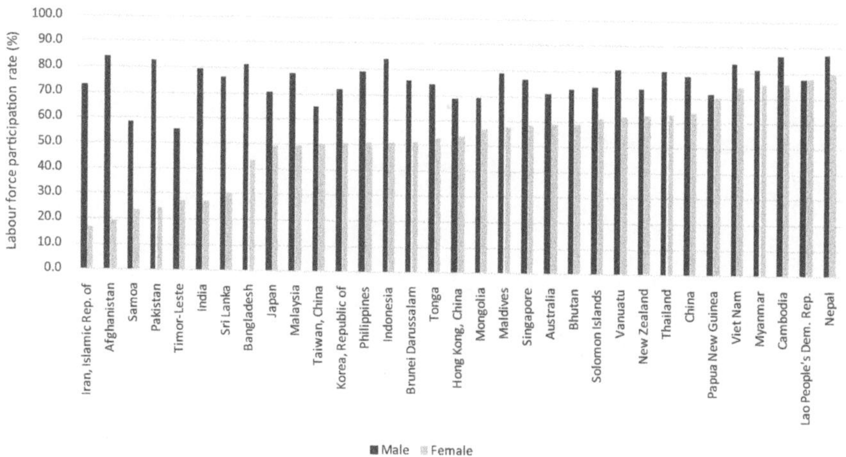

Figure 7.1 Labour force participation rates in Asia and the Pacific, ILO estimates (2015).

Source: *ILO Key Indicators of the Labour Market*, 9th edition; ILO estimates of labour force participation rates.

When compared with other countries in the Asia Pacific region, South Asian countries have some of the lowest female labour force participation rates, which vary much more than the rates for men (Figure 7.1). In South Asia, the lowest rates are in Iran (16.2 per cent), Afghanistan (19.1 per cent) and Pakistan (23.1 per cent). The gender gap in participation rates is the highest in South Asia, along with Samoa and Timor-Leste, while it is very small or non-existent in Nepal, the clear outlier in South Asia and Southeast Asia. While the lowest rates are found in Muslim countries, in majority-Muslim Indonesia the participation rate is 10–30 percentage points higher than in the countries of South Asia other than Nepal and Bhutan. Moreover, in South Asia itself, the majority-Muslim Republic of the Maldives has a much higher participation rate (57.3 per cent) than any of the larger economies to the north.

Beyond levels of participation, there is also considerable variation in the trends in female labour force participation rates in South Asia, especially over the last decade or so (see Figure 7.2). The longer term trends suggest that women have increased their participation in Bangladesh, which has been associated with the growth of the readymade garment sector and an increase in rural female employment, mainly on account of the expansion of micro-credit (Rahman and Islam 2013, 2016). Apart from Nepal and the Maldives, Bangladesh now has the highest participation rate in the region. Female participation has also increased in Pakistan, albeit from a very low starting point, while participation has remained relatively stable in Sri Lanka, despite robust economic growth in recent years (Gunatilaka 2016). However, the most puzzling result for the region as a whole is the falling female labour

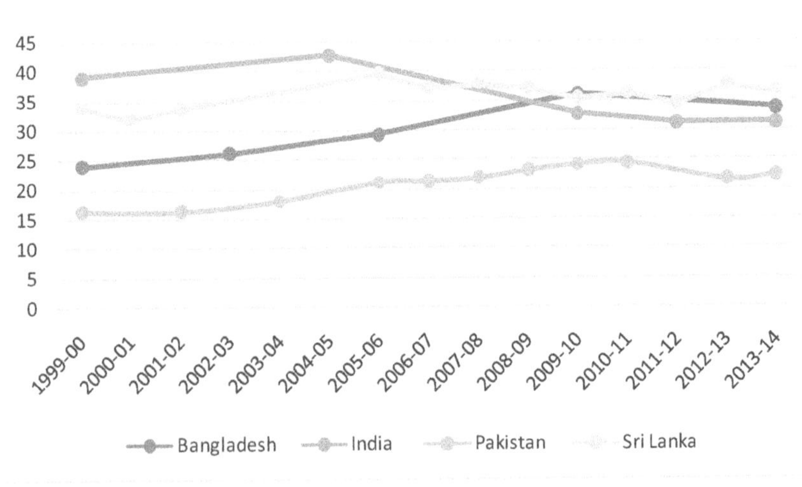

Figure 7.2 Trends in female labour force participation rates in South Asia (per cent) (various years).

Source: Based on data from National Statistical Offices.

Notes: For all countries data is for 15+; Sri Lanka - 10+, and 15+ since 2005–06, excluding North and Eastern provinces; Pakistan - 10+ since 2012-13.

force participation rate in India, which has occurred despite strong economic growth and rising household incomes.

The female labour force participation rate in India has been in steady decline for some decades, with the upturn in 2004–05 an outlier in the overall trend. Most alarming is the decline in the 2000s during the period of strong economic growth. The National Sample Survey's Employment and Unemployment Surveys record labour force participation rates for women aged 15 and above at 42.7 per cent in 2004–05. But by 2009–10 participation had fallen dramatically to 32.6 per cent and by 2011–12 declined further to 31.2 per cent. The latest data from the Labour Bureau for 2013–14 indicates that the participation rate for women has stopped declining and is now stagnant at 31.1 per cent. The unexpected decline in the labour force participation rates of women in India has been largely driven by the withdrawal of women from rural employment even while rates in urban areas have remained largely stagnant for many decades. The participation rate for rural women decreased from 49.0 per cent in 1993–94 to 35.8 per cent in 2011–12, while the rate for urban women fluctuated around 20 per cent over the same period (see Figure 7.3). The labour force participation rate includes both employment and unemployment, though in India's case (as in other developing countries) the rate is largely driven by movements in employment.

In terms of absolute numbers of workers, the trends from the National Sample Survey show that the total workforce in India increased from 459 million in 2009–10 to 472.9 million in 2011–12. In comparison, the increase in employment from 2004–05 to 2009–10 was just 1.1 million. The NSS trends indicate that urban areas have dominated employment growth in India, with rural areas remaining relatively stagnant (see Table 7.1 and 7.2). In 2011–12, there were 101.8 million women workers in rural areas and 27.3 million in

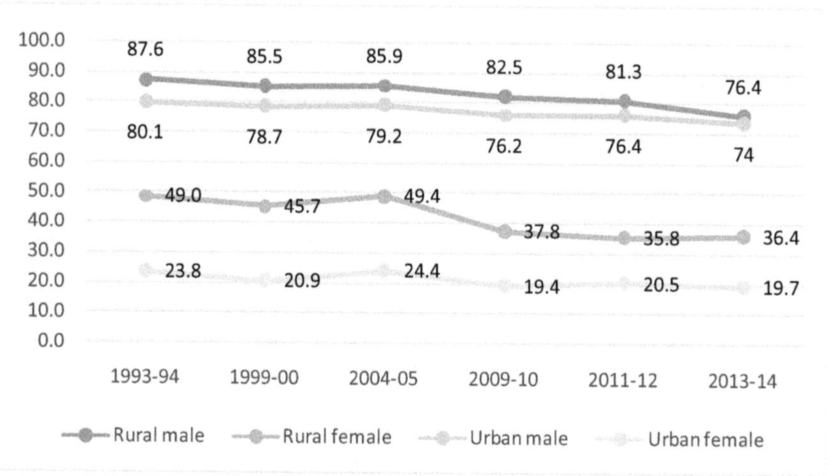

Figure 7.3 Labour force participation rates for 15 years and above (per cent), UPSS.

Source: National Sample Survey, various rounds, and Labour Bureau's data

Note: Data for 2013–14 is from the Labour Bureau.

urban areas. As shown in the trends in participation rates noted above, the number of women workers in rural India registered a significant decline from 2004–05, whereas a reverse trend is evident in the case of urban India. From 2004–05 to 2009–10, the number of women workers dropped by 21.3 million, 19.5 million of whom came from rural areas (Table 7.2).

India is a diverse country with significant variation in economic and social outcomes across its 29 states and 7 union territories. In 2010–11, the per capita net state domestic product ranged from Rs.13,632 in Bihar to over Rs.100,000 in Goa and Delhi (National Capital Territory). Similarly, the poverty rate at the state-level varied from 7.1 per cent in Kerala to 39.9 per cent in Chhattisgarh. On the question of heterogeneity in the labour market, there are considerable differences in the percentage of women in the labour force, despite the overall low rate for India as a whole. In 2011–12, the female employment-to-population ratio ranged from just 5.2 per cent in Bihar to 49.2 per cent in Himachal Pradesh (see Figure 7.4).

Figure 7.4 shows evidence of a positive relationship between the per capita net state domestic product and the female worker population ratio, indicating that in the richer states, more women work outside the home. This positive relationship only holds if the outliers, Goa, Delhi, Puducherry and Chandigarh, are excluded. Nevertheless, it is not possible to attribute causality here. It is

Table 7.1 Number of workers in India (UPSS) (in millions) (all ages)

Category	*1983*	*1993–94*	*1999–2000*	*2004–05*	*2009–10*	*2011–12*
Rural male	153.9	187.7	198.6	218.9	231.9	234.6
Rural female	90.7	104.7	105.7	124.0	104.5	101.8
Urban male	46.7	64.6	75.4	90.4	99.8	109.2
Urban female	12.1	17.2	18.2	24.6	22.8	27.3
Rural persons	244.6	292.4	304.3	342.9	336.4	336.4
Urban persons	58.8	81.8	93.6	115	122.6	136.5
All persons	303.4	374.2	397.9	457.9	459	472.9

Source: NSS, various rounds.

Table 7.2 Net increase in the number of workers in India (UPSS) (in millions) (all ages)

Period	*Rural male*	*Rural female*	*Urban male*	*Urban female*	*All persons*
1983 to 1993–94	33.8	14	17.9	5.1	70.8
1993–94 to 1999–2000	10.9	1	10.8	1	23.7
1999–2000 to 2004–05	20.3	18.3	15	6.4	60
2004–05 to 2009–10	13	−19.5	9.4	−1.8	1.1
2009–10 to 2011–12	2.7	−2.7	9.4	4.5	13.9
1993–94 to 2011–12	46.9	−2.9	44.6	10.1	98.7

Source: NSS, various rounds.

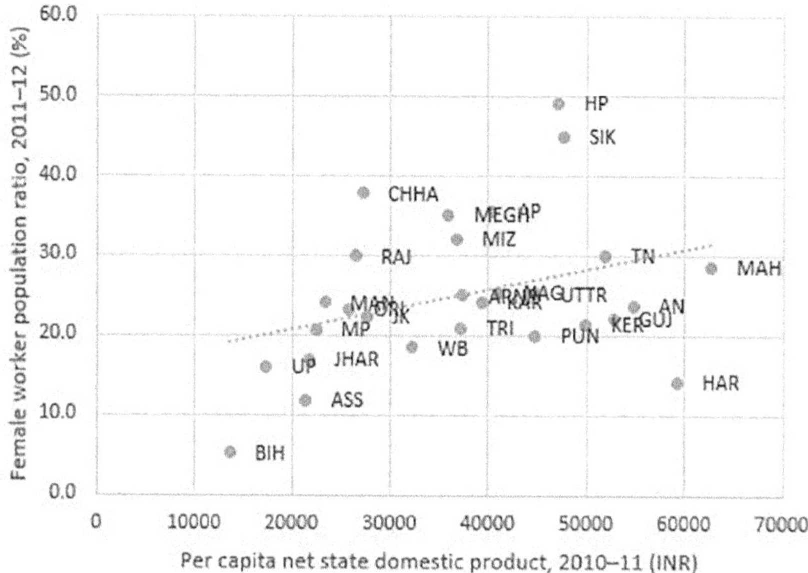

Figure 7.4 State variation in participation of women in the labour force versus per capita net state domestic product.

Source: Central Statistical Office; National Sample Survey.

Note: AN: Andaman & Nicobar Islands; AP: Andhra Pradesh; ARNP: Arunachal Pradesh; ASS: Assam; BIH: Bihar; CHHA: Chhattisgarh; GUJ: Gujarat; HAR: Haryana; HP: Himachal Pradesh; JK: Jammu & Kashmir; JHAR: Jharkhand; KAR: Karnataka; KER: Kerala; MP: Madhya Pradesh; MAH: Maharashtra; MAN: Manipur; MEGH: Meghalaya; MIZ: Mizoram; NAG: Nagaland; ORI: Odisha; PUN: Punjab; RAJ: Rajasthan; SIK: Sikkim; TN: Tamil Nadu; TRI: Tripura; UTTR: Uttarakhand; UP: Uttar Pradesh; WB: West Bengal.

possible that as states become richer, female labour force participation rates increase. Alternatively, however, states may be richer because their female participation rates are higher.

Labour market outcomes vary considerably by levels of educational attainment, which is a major feature of all countries, including emerging economies like India (Cazes and Verick 2013). In India, the participation rates of women vary according to a U-shaped pattern: participation rates are the highest for illiterates, who are poor and forced to work, and tertiary educated women, who have the skills and opportunity to work outside the home. Considered in the longer term, the decline in participation rates in rural areas has been greatest for both the least and the most educated (Table 7.3). However, it should be stressed that the majority of women in rural areas are poorly educated. In urban areas, the participation rates for women of different educational categories have been more or less stagnant since the 1990s, with smaller decreases for both the least and most educated and an increase for women with up to primary education and middle-school education.

Table 7.3 Female labour force participation by levels of educational attainment, ages 15 years and above, UPSS

Educational Attainment	*1993–94*		*1999–2000*		*2004–05*		*2009–10*		*2011–12*		*Change 1993–94 to 2011–12*	
	Rural	*Urban*	*Rural*	*Urban*	*Rural*	*Urban*	*Rural*	*Urban*	*Rural*	*Urban*	*Rural*	*Urban*
Illiterate	54.1	30.1	51.3	27.3	55.2	30.5	43.3	23.2	41.9	24.2	–12.2	–6.0
Up to Primary	41.8	20.9	40.5	18.1	45.5	24.1	38.7	20.7	36.3	22.6	–5.6	1.8
Middle	29.8	14.7	29.9	14.0	38.4	17.5	30.1	16.1	28.3	16.4	–1.5	1.7
Secondary	29.1	15.9	28.5	14.0	33.7	14.2	23.3	11.0	23.5	11.8	–5.6	–4.1
Higher Secondary	29.2	18.2	24.0	14.9	35.9	21.5	24.0	13.8	21.7	14.3	–7.5	–3.8
Graduate & Above	50.4	37.1	44.3	32.0	47.5	34.9	37.4	29.6	36.5	31.9	–13.9	–5.2
Total	49.1	23.8	45.7	20.9	49.4	24.4	37.8	19.4	35.8	20.5	–13.2	–3.3

Source: National Sample Survey.

Note: Primary = grades 1–5; Middle = grades 6-8; Secondary = grades 9–10; Higher secondary = grades 11–12 and includes diploma level.

Chaudhary and Verick (2014) investigate in more detail the relationship between levels of educational attainment and labour market outcomes in India. Based on an econometric analysis of the National Sample Survey data, this study shows that as the level of education rises, the likelihood of being in regular employment increases. For women in the category of "graduate and above", there is a 30 per cent higher probability of being in regular salaried work in rural areas compared to illiterate women, and a 20 per cent higher probability in the case of women in urban areas. At the same time, as the level of education increases, the probability of being self-employed or in casual labour decreases. The results of this study underscore the fact that poorly-educated (illiterate) women are more likely to be in the labour force and working, while only women with tertiary education have an increased probability of being in regular salaried work.

As in most countries, the Government of India has placed considerable emphasis on skill development as a way of ensuring that job seekers and workers are employable. In this context, Chaudhary and Verick (2014) find that vocational training is an important factor determining the employment status of women in India. In particular, having vocational training increases the likelihood that women will be self-employed (though causality is an issue here). Hereditary training received informally through family and other social networks increases the likelihood of self-employment by 38 per cent in rural areas and by 35 per cent in urban areas. On-the-job training appears to be beneficial, as it raises the probability of self-employment by 35 per cent in rural areas and by 31 per cent in urban areas.

Why did women's participation rates fall?

Before delving into the reasons behind the decline in the female labour force participation rate in India, it is important to reflect on why the rate is low to begin with. Overall, the circumstances that determine women's participation in a developing country like India are complex, covering both the demand and supply side of the labour market, and reflecting not only economic forces, but also social and political factors. In India, women's labour market participation is determined to a large extent by caste, religion, marital status, and other sociocultural norms (Dasgupta and Verick 2016; Chaudhary and Verick 2014). These features of society restrict women's mobility and access to wage employment in the formal labour market, in other words whether or not a woman is allowed to work outside the household. In addition to these dimensions, other key factors include a lack of education and skills, both critical determinants of participation (and the nature of employment), as noted above.

Despite the restrictions imposed on women's movements outside the household, it is striking that the proportion of females attending to domestic duties is relatively high in urban areas and among the better educated – the very section of the female population that are likely to face less social constraints on labour participation. In 2009–10, among urban females with tertiary degrees, close to 60 per cent were reported to be attending to domestic duties, almost twice the corresponding proportion for rural females with primary or middle-school education (Thomas 2012). Women's marital status also significantly influences their labour force participation rates. Single women participate in paid work at a higher level than married women (Panda 1999). In their study of female labour in urban Delhi, Sudarshan and Bhattacharya (2009) noted that the decision to work outside the home is usually a household decision and women's household workload and safety concerns are key factors influencing their participation in the labour market. The study also found that family and kinship structures play an important role in determining women's work-life choices.

As a result of these constraints, women often end up outside the labour force or in self-employment in the household or on the family farm. This does not mean, of course, that women are not working. Indeed, women are primarily responsible for household duties and reproduction. Due to the unpaid nature of women's work and the definition of economic activity, women's labour force participation remains statistically under-reported. The role played by women in care activities, predominantly their reproductive work and household maintenance, falls outside the system of national accounts in India. To address this deficiency in measurement, time-use surveys can play a very important role in capturing women's "invisible work" as it covers activities included in the international System of Nationals Accounts (SNA), extended-SNA and also non-SNA activities (Hirway 2002; Hirway and Jose 2011). Though mis-measurement arises from the invisibility of women's work, clearly, women in India are not "hiding" in regular employment in offices and factories. For this reason, the focus in this chapter is on participation in work outside the home.

There are also important economic factors that tend to limit the rate of female labour force participation. In India, as elsewhere, women face various forms of discrimination in the workplace, particularly in terms of wages (Srivastava and Srivastava 2010). In addition, occupational segregation appears to play an important role in holding women back: women in India tend to be grouped in certain industries and occupations such as basic agriculture, sales and elementary services, and handicraft manufacturing. The problem is that these industries/occupations have not seen employment growth in recent years, and this equates to a brake on female employment growth. Female employment in India grew by 8.7 million between 1994 and 2010, but estimates suggest that it could have increased more than three times if women had equal access to employment in the same industries and occupations as their male counterparts (Kapsos, Silberman, and Bourmpoula 2014, 2016).

There has been considerable debate and research on the declining trend in the female labour force participation rate in the 2000s. Analysis has been focused mainly on four possible causes: 1) increased enrolment in secondary schooling; 2) rising household incomes; 3) mis-measurement of women's participation in the labour force; 4) lack of employment opportunities for women in the non-farm sector. In addition, there has been some anecdotal evidence which suggests that the mechanisation of agriculture has played a role in recent years, particularly in poorer states. Each of these will be discussed in turn.

Rising female enrolment in education has meant more young women have been staying out of the labour force. From 2005 to 2013, the gross secondary school enrolment ratio in India increased from 48.7 to 69.2 per cent for girls.[5] At the same time, the ratio for boys increased at a slower rate, from 59.2 to 68.6 per cent. Thus, there are now more girls than boys enrolled in secondary school. When it comes to tertiary education, the gross enrolment ratio for women has grown strongly, from just 8.8 per cent in 2005 to 23.1 per cent in 2013. During the same period, the gross tertiary enrolment ratio for women and men combined rose from 12.5 to 24.6 per cent. This offers an explanation for young women's declining participation in paid work, but does not explain why the labour force participation rate of prime-age women also fell during the 2000s.

One of the arguments put forward suggest some form of mis-measurement in the labour force data. After all, many of the activities women are engaged in are not correctly captured as indicators of economic activity. However, studies such as Kapsos, Silberman, and Bourmpoula (2014) have shown that this explanation cannot account for the bulk of the fall in women's labour force participation. Ultimately, the mis-measurement is most likely to take place in the context of work in the household, that is, whether a woman is classified as being primarily engaged in domestic duties (Natonal Sample Survey codes 92 or 93) or as self-employed, including doing unpaid family labour. Thus, under-reporting is likely to happen in the context of home-based work, not because women are "hidden" in paid employment outside the home in offices and factories.

The third factor that has been considered is the impact of household income. It has been claimed that since the incomes of spouses increased during this period, poor women, especially in rural areas, were able to withdraw from the drudgery of paid work in agriculture and other unskilled occupations. This would appear to be consistent with the fact that the participation rates of women in poor, rural households have decreased the fastest during the 2000s. However, this hypothesis fails to explain why these women continue to live in poor households: is the decline in the participation rate of women in rural India consistent with a neo-classical backward-bending labour supply curve?

Clearly, there are many forces at play in the Indian context, especially in rural areas, which go beyond the standard labour market models. These forces interact to determine the final labour market outcomes. A crucial dimension is the demand-side of the labour market: if jobs are not being created in locations and sectors which women can access, then increased employability and changed social norms will not improve labour market outcomes for women. This explanation is highlighted by Dasgupta and Verick (2016), Chatterjee, Murgai, and Martin (2015) and other researchers as a critical aspect of labour market dynamics in South Asia.

An issue related to job availability is whether the decision of women to engage in domestic duties is entirely voluntary. In this regard, the data from the National Sample Survey tells us that in 2011–12, 34 per cent of women engaged in domestic duties in rural areas and about 28 per cent in urban areas reported their willingness to accept work if they were able to undertake it on their own premises. Tailoring was the most preferred work for women in both rural and urban areas. Among those who were willing to accept work on their own premises, about 95 per cent in both rural and urban areas expressed a preference for work on a regular basis. About 74 per cent in rural areas and about 70 per cent in urban areas preferred "part-time" work on a regular basis, while 21 per cent in rural areas and 25 per cent in urban areas wanted regular "full-time" work.

On the final possible cause of women's declining labour force participation rates – the mechanisation of agriculture and its impact on women's employment in that sector – there is little research evidence. Since the start of the Green Revolution in the 1960s, there has been a rapid increase in the mechanisation of agriculture in India, although the pace has varied in different parts of the country. The agricultural sector in India has a higher density in the use of four-wheel tractors than other similar countries and, as a result, India is also one of the world's largest manufacturers of tractors (Sarkar 2013). Between 2003–04 and 2009–10, the sale of tractors in the domestic market increased at a compound annual rate of growth of 10.5 per cent.[6] The challenge remains to link this growth in the mechanisation and commercialisation of agriculture (not only in terms of tractors, but also harvesters and the use of chemical pesticides and herbicides) to its impact on women's employment in the agricultural sector. This remains an area for further research.

Overall, research on the low and declining levels of female labour force participation in India reveals that this phenomenon is complex and linked to economic and social factors which affect both the demand and supply sides of the labour market. A traditional focus on supply-side dimensions, such as skills development, without a consideration of job creation and women's access to employment will not be sufficient in tackling the barriers women face in joining the labour market.

Employment policies for enhancing women's participation in the labour force

The complexity of factors that drive female labour force participation (and labour market outcomes in general) implies there is no single policy solution to the problem of low female labour force participation in a diverse country like India. As witnessed in the 2000s, very high rates of economic growth failed to increase the participation rates of women in rural areas because new and appropriate forms of employment were not being created. Moreover, women continue to face many barriers to entering the labour market and accessing decent work, including care responsibilities, lack of skills, limited mobility and safety issues. Discrimination against women in the labour market impedes their access to work as well as their career development. Women experience multiple challenges related to access to employment, choice of work, working conditions, employment security, wage parity, discrimination, and balancing the competing demands of work and family responsibilities. But, as a major factor in determining the pace and nature of a country's development path, women's participation in the labour force needs to be taken seriously by economic policymakers, and not seen as an exclusively social issue left to individual ministries and minor agencies. However, the policy goal cannot simply be to increase the female labour force participation rate. It must also involve addressing the quality of employment and removing the work gaps that exist in the sectors and places where women work. It is, therefore, more important to focus on a larger agenda centred on the creation of opportunities for women to enter the labour market. This will support higher levels of participation over the working age portion of a woman's life. Ultimately, this goal is strongly linked to the notion of women's economic empowerment. Participation should be about access to better quality employment, not just employment at any cost.

As Sudarshan (2014) has pointed out, there are specific "transition" points along the life cycle that have special significance for individual and household decisions on women's labour force participation. These include the completion of education and the transition from education to work, as well as marriage and the birth of children. A policy framework that will encourage and enable women's participation through these key transition moments will need to be constructed with an active awareness of the gender-specific constraints facing most women in India. The overarching policy framework needs to focus on removing the constraints to women's work and on encouraging investments that will generate decent jobs accessible to women.

The normative frameworks and observations of the International Labour Organization around the world provide some insights into effective approaches to employment policy.[7] The objective of full and productive employment was stated in the ILO Constitution and the 1944 Philadelphia Declaration, with the Convention on Employment Policy No. 122 (1964), further articulating this goal. In addition, all ILO work on employment derives its current mandate from the Global Employment Agenda (2003), the ILO Declaration on Social Justice for a Fair Globalisation (2008) and the conclusions of the Recurrent Item Discussion on Employment, which took place most recently in 2014 at the International Labour Conference. More specifically, the ILO's Convention 122, one of the four governance Conventions under the 2008 ILO Declaration on Social Justice for a Fair Globalisation, provides a global frame of reference for employment policy. The Convention requires that this policy be positioned as a major macroeconomic goal within the national policy agenda. It also calls for tripartite consultations. The conclusion of the 2010 International Labour Conference reiterated the importance of ILO support for the development and adoption of national employment policies (NEPs). The conclusions concerning the Second Recurrent Discussion on Employment, which took place at the International Labour Conference in 2014, go one step further and invite member states to promote a comprehensive employment policy framework based on a menu of policy choices, which include the pertinent issues covered in this chapter. These broad, comprehensive approaches to employment policy as articulated in Convention 122 and the most recent recurrent item discussion on employment at the International Labour Conference are highly relevant to the challenges outlined above. However, taking a comprehensive approach does not mean that everything is of equal importance and that all policy dimensions should be addressed at the same time. Rather, it is essential that strategic policy entry points are found within a comprehensive understanding of the issues surrounding women's participation in the labour market in a diverse and complex country such as India.

Considering the issues that have been highlighted in this chapter, there are six areas of concern under the broad rubric of employment policy that need to be considered: 1) inclusive growth and job creation; 2) education and skills development; 3) support for reducing the time burden; 4) transport and infrastructure; 5) legal rights and protection; and 6) measurement. These will be discussed in turn.

First, as highlighted above, a crucial policy dimension is the demand side, that is, the creation of jobs and entrepreneurship opportunities for women. In recent decades in India, the majority of jobs have been created in urban areas. There has been no increase in the number of new jobs in rural areas, and employment in these areas has fallen. For this reason, there is a critical need for more emphasis to be placed on promoting investment in smaller towns and rural locations, which would lead to the creation of jobs that women are able to access. Given the poor investment environment in these places, the market has not provided the right incentives for such investments to take place. Therefore, better infrastructure and specific tax and other monetary incentives will be needed to encourage investment in these locations.

Second, as research across different countries shows, good labour market outcomes are dependent on education and skill development.[8] As noted above in relation to India, however, there is no linear connection between educational attainment and women's participation in the labour force. Indeed, the lowest level of participation occurs among women with secondary school education. Thus, a fundamental policy goal should be to increase access to education and skills development beyond secondary schooling for girls and young women. A decent education provides the best foundation for making a successful transition from school to work. In addition to formal education, girls and young women also need greater access to vocational education and training, as a means of broadening their occupational choice.

Third, even if they have the necessary qualifications and skills, women in India struggle to work outside the home because of their traditional responsibilities as primary caregivers for children and elderly parents. Particularly in rural areas, there is very little childcare of a type that households would deem appropriate and trustworthy. This is a key reason why many women prefer to work at home, despite poorer working conditions and lower remuneration. This means that more attention needs to be given to reducing the time burden associated with unpaid household work, which would increase opportunities and enable women to make choices about paid work. Similarly, measures are required to improve the provision of child care and elder care through public policy, as well as through the sharing of care responsibilities between women and men at the household level (Hill and Palriwala 2017). In this context, maternity benefits are essential, as are policies that support married women's work. Flexible work arrangements (but with formal employment benefits) should be offered. In most of rural India, improvements in basic infrastructure (drinking water, sanitation, electricity and cooking fuel) would contribute greatly to the provision of more time for women to engage in paid work.

Fourth, a major challenge for women in India is to be able to access jobs in a safe and secure manner. Further efforts are needed to expand public transport to facilitate the movement of women, especially the poor, as well as the provision of infrastructure such as public toilets and street lighting to improve the safety of Indian women travelling to and from work. Safety in the workplace could be improved by the installation of closed-circuit cameras, which would act as a deterrent to harassment and violence (Sudarshan 2014).

Fifth, to promote women's participation in the labour market and the economy in general, a range of legal rights need to be strengthened. These include the right to own property and land (as well as inheritance rights), protection from violence and sexual harassment, equal pay, safe working conditions, non-discrimination, and representation. India, like most countries, has many rights enshrined in various laws. However, a major challenge is the enforcement (and awareness) of legal rights. As is the case in all countries, including India, the persistence of the gender wage gap arguably acts as a further disincentive for women to participate in the labour market (Deshpande, Goel and Khanna 2015). This indicates the need for firmer measures to improve the implementation of legal provisions for equal remuneration. Better working conditions will, in turn, encourage women to join the labour market and take up employment outside the home. Access to social protection is critical, not only to support household incomes, but also to encourage mobility. Mobility also requires the portability of benefits, something which is largely lacking in India at present as a result of the way most social protection schemes are designed.

Finally, given the challenge of measuring women's work, much of which remains invisible in labour market data, policymakers need to improve the collection of information on different dimensions of women's labour force participation. Particularly important in this regard is the use of time-use surveys. In addition, better trained enumerators (and more female enumerators) would help improve the accuracy of these surveys. More broadly, the Resolution of the 19th International Conference of Labour Statisticians in 2013 provides a foundation for a far more comprehensive approach to measuring women's work.[9]

Conclusion

Given the complexity of these factors and the drivers of employment outcomes, in general, there is no simple policy solution at hand. For this reason, it is important for policy makers in India and other countries to consider a comprehensive employment policy approach. The focus cannot be about participation at all costs; rather, consideration has to be given two principles: 1) promoting access to decent employment and entrepreneurship opportunities that make a difference to the lives of women in terms of economic empowerment; and 2) expanding choice through the diversification of opportunities away from segregated occupations and sectors where women tend to be exploited. Key policy dimensions of such an approach would include creating more jobs that are accessible to women; improving education and skills development beyond secondary schooling; reducing the time burden so women have the chance to work outside the home; enhancing transport and infrastructure; strengthening legal rights and protection; and improving the measurement of women's work to ensure it is accurately analysed and monitored.

Millions of women in India are now better educated and have fewer children than was the case in previous generations. Strong economic growth has helped lift large numbers of households out of poverty. Yet, one of the key remaining challenges is the situation facing Indian women in the labour market. In order to achieve greater equality and give these women more opportunities and real choices in the world of work, policy makers, along with other stakeholders, need to give the issues highlighted above the utmost priority as a central plank of the country's economic and social policy agenda.

Notes

1 See Chatterjee, Murgai, and Martin (2015); Chaudhary and Verick (2014); Das et al. (2015); Dasgupta and Verick (2016); Kapsos, Silberman, and Bourmpoula (2014, 2016); Klasen and Pieters (2015).

2 See, for example, Chatterjee, Murgai and Martin (2015), and Dasgupta and Verick (2016).

3 See Kapsos, Silberman, and Bourmpoula (2014, 2016).

4 ILO estimates; see *ILO Key Indicators of the Labour Market*, 9th edition, http://www.ilo.org/global/statistics-and-databases/research-and-databases/kilm/lang—en/index.htm

5 Source: UNESCO Institute of Statistics (UIS) country profiles, http://www.uis.unesco.org/DataCentre/Pages/country-profile.aspx?regioncode=40535&code=IND

6 Annual Report, Department of Agriculture and Cooperation, Ministry of Agriculture, Government of India, various years.

7 http://www.ilo.org/wcmsp5/groups/public/---ed_emp/documents/publication/wcms_140943.pdf

8 See, for example, Cazes and Verick (2013) for a discussion on the important role of education in determining employment outcomes in emerging economies.

9 See http://www.ilo.org/global/statistics-and-databases/meetings-and-events/international-conference-of-labour-statisticians/19/lang—en/index.htm

References

Cazes, S., and S. Verick. 2013. *The Labour Markets of Emerging Economies: Has Growth Translated into More and Better Jobs?* Geneva and Basingstoke, UK: ILO, Palgrave Macmillan.

Chatterjee, U., R. Murgai, and R. Martin. 2015. *Job Opportunities along the Rural-Urban Gradation and Female Labor Force Participation in India.* New Delhi: World Bank. [Policy Research Working Paper 7412].

Chaudhary, R., and S. Verick. 2014. *Female Labour Force Participation in India and Beyond.* New Delhi: ILO DWT for South Asia and Country Office for India [ILO Asia-Pacific Working Paper Series].

Das, S., S. Jain-Chandra, K. Kochhar, and N. Kumar. 2015. *Women Workers in India: Why So Few among So Many?* Washington, DC: IMF. [IMF Working Paper 15/55, Asia and Pacific Department].

Dasgupta, S., and S. Verick (eds), 2016. *Transformation of Women at Work in Asia: An Unfinished Development Agenda.* New Delhi: SAGE.

Deshpande, A., D. Goel, and S. Khanna. 2015. *Bad Karma or Discrimination? Male–Female Wage Gaps among Salaried Workers in India.* Bonn: Institute for the Study of Labor. [IZA Discussion Paper Series, Working Paper 9485].

Gunatilaka, R. 2016. "Factors Holding Women back from Market Work in Sri Lanka: To Work or not to Work?" In *Transformation of Women at Work in Asia: An Unfinished Development Agenda*, S. Dasgupta and S. Verick (eds), 155–186. New Delhi: SAGE.

Hill, E., and R. Palriwala. 2017. "India: Economic Inequality and Social Reproduction". In *Women, Work and Care in the Asia-Pacific* Marian Baird, Michele Ford, Elizabeth Hill (eds). London: Routledge.

Hirway, I. 2002. "Employment and Unemployment Situation in the 1990s: How Good is the NSS Data?" *Economic and Political Weekly* 37 (21): 2027–2036.

Hirway, I., and S. Jose. 2011. "Understanding Women's Work Using Time Use Statistics: The Case of India." *Feminist Economics* 17 (4): 67–92.

Kapsos, S., A. Silberman, and E. Bourmpoula. 2014. *Why is Female Labour Force Participation Declining So Sharply in India?* Geneva: ILO. [ILO Research Paper 10].

Kapsos, S., A. Silberman, and E. Bourmpoula. 2016. "Decline of Women's Labour Force Participation in India: Explaining the Puzzling Trend." In *Transformation of Women at Work in Asia: An Unfinished Development Agenda*, S. Dasgupta and S. Verick (eds), 75–102. New Delhi: SAGE.

Klasen, S., and J. Pieters. 2015. "What Explains the Stagnation of Female Labor Force Participation in Urban India?" *World Bank Economic Review* 29 (3): 449–478.

Panda, P. K. 1999. *Poverty and Young Women's Employment: Linkages in Kerala.* Thiruvananthapuram: Centre for Development Studies. http://unpan1.un.org/intradoc/groups/public/documents/apcity/unpan010700.pdf

Rahman, R. I., and R. Islam. 2013. *Female Labour Force Participation in Bangladesh: Trends, Drivers and Barriers.* New Delhi: ILO. [ILO Asia-Pacific Working Paper Series].

Rahman, R. I., and R. Islam. 2016. "Women's Employment in Bangladesh: Beyond Garments." In *Transformation of Women at Work in Asia: An Unfinished Development Agenda*, S. Dasgupta and S. Verick (eds), 123–154. New Delhi: SAGE.

Sarkar, A. 2013. "Tractor Production and Sales in India, 1989–2009." *Review of Agrarian Studies* 3 (1): 55–72.

Srivastava, N., and R. Srivastava. 2010. "Women, Work and Employment Outcomes in Rural India." *Economic and Political Weekly* 45 (28): 49–63.

Sudarshan, R. M. 2014. *Enabling Women's Work*. New Delhi: ILO. [ILO Asia-Pacific Working Paper Series].

Sudarshan, R. M., and S. Bhattacharya. 2009. "Through the Magnifying Glass: Women's Work and Labour Force Participation in Urban Delhi." *Economic and Political Weekly* 44 (48): 59–66.

Thomas, J. J. 2012. "India's Labour Market during the 2000s: Surveying the Changes." *Economic and Political Weekly* 47 (51): 39–51.

8 The effectiveness of the Mahatma Gandhi National Rural Employment Guarantee Scheme (MGNREGS) in promoting employment and social inclusion

Salim Lakha

Economic reforms in India since 1991 have accelerated economic growth, but the outcome for employment has been mixed. The boom in the high-tech services sector in the wake of the economic reforms generated considerable growth in urban employment for information technology specialists. However, in rural India, underemployment, poverty and economic insecurity dominate the economic landscape. Poverty declined during the high growth years with 137 million people recorded as rising above the poverty line between 2005 and 2012. Nevertheless, 22 per cent of the population remained poor (World Bank 2013, 8) and more than half the population fell below the more generous poverty lines. At the same time inequality has been on the rise. Between 2005 and 2012 the Gini coefficient climbed from 30.9 to 32.3 (World Bank 2013, 9). More pertinently, around 60 per cent of the population was deemed to be in a precarious state of existence (even though not poor) because it was vulnerable to "minor shocks" that could reduce people to some measure of poverty (World Bank 2013, 9). Under these conditions there is a crucial need for some form of safety net to protect those who are vulnerable to economic pressures and who lack the resources to tide them over a severe economic crisis.

The Mahatma Gandhi National Rural Employment Guarantee Act (MGNREGA) introduced by the United Progressive Alliance (UPA) government in 2005 aimed to ensure that those exposed to economic vulnerability were guaranteed security of livelihood. It was also intended to prevent distress migration from rural areas in times of economic stress. Consequently, the Act guaranteed a legal right of 100 days of employment per financial year to each rural household whose adults were willing to undertake manual work. Thus the employment scheme implemented under MGNREGA (henceforth MGNREGS) operates on the basis of self-selection, without discrimination and rejecting the neoliberal approach which emphasises efficiency (Chopra 2014a, 91). In addition to the provision of guaranteed employment, a major objective of MGNREGS is to promote asset creation through small-scale rural infrastructure works related to water conservation, road construction, afforestation and similar activities. Importantly, it aims to promote the inclusive growth accorded high priority under the 11th National Five Year Plan from 2007–12 (Planning Commission 2006, 56-86).

The scheme stipulates many requirements related to social inclusion, payment to workers and the need for transparency (MoRD 2013). The wages of males and females employed under MGNREGS are equal and of the total beneficiaries at least one-third should be women (Mehrotra 2008, 27, 29). Labourers are to be paid the minimum wage under MGNREGS set by the state where they are employed, and if employment is not provided within 15 days then an unemployment allowance has to be paid to the job seekers. The job seekers are, however, required to register for a job card with their local *gram panchayat* (village council) or GP before they can be provided with work. The details of the work completed by the beneficiaries are recorded in muster rolls, which should be held at the worksite so that workers can check their work activity record. Contractors are barred from engaging in the scheme. This is to avoid any overcharging for materials and services and to ensure that machinery is not deployed in place of labour. The details of the policy are designed to maximise employment. In order to ensure transparency, the scheme also provides for information to be released to the person requesting it within seven days of the lodgement of an application. Minimum wages, an unemployment allowance, gender-sensitivity, participatory democracy, transparency and accountability all form key components of MGNREGS. The scheme is implemented by the village council in consultation with the *gram sabha* (village assembly) and in the financial year 2014-15 provided employment to 41.4 million households (GoI 2015a). Hirway (2012, 47) argues that MGNREGS should be an integral "component of a full-employment strategy for India", as it has the potential to contribute to "labour intensive growth and full employment". This potential, however, is yet to be fully realised.

Despite generating employment for substantial numbers of households, MGNREGS has been criticised strongly by its detractors. The scheme's critics claim that it is riddled with corruption, that it is responsible for the construction of unsustainable, inferior quality public works and that it generally involves wasteful expenditure. For example, one vociferous critic has argued that a major defect of the scheme is the "leakage", or corruption, associated with it, whereby people who are paid under the scheme have either not undertaken the prescribed work or are not poverty-stricken and, therefore, undeserving of the benefits (Bhalla 2014). Echoing the concerns of the critics, Prime Minister Narendra Modi famously declared just a day prior to the release of the 2015–16 Budget that MGNREGS was a "living monument" to the failings of the previous UPA government (Tewari 2015). While claims of corruption are in some instances valid, viewing the scheme solely through the prism of corruption underestimates some of its achievements. Despite Prime Minister Modi's strong reservations regarding the benefits of MGNREGS, the continuation of funding for the scheme under the Budget for 2015–16 underlined its importance, although some claim this funding is inadequate for the effective functioning of the scheme. Both the economic benefits of the scheme, especially for economically marginalised sections of the rural population, and the political ramifications that would result from the termination of the scheme have ensured its continuation.

In contrast to the detractors of MGNREGS, the scheme's supporters argue that it has generated much needed employment and benefited large sections of the marginalised population in rural India (Dreze and Khera 2011, 51–62). It is now evident from a cross-section of scholarly and other studies of MGNREGS that despite the many criticisms associated with its implementation, the scheme has promoted a significant measure of social inclusion. Further, it has empowered some women through improvements in different aspects of their lives, including their status within the household, their consumption of consumer goods and access to essential services like health, and their greater involvement in local institutions like the *gram sabha* (Pankaj and Tankha 2012, 282–289). It has also benefited many members of the Scheduled Castes (SCs) and Scheduled Tribes (STs), substantial numbers of whom are marginal landholders and agricultural labourers. Even criticisms about the poor quality of public works are only partially valid, and there are a number of evaluations that have demonstrated the benefits flowing to the villagers from public works initiated under the scheme (Dhananjaya and Prathibha 2011, 277–278). Thus Aiyyar (2014) has argued that the debate over MGNREGS has largely been defined by an ideological battle over the involvement of the state in the provision of social welfare. Those who are less inclined to support state investment in welfare are quick to dismiss the employment benefits of the scheme, by highlighting the prevalence of corruption in its implementation. As others have pointed out, however, corruption can be tackled by existing provisions within MGNREGS, which require regular social audits of the scheme. In many cases these audits have not been conducted effectively, sometimes because of manipulation and opposition from dominant social forces like state politicians and officials at the district and village levels (Afridi 2008; Lakha, Rajasekhar, and Ramachandra 2015).

This chapter specifically evaluates the contribution of MGNREGS to employment creation, social inclusion, and skill development. An assessment of the scheme is important, considering that it represents the most extensive social protection programme in existence both nationally and internationally. Further, it accounts for as much as 38 per cent of the total social protection expenditure in India (ADB 2013, 34). The chapter argues that while MGNREGS has contributed to social inclusion and has been responsible for a degree of empowerment amongst marginalised and vulnerable groups, there is still considerable potential for increasing the level and quality of employment under the scheme. Further, more emphasis on skill training is necessary in order to enhance both the quality of projects implemented under the scheme and the future employment prospects of the scheme's beneficiaries.

The chapter is divided into three sections. It begins with a discussion of the contribution of MGNREGS to employment creation in India, taking into account variations in employment generation between the states. The second section examines the extent to which MGNREGS has led to social inclusion and the empowerment of women. Finally, the chapter considers how skill training could contribute to more productive and longer-term benefits for the beneficiaries of the scheme. The discussion is based primarily on an analysis of primary and secondary sources, including newspaper reports related to the implementation of MGNREGS. It is also informed by two fieldwork visits (in 2011 and 2012) to Bangalore and Chitradurga District of Karnataka. During the second field visit in 2012 two interview surveys of beneficiaries of the scheme and members of Vigilance and Monitoring Committees (VMCs) in five *gram panchayats* were conducted jointly with research collaborators from the Institute of Social and Economic Change in Bangalore. The field visits also included interviews with officials at the state, district, sub-district and *gram panchayat* levels and discussions with other key informants.

Employment creation

It is clear from various studies that MGNREGS is not performing at its full potential, especially where the provision of employment is involved (Alam and Alam 2014, 8). For example, in 2009–10, of the total percentage of rural households seeking work, only 56 per cent managed to obtain employment under the scheme (Dutta et al. 2012, 57). Also, the data for the nine months of each of the periods 2009–2010 and 2011–2012 reveal that nationally there was a drop in employment between the two periods when measured in terms of the average person days of work per household, from 46.83 to 32 (Jha and Gaiha 2012, 19). Subsequent estimates for the financial year 2012–13 showed the average workdays per household rose to just over 46 (Tewari 2014; GoI 2015a), but in the financial year 2014–15 the average days of employment per household dropped back to 40.17 (GoI 2015a). It is evident from these statistics that progress as far as employment is concerned has not been consistent. These figures are also much lower than the maximum employment allowed to a household under the scheme, which is 100 days per year. Significantly, the total number of households obtaining 100 days of wage work under the scheme declined from over 5.17 million in the financial year 2012–2013 to around 2.49 million in 2014–2015 (GoI 2015a). As stated above, the demand for work is higher than the work delivered under the scheme, so this decline cannot be explained by a lack of demand.

There are also wide variations in employment creation across the different Indian states. Table 8.1 indicates the top 10 states in terms of the average number of days of employment per household over the three financial years from 2012–13 to 2014–15.

Remarkably, of the top ten states represented in Table 8.1, four are located in north-eastern India: Tripura (ranking highest), Mizoram, Sikkim and Meghalaya. There are three southern states (Andhra Pradesh, Kerala and Tamil Nadu) and another three are in northern and western India. Excepting Tripura, none of the states reached an average over the three years that was close to the maximum of 100 days allowed under MGNREGS. Significantly, the more populous northern states with comparatively low per capita incomes and higher poverty rates generated a lower level of employment. In the case of Uttar Pradesh the three year average was only 32.3 days per household

Table 8.1 Top 10 states ranked by the average days of employment provided per household over three financial years

Rank	*State*	*FY 2014–15*	*FY 2013–14*	*FY 2012–13*	*Three FY Average*
1	Tripura	87.96	88.91	87.35	88.07
2	Mizoram	22.47	75.29	87.81	61.85
3	Sikkim	42.51	69.58	64.12	58.73
4	Tamil Nadu	47.36	58.67	57.8	54.61
5	Meghalaya	47.65	59.31	52.43	53.13
6	Kerala	42.65	56.83	54.89	51.45
7	Andhra Pradesh	47.18	49.58	55.92	50.89
8	Maharashtra	52.93	45.23	53.7	50.62
9	Rajasthan	45.74	50.86	52.25	49.61
10	Himachal Pradesh	42.14	52.39	50.92	48.48

Source*:* Table constructed by the author from Government of India (2015b).

and in Bihar the figure was just 40.3 days per household (GoI 2015b). The relatively populous state of West Bengal in eastern India generated a three year average of a mere 35.07 days employment per household (GoI 2015b). The performance of MGNREGS differs enormously across the regions. What is disturbing is that in all the top 10 ranked states the average number of days of employment declined in the 2014–15 financial year compared to 2012-13, except in Tripura, where it climbed very slightly. Among the other states (ranked outside the top ten) only Odisha (Orissa), Uttar Pradesh, Goa and Chandigarh experienced a rise in 2014–15 compared to 2012–13 (GoI 2015b). Overall, employment creation in the three years from 2012–13 to 2014–15 was not positive.

Several factors influence the provision of work under the scheme, including state government support for implementation, the willingness of the *gram panchayat* officials to issue job cards to those seeking work, and the dedication of officials at various levels of administration to promote awareness about the scheme. In Karnataka, for instance, the promotion of awareness of MGNREGS was not a significant priority for local government officials (at the district, sub-district and *gram panchayat* levels) who complained that they already suffered from an onerous workload and did not have sufficient time for the additional demands the scheme placed on them (Pani and Iyer 2011, 85). This situation is in stark contrast to the official view espoused by the central government, according to which a "much greater emphasis is needed on spreading awareness among MGNREGS workers about their legal entitlements and procedures of the Act" (MoRD 2011, 5). Where complaints about workload and capacity constraints are concerned, Karnataka is not an isolated example. Similar complaints were also raised by local level bureaucrats in Rajasthan (Chopra 2014b, 14–15). Other factors have also influenced the provision of work under the scheme, such as the requirement that job seekers should be paid an unemployment allowance if they do not find work within 15 days of a request. In Rajasthan this has led some officials to refuse to register workers, thus absolving the state from paying them the unemployment allowance (Chopra 2014b, 15).

According to a study of four states, the achievements of MGNREGS are substantially dependent upon the "'commitment" of stakeholders involved in executing the scheme. [1] The 2015 ESID study found Andhra Pradesh and Chhattisgarh did well because there was a substantial degree of commitment, whereas Bihar and Assam did comparatively less well because of an insufficient level of commitment.[2] In the case of Andhra Pradesh the scheme initially had strong support from the chief minister, who was keen to implement welfare schemes in his state as a means of extending his political support, something which he did quite successfully (Maiorano 2004, 96). In addition, state-supported institutions combined with civil society actors such as non-government organisations (NGOs) reinforced the efforts of the Andhra Pradesh state government to ensure the success of the scheme (Galab and Revathi 2012, 150–151). Similarly in Tamil Nadu, where the scheme has been comparatively successful, strong state government support combined with close monitoring of the scheme by different chief ministers has played an important part in its effective implementation (Carswell and De Neve 2014). Interestingly, the ESID study revealed that the political party affiliation of state governments was not a significant factor in the successful implementation of the scheme, although the chief minister of Andhra Pradesh belonged to the Indian National Congress which, together with its coalition partners, introduced MGNREGA when it led the national government. In the case of Chattisgarh, however, the state government is affiliated with the Bharatiya Janata Party (BJP) which was in opposition when MGNREGA was enacted (ESID 2015).

Social inclusion and empowerment of women

Despite various criticisms of MGNREGS, in some states the outcomes for social inclusion and social development have been quite significant. For the financial year 2014–2015 the national level share of employment for marginalised groups, namely, SCs, STs and women, was 22.27 per cent, 18.44 per cent and 50.22 per cent respectively (GoI 2015a). Women's share of employment was well above the stipulated requirement under MGNREGA, which is 33 per cent. Further, the employment for SCs and STs under the scheme was proportionately much higher than their total population at the national level. The scheme also provides for SCs and STs who own land to implement works connected with agriculture, sanitation, and drinking water on their lands, in order to promote their social and economic well-being (Manjula and Rajasekhar 2015, 5–6). Though some measure of social inclusion has been achieved through the higher proportional representation of SCs and STs and the provision for improvements to their lands, the employment benefits of MGNREGS have not been evenly spread among different caste groups. In the case of Karnataka there was an uneven distribution of work along caste lines, with proportionately more people from Other Backward Castes (OBCs) households receiving employment in the bracket of 50 to100 days annually, compared to the majority of SCs and STs who received only 20 days of employment under the scheme (Manjula and Rajasekhar 2015, 10–11).

The minimum mandatory quota for women under MGNREGS has also ensured the social and economic inclusion of women. According to one sample study of six Indian states, there were significant benefits for women in the form of improved and safer work conditions, greater income earning opportunities and the localised nature of work, which suited their needs (Khera and Nayak 2009). However, there were wide variations in levels of female employment between the states. In the southern states of Tamil Nadu and Kerala, for example, female participation measured as a "share of total person days" in 2009–2010 was over 80 per cent, whereas in Karnataka it was only 37 per cent (Sudarshan 2011, 4). Both Tamil Nadu and Kerala have maintained an overwhelming representation of women in the total employment created under MGNREGS, with women in these states accounting for 85.36 per cent and 92.16 per cent of person days worked in 2014–15 respectively (GoI 2015b). While Karnataka increased its share of female participation, it still remained far behind, at 46.86 per cent (GoI 2015b). In another southern state, Andhra Pradesh, women's share of employment remained consistently above 58 per cent between 2012–13 and 2014–15 (GoI 2015b). In some of the more populous states in the north with lower levels of social development, the female participation rate was relatively low in 2009–10, at 30 per cent in Bihar and 21.6 per cent in Uttar Pradesh (Sudarshan 2011, 4). By 2014–15 women's share of total person days of employment had risen fairly significantly in Bihar, to 37.32 per cent, but in Uttar Pradesh the increase was more modest, at 24.77 per cent (GoI 2015b). The full potential of the scheme, as far as the provision of employment and social inclusion are concerned, is yet to be realised in these two populous states. Women's lower share of employment is a reflection of the lower status of women in those states, which results in gender inequality in the distribution of resources. Importantly, during the financial year 2011–12 Tamil Nadu and Kerala allocated a much higher proportion of their MGNREGS funds to wages (99.7 per cent and 96.2 per cent respectively) in order to maximise employment. At the same time, they spent less on materials compared to states such as, for example, Karnataka, where the expenditure on wages was much lower, at 60.1 per cent (GoI n.d., 63).

Several studies have confirmed that the achievements in social inclusion have improved the economic and social conditions of women, especially those of the lower classes (Narayanan 2008; Jandu n.d.; Sudarshan 2011). A survey of 104 women in Viluppuram district in Tamil Nadu revealed that the scheme was of particular benefit to women (Narayanan 2008, 10). This study revealed that 87 per cent of the female beneficiaries belonged to lower socio-economic groups like SCs, STs, "backward classes" or "most backward classes" and 60 per cent were from landless households. For many of these beneficiaries, work provided under MGNREGS was their sole means of earning an income during the slack agricultural season. Consequently, it was an important source of economic security, allowing them to stay in their home districts rather than migrate long distances to neighbouring states in the south (Narayanan 2008, 11). Other studies have reported similar benefits for women. Jandu's survey (n.d.) of four districts in the states of Chattisgarh, Madhya Pradesh, Orissa and Tamil Nadu also found that the majority of respondents claimed that the scheme meant they were not forced to migrate in search of work. In some districts a very large proportion of the women obtained their wages "in person" instead of through intermediaries like their husbands or other males (Jandu n.d., 6). This practice, however, is not uniform across different states, as another study revealed that in Gaya (Bihar) and Ranchi (Jharkhand) only 33.3 per cent and 38.6 per cent of women respectively obtained their wages personally instead of relying on male relatives or male intermediaries (Pankaj and Tankha 2012, 284). Where women did collect their own wages it was a demonstration of their increased independence and confidence in the public domain (Jandu n.d., 4-5). To that extent, the scheme was helping to empower some women because it allowed them more authority over the income they earned and how it was spent (Pankaj and Tankha 2012, 284–285).

Research suggests that the scheme is empowering women in other respects as well. During fieldwork in Karnataka in 2012, an informant who worked as a resource officer with a local NGO reported a revealing case of empowerment achieved through the convergence of social mobilisation and mobile phone technology. One of the women working on the scheme, who protested against the deployment of machinery by a contractor at the worksite, approached the *panchayat* development officer (PDO) to complain, on the grounds that neither the use of machinery nor contractors are allowed under the scheme. She was rebuffed by the PDO, who denied that machinery had been deployed. Undeterred, the woman photographed the machine operating at the worksite with her mobile phone and presented the image to the PDO to prove her case. Collective social mobilisation through NGO activity, combined with creative application of mobile phone technology, gave this female labourer the confidence to confront a male official. In Karnataka, where even female *gram panchayat* members often let their husbands act as their proxies at official meetings, this was a significant reversal of unequal gender relations.

Sudarshan's survey of the states of Himachal Pradesh, Kerala and Rajasthan also confirms the benefits for women and their empowerment through the work provided under the employment scheme, even though the degree of women's empowerment varied. In Kerala the scheme is implemented through *Kudumbashree,* or the state's "poverty eradication mission", where women are organised into self-help groups (SHGs). As a result there is a high level of self-mobilisation of women involved in MGNREGS, and it is the women themselves who manage the worksites. This has led to a strengthening of women's status in the scheme (Sudarshan 2011, 10–11). In Rajasthan, by contrast, a similar self-mobilisation does not exist; here, *gram panchayats* are in charge of implementing MGNREGS. Though youth organisations have mobilised women in Rajasthan, women are not actively engaged in implementing the scheme or participating in the social audits, which are left to *gram panchayats* to conduct. The gram panchayats, however, have vigorously opposed any "independent audits" (Sudarshan 2011, 11). The local level institutions, therefore, can have a significant bearing on the degree to which the scheme delivers benefits in the form of women's empowerment.

Skills training

An important means of empowering both male and female participation in MGNREGS has been the implementation of skill training programmes. The acquisition of new skills facilitates participation in the wider employment market and builds self-confidence among the scheme's beneficiaries. Until recently, however, insufficient consideration has been given to the implementation of skill training programmes on a coordinated nationwide basis, even though such programmes have proved quite successful in some other countries (World Bank 2012). This official oversight may partly be explained by the different qualitative approach to social protection in India compared to, for example, East Asia. Rudra distinguishes two separate paradigms: the productive welfare state and the protective welfare state (2008, 86–87). Protective welfare states like India are identified with protected markets, import-substitution, and a "protective" labour market combined with the expansion of public sector employment (Rudra 2008, 86, 111). For a long time India followed this trajectory, before gradually introducing economic reforms in 1991. Reform of the labour market, however, has been slow. By contrast "productive" welfare states like South Korea, which are export-oriented, do not incorporate public employment programmes in their social protection approach instead placing greater emphasis on the enhancement of human capital through education and training (Rudra 2008, 147–149).

Under the productive welfare state paradigm "social policy is strictly subordinate to the overriding policy objective of economic growth" (Kwon and Holliday 2008, 243). Importantly, in relation to unemployment, social policy is aimed not only at providing unemployment benefits but also the provision of training for workers in order to promote "job capability" instead of merely "job security" (Kwon 2005, 493). In this respect, Singapore's experience is instructive for India because one means of promoting "job capability" in Singapore is through the education system. Technical institutes prepare students for the needs of the labour market through the design of appropriate curriculum and provision of on-the-job training (Advani 2015, 9). This emphasis on job capability is in stark contrast to the situation in India, where job security has dominated the state's economic and employment agenda.

The potential benefits of MGNREGS could be expanded significantly by incorporating measures that promote job capability through skills training. However, in India the skills gap is a national malaise. This is reflected in the very low level of formal vocational training among adults – only 2.2 per cent, compared to 75 per cent of the working population in Germany, 80 per cent in Japan and almost 50 per cent in China ("The Challenge" 2015). While the current BJP-led government has enthusiastically committed itself to skilling the nation, tangible outcomes of this commitment are yet to emerge. In the past, there have been insufficient attempts to promote skills development under MGNREGS, although in 2010, under the UPA government, it was proposed that training be offered to workers from families where two people had completed over 50 days of employment for two successive years (Tewari 2010). This proposal aimed to link MGNREGS to another scheme, *Swarnajayanti Gram Swarozgar Yojana* (SGSY), which since 1999 has been available to families identified as "Below Poverty Line" and which has been quite successful in providing employment through training.

Without the provision of training there are serious questions about the longer-term outcomes for the beneficiaries of MGNREGS. There are some longer-term benefits for those beneficiaries who are landowners and able to utilise MGNREGS funds for works on their own land, but for landless participants the benefits are confined to a supplementary income that improves personal consumption and access to services like health. If, however, job security were to be combined with the promotion of job capability, both the productivity of labour and the quality of works promoted under the scheme could be improved (Hirway 2012, 47). If works completed under MGNREGS are to result in sustainable development then the introduction of a skills training component into the scheme is vital. Considering the low levels of literacy and the skills gap among the labour force in rural India, the critics of MGNREGS would be better advised to direct their efforts at demands for skills development under the scheme rather than the scheme's termination.

The need to enhance labour productivity and long-term employment opportunities through training has also been emphasised by the World Bank (2012, 269–270). Countries as diverse as Bangladesh, El Salvador, Liberia and Papua New Guinea have combined public works schemes with training in order to enhance the employability of workers in the wider labour market (World Bank 2012, 270). These models suggest that there are several different approaches to training that could be implemented to suit the needs of the different categories of workers employed under MGNREGS. In Sierra Leone the focus is upon the promotion of literacy and numeracy, an approach which could prove suitable for those MGNREGS participants who have had either limited or no opportunity for schooling. Liberia offers participants in public works programmes training in life-skills, while El Salvador and Papua New Guinea supplement life-skills with technical training. Appropriate forms of technical training for some of the beneficiaries of MGNREGS would significantly improve the quality of the works they are engaged in. Technical training connected with, for example, construction work, forestry, and water resources management is particularly relevant to the activities promoted under the scheme. Bangladesh offers yet another pathway to participation in the wider economy. There, the participants in public works programmes are directed to micro-finance organisations for training in operating micro-enterprises, a skill which most of the participants acquired successfully. Training in micro-finance has the potential to contribute to the development of sustainable livelihoods and provide households with opportunities to supplement their incomes. In India, where there is an extensive network of NGOs and government-supported agencies, training in micro-finance could be delivered effectively across the country.

Recently, however, a more concerted effort at skills training has been made through the "Project for Livelihoods in Full Employment", or Project LIFE-MGNREGA (GoI 2015c). Guidelines for this project were announced in April 2015, with the aim of promoting self-reliance and enhancing the skills of those employed under MGNREGS so that they are able to make the transition from part-time employment to full-time employment. The project is undertaken in conjunction with *Deen Dayal Upadhyaya Grameen Kaushalya Yojana* (DDU-GKY), a scheme that provides training programmes of varying length at the national level for over 250 trades spanning more than 50 sectors (PIB 2015).[3] Importantly, it is mandatory for the DDU-GKY to find placements for 75 per cent of the students it trains.

Eligibility for training under LIFE-MGNREGA is confined to people aged 15–35 years who belong to households where persons have worked for a minimum of 15 days during the preceding financial year. The age limit is extended to 45 years for women and groups belonging to certain categories like vulnerable members from STs, persons suffering disability, the transgender population, and some others (GoI 2015c). Eligibility for training also requires sitting an aptitude test for the chosen occupation. However, the number of applicants accepted for training is limited. If the numbers of those passing the aptitude test exceeds available places then priority is accorded to applicants from households whose members have completed 100 days of work in the preceding financial year (GoI 2015c). In 2015 it was estimated that there were 14 lakhs (or 1,400,000) households with members who had worked 100 days in the previous financial year and with workers who were below the age of 35 years ("14 Lakh Households" 2015). On completion of the programme, the beneficiaries of the training will be placed in employment in urban areas. It is still too early to assess the effectiveness of LIFE-MGNREGA, but this project is a step in the right direction, because its aim is to ensure job capability for at least some MGNREGA beneficiaries who are eligible under the scheme.

Conclusion

It is evident from the functioning of MGNREGS that the provision of employment in India is not commensurate with the demands for work. Employment creation is regionally uneven and in 2014–15 declined in comparison to the previous two years. None of the states have achieved the maximum employment allowable per household annually, which is 100 days. The scheme has therefore been only partially successful in achieving its objectives. Further growth in employment creation will depend upon a variety of factors, including collective pressure from below through a rise in workers' awareness of their entitlements. Raising awareness is an important requirement for the full potential of the scheme to be realised. The effectiveness of the scheme is also reliant upon the commitment of political actors in the individual states involved and adequate funding by both the state and central governments. The scheme's significance in providing a safety net for the poor and the marginalised is recognised by some at the official level. The Economic Survey 2014–15 argues that as the terms of trade for agriculture deteriorate, there will be increasing demand for assistance, especially for "vulnerable" sectors of the population like agricultural workers and small farmers. The Survey supports MGNREGS because the scheme is quite "well-targeted" and provides for rural infrastructure development at the same time as it protects incomes (GoI 2014). There is consequently a strong case for strengthening the scheme rather than weakening or dismantling it.

Social inclusion under the scheme is also taking place unevenly, at both the social and spatial levels. While the SCs and STs are well-represented nationally in the scheme, evidence, from Karnataka at least, suggests that it provides these groups with less work compared to OBCs. Regionally, the social inclusion of women is very uneven, with Tamil Nadu and Kerala attaining considerably high rates of female participation while the more populous states of Bihar and Uttar Pradesh lag far behind. To some extent, the greater inclusion of women is dependent upon self-mobilisation and the ability of local level institutions to foster an enabling environment that promotes self-confidence and empowerment amongst women. While there are many different dimensions to the concept of empowerment, in relation to MGNREGS it can be observed at three levels: personal, social and economic. At the personal level, some women are gaining more confidence through independent income earning opportunities as well as through their interactions with government officials and other social actors outside their homes. Socially, women are improving their status within the family and the household because of their ability to contribute to household income. Income earning opportunity also enables women's economic empowerment, as it allows them to ameliorate both their own consumption standards and that of their families, especially where they exercise independent control over their earnings.

The economic empowerment of the beneficiaries of MGNREGS could be increased substantially through the implementation of nationwide skills training programmes. The introduction of Project LIFE-MGNREGA represents an opportunity for a significant shift from short-term income security to better paid, longer-term employment through the acquisition of skills. While this project is welcome, its scope is rather limited since, according to some reports, its beneficiaries will be younger members of households that have completed 100 days employment. Statistics reveal that proportionately not many households have completed this number of days of employment. The project needs to be supplemented with other training programmes that take account of the aptitude and needs of different categories of beneficiaries. As the experience of other countries demonstrates, training may take one of a number of different pathways.

Many workers employed under MGNREGS lack basic literacy and numeracy skills. Improvements in these areas would go a long way towards raising awareness of entitlements, increasing levels of personal confidence and facilitating incremental change in employment prospects. An experiment in literacy promotion was undertaken on the initiative of the district collector in Jhalawar district of Rajasthan, where 18,000 workers, mostly women, employed under MGNREGS successfully completed 50 days of the literacy programme offered on worksites (Parmar 2012). Remarkably, many of these workers made rapid progress, and the skills they acquired allowed them to deal effectively with the middlemen who in the past had exploited them. Part of the reason for the success of this scheme lay in its recognition that labourers have very little time available for personal development. Locating training programmes at worksites made it possible to overcome this time constraint and respond effectively to workers' immediate needs. There is, therefore, considerable scope for promotion of literacy and numeracy if it is attempted on a coordinated, nationwide basis, and is tailored to suit the requirements of workers at the local level.

According to Jean Dreze (2015) on-the-job learning is an ongoing process under MGNREGS. In a review of the scheme, Dreze found that hundreds of thousands of "women and men are learning technical, administrative and social skills as *gram rozgar sevaks*, programme officers, worksite mates, barefoot engineers, data entry operators and social auditors" (4). These skills can be transferred to other sectors of the economy, as many of the workers move on to other jobs after completing their contracts under the scheme. Skills could also be disseminated more systematically to the beneficiaries of MGNREGS through formal training programmes. This would equip them with the skills required to implement the public works and conduct the social audits which are mandatory under MGNREGS. Fieldwork in Karnataka demonstrated that these types of skills were in short supply among the beneficiaries of the scheme, hindering their ability to execute their duties effectively. Ultimately human capital is as important as other forms of capital in the promotion of economic development. Skills formation is integral to this process and an essential part of a successful employment guarantee scheme such as the MGNREGS.

Notes

1 "Commitment" is defined as "the willingness and intent of actors to undertake sustained actions to achieve a set of objectives" (ESID 2015).

2 While Chattisgarh did not rank in the top ten states in Table 8.1, its record of employment creation (three years average) was much better than those of many other states.

3 The scheme is a continuation of a previous skills development scheme called *Aajeevika*, which was rebranded after the BJP-led government gained power in 2014 ("BJP to Rename" 2015).

References

"14 Lakh Households to be Provided Skill Development Training under LIFE." *The Economic Times.* May 10, 2015. http://articles.economictimes.indiatimes.com/2015-05-10/news/62001693_1_skill-development-training-households-mgnrega

ADB. 2013. The *Social Protection Index. Assessing Results for Asia and the Pacific.* Manila: Asian Development Bank (ADB). http://www.adb.org/sites/default/files/pub/2013/social-protection-index.pdf

Advani, Rahul. 2015. "Skills Development in India: Prospects of Partnership with Singapore and Japan." National University of Singapore, Singapore [ISAS Working Paper No. 207].

Afridi, F. 2008. "Can Community Monitoring Improve the Accountability of Public Officials?" *Economic and Political Weekly* 43 (42): 35–40.

Aiyyar, Yamini. 2014. "Re-framing the MGNREGA Debate." *The Hindu*, Nov. 8. http://www.thehindu.com/opinion/lead/reframing-the-mgnrega-debate/article6575483.ece

Alam, Shabbir, and Mohamed Noor Alam. 2014. "Good Governance and Employment Generation through MGNREGA." *International Journal of Economics, Commerce and Management* II (9): 1–17.

Bhalla, Surjit S. 2014. "Column: Do Not Reform NREGA, Junk it." *The Financial Express*, Dec. 12. http://www.financialexpress.com/article/fe-columnist/column-do-not-reform-nrega-junk-it/18180/

"BJP to Rename UPA Scheme after Deen Dayal Upadhyaya." *The India Express.* Sept. 24, 2015. http://indianexpress.com/article/india/india-others/bjp-to-rename-upa-scheme-after-deen-dayal-upadhyaya/

Carswell, Grace, and Geert De Neve. 2014. "MGNREGA in Tamil Nadu: A Story of Success and Transformation?" *Journal of Agrarian Change* 14 (4): 564–585. DOI: 10.1111/joac.12054.

"The Challenge of Skills and Jobs." *The Hindu.* Editorial. Sept. 28, 2015. http://www.thehindu.com/opinion/editorial/the-challenge-of-skills-and-jobs/article7695056.ece

Chopra, Deepta. 2014a. "The Indian Case. Towards a Rights-based Welfare State?" In *Development and Welfare Policy in South Asia*, edited by Gabriel Koehler and Deepta Chopra, 85–105. London: Routledge.

Chopra, Deepta 2014b. "'They Don't Want to Work' versus 'They Don't Want to Provide Work': Seeking Explanations for the Decline of MGNREGA in Rajasthan." Manchester: University of Manchester. [*ESID (Effective States in Development) Working Paper No. 31*].

Dhananjaya, K., and M. S. Prathibha. 2011. "Role of Mahatma Gandhi National Rural Employment Guarantee Act (MGNREGA) in Rural Asset Creation in India – An Analysis." *Journal of Global Economy* 7 (4): 275–295.

Dreze, Jean, and Reetika Khera. 2011. "The Battle for Employment Guarantee." In *The Battle for Employment Guarantee*, edited by Reetika Khera, 43–80. New Delhi: Oxford University Press.

Dreze, Jean. 2015. "The Digging-holes Myth." *Indian Express*, Jul.1. http://indianexpress.com/article/opinion/columns/the-digging-holes-myth-2/

Dutta, Puja, Rinku Murgai, Martin Ravallion, and Dominique van de Walle. 2012. "Does India's Employment Guarantee Scheme Guarantee Employment?" *Economic and Political Weekly* 42 (16): 55–64.

ESID. 2015. *How Commitment and Class Relations Shape MGNREGA Implementation in India.* Manchester: Effective States in Development (ESID). [ESID Briefing No. 11]. http://www.effective-states.org/wp-content/uploads/briefing_papers/final-pdfs/esid_bp_11_MGNREGA_implementation.pdf

Galab, Shaik, and E. Revathi. 2012. "MGNREGS in Andhra Pradesh: Examining the Role of State-enabled Institutions." In *Right to Work and Rural India. Working of the Mahatma Gandhi National Rural Employment Guarantee Scheme (MGNREGS)*, edited by Ashok K. Pankaj, 149–168. New Delhi: Sage.

GoI. n.d. *Outcome Budget of Department of Rural Development 2013-2014.* New Delhi: Ministry of Rural Development, Government of India. http://rural.nic.in/sites/downloads/budget/Outcome_Budget_2013_14Eng.pdf

GoI. 2014. *Economic Survey 2014–15, Vol. I.* New Delhi: Ministry of Finance, Government of India.

GoI. 2015a. *At a Glance.* New Delhi: Ministry of Rural Development, Government of India. http://www.nrega.nic.in/netnrega/home.aspx

GoI. 2015b. *States.* New Delhi: Ministry of Rural Development, Government of India. http://nrega.nic.in/Netnrega/stHome.aspx

GoI. 2015c. *Guidelines for Securing Full Employment Status to MGNREGA Workers through Project for Livelihoods in Full Employment (Project LIFE-MGNREGA).* New Delhi: Ministry of Rural Development, Government of India. http://nrega.nic.in/Netnrega/WriteReaddata/Circulars/1040Guideline_Special_project_for_LIFE_0415.pdf.

Hirway, Indira 2012. "MGNREGS: A Component of Full-Employment Strategy for India." In *Right to Work and Rural India. Working of the Mahatma Gandhi National Rural Employment Guarantee Scheme (MGNREGS)* edited by Ashok K. Pankaj, 47–71. New Delhi: Sage.

Jandu, Navjyoti. n.d. "Employment Guarantee and Women's Empowerment in Rural India." http://www.righttofoodindia.org/data/navjyoti08_employment_guarantee_and_women's_empowerment.pdf

Jha, Raghbendra, and Raghav Gaiha. 2012. "NREGS: Interpreting the Official Statistics." *Economic and Political Weekly* 47 (40): 18–22.

Khera, R., and N. Nayak. (2009). "Women Workers and Perceptions of the National Rural Employment Guarantee Act." *Economic and Political Weekly*, Vol. 49 (43): 49–57.

Kwon, Huck-ju. 2005. "Transforming the Developmental Welfare State in East Asia." *Development and Change* 36 (3): 477–497. DOI: 10.1111/j.0012-155X.2005.00420.x.

Kwon, Soonman, and Ian Holliday. 2007. "The Korean Welfare State: A Paradox of Expansion in an Era of Globalisation and Economic Crisis." *International Journal of Social Welfare* 16 (3): 242–248. DOI: 10.1111/j.1468-2397.2006.00457.x.

Lakha, Salim, Durgam Rajasekhar, and Ramachandra Manjula. 2015. "Collusion, Co-option and Capture: Social Accountability in Karnataka, India." *Oxford Development Studies* 43 (3): 330–348.

Maiorano, Diego. 2014. "The Politics of the Mahatma Gandhi National Rural Employment Guarantee Act in Andhra Pradesh." *World Development*, 58 (C): 95–105. http://dx.doi.org/10.1016/j.worlddev.2014.01.006.

Manjula, R. and D. Rajasekhar. 2015. *Participation of Scheduled Castes in MGNREGS: Evidence from Karnataka.* Bangalore: Institute for Social and Economic Change. [Working Paper No. 339].

Mehrotra, Santosh. 2008. "NREG Two Years On: Where do we go From Here?" *Economic and Political Weekly,* Vol. 43, (31): 27–35.

MoRD. 2011. *Reforms in MGNREGA Implementation*. New Delhi: Ministry of Rural Development, Government of India.

MoRD. 2013. *Mahatma Gandhi National Rural Employment Guarantee Act 2005 (Mahatma Gandhi NREGA, Operational Guidelines 2013*, 4th ed. New Delhi: Department of Rural Development, Government of India.

Narayanan, Sudha. 2008. "Employment Guarantee, Women's Work and Childcare." *Economic and Political Weekly* 43 (9): 10–13.

Pani, Narendra, and Chidambaran G. Iyer. 2011. *Evaluation of the Impact of Processes in the Mahatma Gandhi National Rural Employment Guarantee Scheme in Karnataka*. Bangalore: National Institute of Advanced Studies.

Pankaj, Ashok K., and Rukmini Tankha. 2012. "Empowerment Effects of the MGNREGS on Women Workers" In *Right to Work and Rural India. Working of the Mahatma Gandhi National Rural Employment Guarantee Scheme (MGNREGS)*, edited by Ashok K. Pankaj, 273–297. New Delhi: Sage.

Parmar, Ajay. 2012. "NREGA ki pathshala makes Labourers Study at Work." *Times of India*, Dec. 3. http://timesofindia.indiatimes.com/india/NREGA-ki-pathshala-makes-labourers-study-at-work/articleshow/17457859.cms

Planning Commission. 2006. *Towards Faster and More Inclusive Growth. An Approach to the11th Five Year Plan (2007–12)*. New Delhi: Government of India. http://planningcommission.nic.in/plans/planrel/app11_16jan.pdf

PIB. 2015. "Deen Dayal Upadhyaya Grameen Kaushalya Yojana (DDU-GKY) – Skill Development for Inclusive Growth." New Delhi: Press Information Bureau, Ministry of Rural Development, Government of India. http://pib.nic.in/newsite/efeatures.aspx?relid=115288

Rudra, Nita. 2008. *Globalization and the Race to the Bottom in Developing Countries. Who Really Gets Hurt?* Cambridge: Cambridge University Press.

Sudarshan, Ratna M. 2011. *India's National Rural Employment Guarantee Act: Women's Participation and Impacts in Himachal Pradesh, Kerala and Rajasthan*. Brighton: Institute of Development Studies. [CSP Research Report 06].

Tewari Ruhi. 2010. "NREGA May be Linked to Skill Development." *Livemint*, Apr. 14. http://www.livemint.com/Politics/fozP300epjFvNfUaL1lMPP/NREGA-may-be-linked-to-skill-development.html

Tewari, Ruhi. 2014. "Workdays: MNREGS Short of Even Halfway Mark." *The Indian Express*, March 17. http://indianexpress.com/article/india/india-others/workdays-mnregs-short-of-even-halfway-mark/

Tewari, Ruhi. 2015. "Despite Modi Criticism, Jaitley Gives NREGA a Slight Nudge." *The Financial Express*. March 1. http://indianexpress.com/article/business/budget/despite-modi-criticism-jaitley-gives-nrega-a-slight-nudge/

World Bank 2012. *World Development Report 2013. Jobs*. Washington D.C.: World Bank.

World Bank 2013. *India Development Update*. Washington D. C.: World Bank. [Report No: AUS5757]. http://documents.worldbank.org/curated/en/595561468293126072/pdf/AUS57570WP0P140Box0379846B00PUBLIC0.pdf

9 Jobs in India

The crisis of less and loss

Amitendu Palit

None other than the Indian President Pranab Mukherjee has expressed serious concern over India's inability to create enough jobs for its burgeoning workforce. Addressing the National Student Startup Policy on November 16, 2016, President Mukherjee stated:

> We must turn our evolving demographic configuration into strength. For that, adequate job creation is a priority. The job creation figures of 1.35 lakh in 2015, which is the lowest in seven years, are not encouraging. With machines fast replacing men, we have to look at a paradigm shift. We have to prepare our youth, who are buzzing with innovative ideas, to turn into entrepreneurs. We also have to enable our students-turned innovators-turned entrepreneurs to be able to successfully harness the market.[1]

President Mukherjee's concerns highlight one of the biggest challenges facing policymakers in India: reversing the rapid pace of job loss and inadequate job creation.[2]

With India's expanding population and the World Bank's estimate that one of out of five Indians is poor, low levels of job creation and a lack of sufficient livelihood opportunities can accelerate poverty.[3] Contrary to earlier estimates, India appears to be on track to replace China as the world's most populous country. While India was previously expected to catch up with China by 2028, the latest UN projections point to the possibility of the catch-up as early as 2022.[4] The projections indicate that more and more people will figure in the working-age population within a remarkably short period of time. As the new entrants to the workforce seek gainful employment, job seekers are expected to significantly outnumber job-holders—a scenario made gloomier by the fact that job creation in India stands at one of the lowest levels ever recorded.

Concerns expressed by the Indian President pertain to two significant supply-side aspects of India's labour market. The lack of growth in job creation is compounded by a loss of jobs to automation. This is certainly not what policymakers in an economy aiming to capitalise on the demographic dividend of a large young population want to see. India stands to benefit significantly from a steady supply of labour for its expanding economy; in turn, the gainfully employed young are expected to save and invest productively, placing India on a trajectory of high economic growth made possible by its young workforce as drivers of both the supply- and demand-sides of the economy. This demographic dividend, however, will remain largely unrealised if the economy is unable to create an adequate number of jobs for these young people. In other words, if labour-intensive industrialisation does not deliver on the expectations attached to it (see Hill, this volume), national economic aspirations and development plans in a labour surplus emerging market economy like India will encounter major obstacles. It is in this context that the dual challenge of low job creation and job losses faced by India's economic policymakers become significant. The next section looks at the broader economic and structural changes India has experienced since the 1990s and contextualises these two challenges.

Structural change and jobless growth

The introduction of economic reforms in India since 1991 has produced major structural changes in the Indian economy. These include a greater external orientation, visible in the significant increase in the external trade–GDP ratio and the rise in long- and short-term cross-border capital inflows. At the same time, there has been a significant increase in the contribution of services to economic growth and India's GDP. Services now comprise more than 60 per cent of the Indian economy. According to the quarterly estimate of national income for April–June 2016–17 by the Central Statistical Organization of India (CSO) (measured at 2011–12 prices),[5] the shares of agriculture (including forestry and fishing) and manufacturing in India's total economy are 14.4 per cent and 17.6 per cent respectively, yielding a combined share of 32.0 per cent. If all the remaining sectors are included within services, i.e. mining and quarrying; electricity, gas, water supply and other services; construction, trade, hotel, transport, communication and services related to broadcasting; financial, insurance, real estate and professional services; and public administration, defence and other services, the aggregate share of services increases to 68 per cent. Among all these services, the latter three account for 53 per cent of the total economy, a significant rise from 38.5 per cent in 1991–92.

The greater contribution of services to the economy has been accompanied by a reduction in the contribution of agriculture, which now accounts for only 17 per cent of the total economy, compared with almost 30 per cent in early 1990s. The contribution of manufacturing (exclusive of mining and quarrying, electricity and construction) has increased only marginally during this period, from around 14 per cent in 1991–92 to 18 per cent in 2015–16.[6] The higher contribution of services to the national economy has been accompanied by a reduction in the share of agriculture and manufacturing, whose combined contribution to GDP has declined from 43 per cent in 1991–92 to 32 per cent in 2015–16.

The progressively greater role of services in the economy has been precipitated by several factors, including deregulation, urbanisation and the increasing role of private players in the provision of modern services like finance, hospitality, education, health, real estate, retail, entertainment, transport, communication and IT. While many service industries have generated new employment, the overall contribution of services to employment has not been commensurate with their contribution to the national economy. In this respect, services contrast with manufacturing and agriculture, particularly the latter, which, notwithstanding its declining share in national output, continues to provide significant employment to both rural and urban India.

The 46th annual survey of the National Sample Survey Organization (NSSO), conducted between July 1990 and June 1991, recorded the highest levels of rural employment for both males and females in the primary sector (agriculture and allied activities), followed by secondary (manufacturing, mining, electricity and construction) and tertiary (trade, hotel, transport, storage communication and other services) sectors.[7] Roughly two decades later, the 68th annual survey of the NSSO, covering the period July 2011–June 2012, still found that the primary sector was the largest provider of employment for rural males and females. The result points to the inability of the tertiary sector, or services, to replace agriculture as the main source of jobs for rural India. However, the tertiary sector was the largest employment provider for both urban males and females in 2011–12, much as it was two decades earlier. The rural–urban dichotomy is indeed conspicuous in the role of services in generating employment in the Indian economy, with services exhibiting a predominantly urban bias. The low employment creation by services in rural India needs to be viewed alongside the fact that while the primary sector, particularly agriculture, remains the largest source of employment for rural men and women, it is now employing far fewer of both than in the early 1990s. More rural jobs have been created in both secondary and tertiary sectors over the last two decades but not enough to displace agriculture as the largest provider of employment in rural India. At the same time, the centrality of services and the tertiary sector as providers of jobs in urban India has increased rapidly, particularly for women, mainly due to the greater employment of women in various urban-based services such as the construction industry, retail trade, IT-based call centres and business process outsourcing (BPO) establishments, hotels, restaurants and hospitality establishments, financial enterprises and educational institutions.

The current crisis in India's labour market has much to do with the inability of services to become as significant in the provision of jobs as it is in contributing to the national economy. This mismatch has given rise to the disconcerting notion of "jobless growth" which has become a huge concern for policy makers. Indeed, the failure of services to yield job-intensive growth is far more noticeable in India than in other emerging markets. During 2001–2014, the share of services in India's overall employment increased by only 4.7 per cent,[8] which was in marked contrast to the figures for China,

Russia and Brazil, which, together with India and South Africa, make up the BRICS group of emerging market economies. In the same 2001–2014 period, the increases in the share of services in employment for China, Russia and Brazil were 34.3 per cent, 7.2 per cent and 17.2 per cent respectively.[9] The stunted performance of services in creating jobs in India is particularly stark given that the sector itself grew faster than services in Russia and Brazil during the entire period (2001–2014) and faster than services in China during the latter part of the period.[10]

Services-led growth in India during the last two decades has imparted the unfortunate characteristic of "jobless growth" to the economy. This phenomenon portends grim prospects for future employment generation given the declining share of agriculture and the almost stagnant share of manufacturing in India's GDP, and the inability of both to generate jobs.

Disturbing trends in the labour market

The tightening of the labour market in India is visible from several fundamental parameters, including the Labour Force Participation Rate (LFPR).[11] The 5th Annual Employment–Unemployment Survey conducted by the Labour Bureau for 2015–16 indicates a lower LFPR of 50.3 per cent compared with the 52.5 per cent noted in the 4th Survey for 2013–14.[12] Assuming a population of 1.2 billion, the more than two percentage point reduction in LFPR within two years reflects a drop of more than 20 million in the number of new entrants to the labour force. The comparable estimates for the unemployment rate[13] between the two surveys are also important to note. The latest survey reveals an overall unemployment rate of 5.0 per cent, with rural and urban unemployment rates of 5.1 per cent and 4.9 per cent respectively. The overall unemployment rate is marginally higher than the 4.9 per cent in the previous survey that had rural and urban unemployment rates of 4.7 per cent and 5.5 per cent respectively. A lower LFPR is therefore accompanied by higher unemployment, with a proportionally greater increase in rural unemployment. This needs to be seen alongside a parallel trend underscoring lower urban unemployment, with marginally decreased unemployment for urban females compared with an increase in unemployment for rural women.[14] This trend largely reflects the increase in tertiary sector employment for urban women along with a reduction in employment opportunities for rural women.

The reduction in the LFPR reflects the lower participation rate of women in the labour force. Socio-cultural factors like women's preoccupation with household responsibilities and a lack of encouragement to take up work outside the home continue to hamper the entry of women into the labour force. The LFPR for women declined by almost two percentage points, from 25.8 per cent to 23.7 per cent, between the two surveys. Lower participation of women in the labour force continues to remain a chronic characteristic of the Indian labour market and is now an even greater drag on the overall LFPR, given the decline in the male LFPR as well.

Apart from socio-cultural issues, the low female LFPR in India has also been related to the time being spent by women in higher education, which is delaying their entry into the labour force. At the same time, the rise in overall household incomes, particularly in urban India, might also have reduced the need for women to enter the labour force in search of subsistence jobs. Empirical evidence also points to the low female LFPR being driven by a "jobs deficit" in the form of a lack of an adequate number of "suitable" jobs offering women the flexibility to manage domestic and professional responsibilities simultaneously.[15] This again is a structural limitation of the services-led growth process in India where many modern service industries are unable to generate the flexible part-time jobs that are sought after by many urban women. This limitation, apart from influencing the low LFPR, also contributes to a high urban female unemployment rate, as much as 12.1 per cent according to the latest survey.

India's unemployment rate, however, compares relatively favourably with peer economies in other emerging markets. The ILO's estimates for unemployment in other BRICS economies for 2014 were: Brazil 6.8 per cent, China 4.7 per cent, Russia 5.1 per cent and South Africa 25.1 per cent.[16] The ILO's comparable estimate for India was 3.6 per cent. Nonetheless, the twin crisis of decreased job growth and the loss of many jobs is a matter of concern for India, along with the problem of under-employment. The Labour Bureau's Report on Employment–Unemployment Survey for 2015–16 notes:

> It is pretty well-known that many of the persons who are reported as "employed" or "workers" in official publications do not get work for the entire duration of their stay in the Labour Force. And even those who get some work or the other for the entire duration may be getting work for only a small fraction of the time they are available for work. This apart, some may be working on jobs which do not allow them to fully utilise their abilities or from which they earn very low incomes. All this constitutes under-employment, which remains a worrying aspect of the employment –unemployment scenario in the country.[17]

Under-employment is particularly relevant for female workers given the jobs deficit for women alluded to earlier. The combined problems of fewer people entering the work force, growing unemployment and prevailing under-employment are accentuated by issues related to quality of employment. The Labour Bureau's observations in this regard, noting the unhappiness among graduates and post-graduates over remuneration, lack of written contracts and absence of social security benefits, convey a disturbing trend.[18]

Fewer and fewer jobs

The concern alluded to at the beginning of this chapter regarding the reduction in the number of new jobs being created in the economy is perhaps best

Table 9.1 Results from Labour Bureau's Quarterly Employment Surveys (QES)

Survey	*Period*	*Change in Employment (in 100,000)*
1	Oct–Dec, 2008	5.00 (–)
2	Jan–Mar, 2009	1.17 (–)
3	Apr–Jun, 2009	1.31 (–)
4	Jul–Sep, 2009	4.97 (+)
5	Oct–Dec, 2009	6.40 (+)
6	Jan–Mar, 2010	0.61 (+)
7	Apr–Jun, 2010	1.62 (+)
8	Jul–Sep, 2010	4.35 (+)
9	Oct–Dec, 2010	2.07 (+)
10	Jan–Mar, 2011	1.74 (+)
11	Apr–Jun, 2011	2.15 (+)
12	Jul–Sep, 2011	3.15 (+)
13	Oct–Dec, 2011	2.26 (+)
14	Jan–Mar, 2012	0.81 (+)
15	Apr–Jun, 2012	0.73 (+)
16	Jul–Dec, 2012	1.68 (+)
17	Jan–Mar, 2013	1.07 (+)
18	Apr–Jun, 2013	0.86 (+)
19	Jul–Sep, 2013	1.43 (+)
20	Oct–Dec, 2013	0.83 (+)
21	Jan–Mar, 2014	0.36 (–)
22	Apr–Jun, 2014	1.82 (+)
23	Jul–Sep, 2014	1.58 (+)
24	Oct–Dec, 2014	1.17 (+)
25	Jan–Mar, 2015	0.64 (+)
26	Apr–June 2015	0.43 (–)
27	July–Sep 2015	1.34 (+)

Source: Table 1.1, p. 5, *Quarterly Report on Changes in Employment in Selected Sectors* (July 2015–September 2015); Government of India, Ministry of Labour and Employment, Labour Bureau, Chandigarh, March 2016.

observed in the creation of jobs in typically employment-intensive industries. The findings from the Labour Bureau's quarterly employment surveys for the last seven years (Table 9.1) shed valuable light on this issue.

These quarterly employment surveys throw light on India's employment scenario after the onset of the global financial recession of 2008. While the Indian economy was not severely affected by the recession, primarily due to the limited exposure of its banks and financial institutions to toxic assets of financial institutions in the US and Europe, India's overall economic growth decelerated in the wake of the crisis, as its economy tried to adjust to the global downturn and overcome some of the adverse impacts, such as reduced demand for goods and service exports and volatility in capital flows. These impacts were unavoidable because the Indian economy, much like several other emerging markets, has over time become more integrated with global trade and investment. Thus some of the implications of the financial crisis influenced the Indian economy as well, with consequences for the country's labour market.

The post-financial crisis Indian labour market reflects the contemporary characteristics and challenges of global employment in more than one respect. As Table 9.1 indicates, in the immediate aftermath of the crisis, employment declined for three successive surveys. The total job loss reported in these three surveys was around 750,000. Fairly robust growth in employment was recorded in several of the subsequent surveys, between April–June 2009 and October–December 2011. Since then, employment growth has fluctuated, with a progressive decline having set in from the 22nd survey onward. This culminated in negative growth in employment in the 26th survey (April–June 2015), for the first time since April–June 2009. However, the latest survey, for July–September 2015, shows a reversal of this trend and positive growth in employment. The results of the next few surveys will be critical in determining whether the result of the last survey marks the beginning of a new positive trend in employment growth. At this point any conclusions would be premature. As indicated earlier, the problem of under-employment also needs to be noted in all employment estimates.

The latest QES survey results indicate the salience of two industries—textiles and IT/BPO—in accounting for the improvement in employment. Between them, these industries accounted for 293,000 additional jobs between September 2014 and September 2015. But the net overall employment gain during this period was only 272,000, due to a loss of jobs in automobiles, gems and jewellery and handloom industries.[19] Broad-based employment prospects are hardly encouraging if among eight major employment-intensive sectors, only two generate new employment. Industries like gems and jewellery have been traditional foreign exchange earners and an important source of jobs, as India's Commerce Minister Nirmala Sitharaman observed in late 2016.[20] The loss of employment in significant industries like gems and jewellery, automobiles and leather, is a worrying development.

The impact of automation

India's labour market is increasingly experiencing a trend visible in several parts of the world, which is a source of major concern for national governments and policymakers. This is the rapid onset of automation replacing human jobs in a large number of industries. The loss of jobs in India's automobile industry is a typical example.

The tremendous impact of automation on traditional jobs is an inevitable consequence of economic globalisation and the technological advancement that has accompanied it. The consequences have been aptly highlighted by the celebrated physicist and thinker Stephen Hawking: "The automation of factories has already decimated jobs in traditional manufacturing, and the rise of artificial intelligence is likely to extend this job destruction deep into the middle classes, with only the most caring, creative or supervisory roles remaining."[21] Elaborating on the social and political impact of automation in the context of major recent developments like the decision of the United Kingdom to separate from the European Union (EU) and the election of Donald Trump as the President of the United States, Hawking argues the effect of automation on jobs will "accelerate the already widening economic inequality around the world".[22] The apprehension expressed by Hawking resonates with the concerns articulated by President Mukherjee and alluded to at the beginning of this chapter. The destructive impact of automation on jobs is not limited to developed country economies but has impacted on emerging markets as well.

The global labour market is grappling with the adverse "substitution effect" of technological innovations like industrial robots and artificial intelligence replacing human labour. From a business or firm perspective, greater use of IT, software and digital operations is justified on the grounds of efficiency. But the impact of these changes on employment is profound, particularly at a time when global economic growth is low and the share of wages in national incomes is declining (Basu 2016). Indeed, automation as a labour-displacing force has advanced to the developing countries and is a significant threat to employment prospects. As automation swallows human jobs, labour-abundant developing countries can no longer hope to ride the trajectory of economic growth through shifting surplus labour from agriculture to manufacturing.[23] Premature deindustrialisation precipitated by automation is an enormous challenge for emerging markets, particularly in populous countries like India.

The World Bank (2016, 126) estimates that two-thirds of all jobs in the developing world are vulnerable to automation, broadly defined as the greater use of artificial intelligence, IT and robotics by businesses. China and India are at risk of losing 77 per cent and 68 per cent of their current jobs to automation (Table 9.2). These two are the world's most populous economies, in which modern industries producing sophisticated goods and services coexist with industries employing primarily labour-intensive technologies and engaging low-skilled workers. The impact of automation in these countries is significant for both these sectors of employment. In addition to China and India, developing countries with a comparative advantage in moderately skilled labour-intensive production, such as Ethiopia, Nepal, Cambodia, Bangladesh and Guatemala, are also at significant risk from automation.

While progress on automation varies between industries and countries, the employment trends and industrial strategies being adopted by major businesses in India's automobile and engineering industries are indications that the process is accelerating. From the Indian perspective, the inability to generate enough jobs due to a loss of jobs to automation is probably best exemplified by the automobile industry. As an industry that has been at the forefront of automation and cutting-edge technological innovation for reducing costs and improving operational efficiency, the global automobile industry has been shedding jobs and shifting to more automated production. The latest data

Table 9.2 Countries and their jobs at risk (%) due to automation

Country	*Unadjusted*	*Adjusted*
Ethiopia	84	43
Nepal	79	41
Cambodia	78	40
China	77	55
Bangladesh	76	47
Guatemala	75	46
El Salvador	75	46
Angola	73	53
Albania	72	52
Thailand	72	51
India	68	42
Romania	68	49
Ecuador	68	49
Costa Rica	68	49
Macedonia	68	49

Source: World Bank (2016) and http://www.businessinsider.com/countries-where-robots-will-take-jobs-2016-3?IR=T&r=US&IR=T/#15-macedonia-1

Note: Unadjusted and adjusted projections differ in terms of the latter being adjusted for slower pace of technology adoption; the former estimates do not account for such adjustment.

from India shows that the industry shed 18,000 jobs between September 2014 and September 2015.[24] The substitution effect of labour-saving technological changes is also being experienced in industries and sectors connected to automobiles, such as transport services, where 4,000 jobs were lost in the September 2014–September 2015 period. Job losses have also been reported from elsewhere in the industry. The Indian engineering giant Larsen and Toubro (L&T) recently shed 14,000 jobs through digitalizing operations and cutting costs in response to lower than expected economic growth. The company declared upfront: "'If we needed 10 people for a job we tried to bring it down to five" and explained that lay-offs had taken place across various parts of the organisation, including financial services, minerals and metals.[25] Telecommunications, healthcare and entertainment are some of the other industries in India that have experienced job losses due to automation. The problem is exacerbated at a time when several industries are being forced to downsize due to weak demand and gloomy business prospects.[26]

Information technology (IT) is another industry reeling from the impact of automation in India. Industry experts predict a loss of 25,000–50,000 of the new jobs being created in the IT sector to automation each year, along with the displacement of a significant number of middle-level managerial jobs.[27] Other studies of employment prospects in the IT industry point to similar conclusions, underscoring a shrinkage of around 14 per cent of the IT and BPO industry's current work force (Narayana 2016). Identical concerns have been voiced by NASSCOM, the national IT industry association in India, highlighting the possibility of a large number of existing jobs being lost as skills become irrelevant in an environment where technological improvement is the key driver of productivity, as opposed to greater labour intake.[28] The projections are alarming in the light of the important role that the IT/BPO industry has been playing in advancing employment in India, as the quarterly employment surveys discussed in the previous section indicate.

Globally, the advance in automation has been accompanied by the increasing redundancy of multiple skills. Again, India's automobile and IT/BPO sectors are major examples. Greater digitalisation of functions, apart from displacing jobs, has generated a demand for new skills that are consistent with, and required by, digitally run and managed industrial processes. Most clerical and low technology-intensive skills are becoming redundant as a result. From an IT industry perspective, entry-level candidates with graduate degrees in engineering (Bachelor of Technology) are expected to become increasingly unattractive to companies as they move to a focus on more specialised skills (Basu 2016). In emerging market economies like India, it is becoming increasingly evident that automation's adverse impact is not limited to low-skill manual blue collar jobs, but is gradually extending to jobs requiring more skills. While on the one hand this confirms the onset of premature deindustrialisation, on the other it creates new supply-side challenges for skilling the new entrants to the workforce, as well as those displaced from existing jobs. Indeed, the growing irrelevance of multiple skills augments the challenge of managing employment prospects in an economy that is adding large numbers of young people to its workforce as skills obsolescence diminishes the employability of job-seekers.

Looking ahead

India's labour market and employment prospects have been significantly influenced by the structural changes that have taken place in the country's economy over the last twenty-five years. The most important of these changes is the increasing contribution of services to the national economy. A progressive reduction in the share of agriculture in national output and a marginal improvement in the share of manufacturing reflects the inability of both sectors to create and sustain new jobs. Nonetheless, both sectors, particularly agriculture, continue to remain major sources of livelihood, particularly for rural workers. On the other hand, the tertiary sector, while expanding its presence in the national economy, has not proved capable of generating the number of jobs required to absorb the ever-increasing workforce in one of the world's largest and populous economies. The outcome of all these changes has been the accentuation of "jobless growth". The current high trajectory of more than 7 per cent in GDP growth is capital-intensive and technological innovation-driven, and as a result is not producing enough jobs. Most labour market parameters like the LFPR and the unemployment rate point to a situation where lower participation in the labour force is accompanied by an increase in unemployment. The trend has particularly affected female employment. For women, the problem is not only a lack of jobs, but also a significant absence of suitable jobs. The poor quality of available jobs is one of the deterrents to women's increased participation in the labour force and employment.

In recent months, the issue of inadequate job creation has become critical, with several high employment industries like automobiles, gems and jewellery, transport and metals proving unable to generate jobs. Job creation is now largely limited to IT and textiles. The IT industry is vulnerable to the risk of job loss from automation, as discussed in the previous section. Indeed, India, along with China and other developing countries, is at risk of losing jobs to greater automation throughout its economy. Apart from the fact that greater automation reduces job creation, it is also making existing skills redundant. India's problems are further accentuated by the fact that low demand for its exports, due to the persistence of an economic slowdown in its major consumer markets, is affecting employment prospects in its major export industries such as gems and jewellery, leather, textiles and automobiles. These pressures are further compounding the problem of employment in a shrinking job market.

From the perspective of policymakers, the complexities of the labour market underline the need to recognise demography, quality and gender as the three substantive challenges facing India's employment prospects (see Hill, this volume). Simply put, the policy dilemma boils down to a single question: How can India create more employment for its young population that is qualitatively "decent" and gender-friendly, at a time when jobs are being lost to automation?

The government's effort to encourage start-ups through the "Start-Up India" initiative is an important response to the challenges India is facing. The key objective of this initiative is to encourage talented youth to mature as entrepreneurs, rather than seek a career in salaried or wage employment. The positive impact of more entrepreneurs and new businesses on overall employment prospects is undeniable. The emphasis marks a significant departure in India's outlooks and strategies for employment. Historically, for four decades after independence, the public sector was the largest provider of employment in India. Large state-owned enterprises, in addition to pursuing the objective of self-reliance in industrial production, also focused on employment. Alongside these large enterprises, small-scale industrial units were also considered essential for creating more employment opportunities in a labour-surplus economy. Notwithstanding the importance of small enterprises, which were allowed to develop in a protected industrial eco-system cushioned from competition from imports and large enterprises, incentivizing start-ups was never a conscious strategy, even for several years after the introduction of economic reforms in the 1990s. This might have been due to the assumption that private investment—both foreign and domestic—would generate enough projects and sector-specific employment opportunities. There was also the expectation that sooner or later, manufacturing would take off and begin absorbing more and more workers from agriculture. At the same time, services were also expected to generate more employment than has been the case till now, under the influence of the phenomenal growth of the financial, IT, telecom and real estate sectors. But these expectations have clearly not been met, forcing a rethink on employment strategies.

Manufacturing is still at the forefront of the government's strategy for industrial and economic growth. The "Make in India" initiative places heavy emphasis on manufacturing, with several of its designated industries—automobiles, automobile components, biotechnology, chemicals, electrical machinery, electronics, defence production, pharmaceuticals, oil and gas and renewable energy—being primarily capital-intensive.[29] Looked at from the perspective of job growth and employment, these industries are hardly the answer, as they are clearly dependent on labour-saving technological innovations for productivity gains and are likely to take every opportunity for increased automation. However, "Make in India" does encompass industries like construction, textiles and garments, leather, and food processing, which are relatively more labour-intensive. Employment prospects in some of these industries like textiles, leather, and food processing, which are among India's major exports, are sensitive to global demand. Nevertheless, these are industries relatively less affected by automation. If, over time, "Make in India" succeeds in increasing the share of manufacturing in India's GDP, the quantum and quality of the new jobs created will depend significantly on the performance of these labour-intensive sectors. Apart from offering specific incentives to these sectors for encouraging more employment, it is also important to work on options for increasing exports, as more exports should generate more jobs. In this regard, the conclusion of India's Free Trade Agreement (FTA) with EU and the Regional Comprehensive Economic Partnership (RCEP) among sixteen Asia-Pacific countries including India are essential.[30]

"Make in India" also includes some major service industries—aviation, IT and BPO, media and entertainment, tourism and hospitality, railways, ports and shipping, roads and highways and wellness.[31] During the last two decades, the IT industry has been a major source of urban employment, but it is now struggling hard to retain jobs under the onslaught of automation. The industry is likely to shed more jobs given the efforts of major OECD economies like the US and the UK, that are key business hubs of Indian IT firms, to control immigration. Coupled with automation, immigration restrictions have the potential to seriously impair the Indian IT industry's long-term contribution to jobs and employment. Aviation, media and entertainment, tourism and hospitality and wellness are emerging sectors creating new job prospects, though primarily in urban areas. "Make in India" does not include the retail sector, which not only accounts for a tenth of India's GDP but also around 8 per cent of total employment.[32] The retail sector's employment-generating capacity needs to be looked at in conjunction with the rapid growth of e-commerce in India and the multiple domestic and foreign e-commerce service providers (Amazon, Ikea, Walmart, Flipkart, Snapdeal) expanding their presence and distribution networks in the country. Aided by new-generation digital financial transaction modes like "mobile wallets"[33] and the government's determination to transform India into a less cash and more digital payments-enabled economy, e-commerce and retail are not only destined to expand in economic size, but should also create new jobs. Government focus in facilitating the growth of the sector as a source of more jobs should be a priority.

It is also important to note the occupations being taken up by people in the absence of jobs of their choice. There are examples of engineering graduates and trained interior designers taking to driving Uber cabs through a lack of other employment opportunities.[34] As urbanisation expands and public transport capacities struggle to keep pace, Uber and Ola are becoming preferred transport options for many people in Indian metropolises and state capitals. These companies also represent a new generation of employment providers for many technically qualified new entrants to the job market. While they are inferior options, these jobs are nonetheless taking some pressure off the labour market by chipping away chunks of incremental unemployment. More attention to the formalisation of these jobs would help increase their attractiveness as employment options. Similarly, as discussed earlier in the context of lower female participation in the labour force and growing unemployment, encouraging more flexible work arrangements within the formal sector should result in an increase in female employment, particularly if they include options for working at home.

India faces the exceptionally difficult challenge of creating more jobs in the face of rising automation. The situation is being made more difficult by the "hard" measures being taken by the government, such as the demonetisation of almost 90 per cent of the Indian currency in circulation announced on November 8, 2016, in an effort to curb the circulation of black money and give the Indian economy a more cashless character. The unexpected withdrawal of currency is likely to affect several types of employment, particularly daily wagers, in many labour-intensive industries.[35] More structural adjustments, such as the introduction of a countrywide Goods and Services Tax (GST), are also in the pipeline. These adjustments are disruptive for the economy, at least in the short run and can have repercussions in the job market.

Two further issues are important in the context of India's employment challenges. Rural employment opportunities are unlikely to expand in the future, given premature deindustrialisation and the difficulty of shifting low-skill rural workers to manufacturing. In this respect, there is little option for the government other than to continue allocating large resources to employment guarantee programmes such as the MGNREGA, which supports seasonal rural employment.[36] While this would mean increasing the pressures on a public exchequer already strained by previous borrowings, it is likely that government expenditure will have to accommodate an upward rise in the minimum wages for unorganised sector workers.[37] The increase in minimum wages has long been a pending demand of unorganised sector workers and trade unions. An increase in such wages is important for improving the quality of employment for informal sector workers in labour-surplus emerging market economies. But like India, most of these economies suffer from problems of fiscal unsustainability. This is due to their inability to mobilise sufficient revenues for meeting development expenditures, including those targeted at qualitative and quantitative aspects of employment such as minimum wages and employment guarantee programmes. In the long run, the success of efforts to address employment challenges will depend significantly on the ability of these economies to mobilise resources for funding development and social security for the informal workers.

India and other emerging market economies have little choice but to adjust to both "inevitable" technological changes and "necessary" structural measures while at the same time protecting employment. The latter will entail both short-term measures like specific packages for helping employment-intensive sectors during periods of policy adjustment as well as medium-term measures like greater outlays for employment programmes and higher wages. In the long run, however, the focus must be on protecting and sustaining jobs in industries—both old and new—that are providing employment notwithstanding the advent of automation. Indeed, automation makes the test of addressing the challenges for employment identified in this discussion far more onerous for countries like India and other emerging market economies.

Notes

1 Speech by the President of India Shri Pranab Mukherjee at the Inaugural Session of the Visitor's Conference 2016, November 16, 2016. http://presidentofindia.nic.in/speeches-detail.htm?568
2 Mehta and Kulkarni (2016) argue India is losing 550 jobs per year, placing it behind Bangladesh and Vietnam in job creation.
3 "India's Poverty Profile." World Bank, May 27, 2016. http://www.worldbank.org/en/news/infographic/2016/05/27/india-s-poverty-profile
4 "India will become the world's most populous country by 2022, UN says," *Time*, July 30, 2015. http://time.com/3978175/india-population-worlds-most-populous-country/
5 Press Note on Estimates of the Gross Domestic Product for the First Quarter (April–June) 2016–17, Central Statistics Office, Ministry of Statistics and Programme Implementation, Government of India, August 31, 2016. http://mospi.nic.in/sites/default/files/press_release/nad_PR_31aug16.pdf
6 Computed from CSO national account statistics.
7 Employment Situation in India per 1000 Distribution of Usually Employed by Broad Groups of Industry for Various Rounds, September 16, 2016, Table 163, *Handbook of Indian Statistics*, Reserve Bank of India. https://rbi.org.in/Scripts/PublicationsView.aspx?id=17296
8 Economic Survey 2015–16, Ministry of Finance, Government of India; Chapter 7, Volume II, pp. 153–154; http://indiabudget.nic.in/es2015-16/echapvol2-07.pdf
9 Ibid.
10 During 2001–2008, China, Brazil, India and Russia experienced CAGR (Compounded Annual Growth Rate) of 11.7 per cent, 3.9 per cent, 9.3 per cent and 7.6 per cent respectively. The corresponding CAGR for 2010–14 for the four countries were 8.4 per cent, 6.9 per cent, 8.6 per cent and 2.6 per cent. Table 7.1, Ibid.

11 LFPR is defined as the number of persons in the labour force per 1,000 head of population. Report on Employment-Unemployment Survey, Volume 1, 2015–16, Government of India, Ministry of Labour and Employment, Labour Bureau, Chandigarh; Box 3.1, p. 25. http://labourbureau.nic.in/EUS_5th_Vol_1.pdf
12 *Economic Survey 2015–16*, Ministry of Finance, Government of India; Volume II, Chapter 9, Table 9.3, p. 194 and Report on Employment–Unemployment Survey, Volume 1, 2015–16, Government of India, Ministry of Labour and Employment, Labour Bureau, Chandigarh.
13 The unemployment rate is defined as the number of unemployed persons per 1000 persons in the labour force (employed and unemployed). The definition is provided in the source mentioned in endnote 9.
14 Rural unemployment increased from 4.7 per cent to 5.1 per cent between the fourth and fifth surveys, while rural female unemployment increased from 6.4 per cent to 7.8 per cent between the two surveys. Urban female unemployment declined from 12.4 per cent to 12.1 per cent during this period. This data is drawn from the sources mentioned in endnote 10.
15 See Afridi, Dinkelman, and Mahajan (2016) and Chatterjee, Murgai, and Martin (2015) for more details and discussion.
16 Unemployment, total (percentage of labour force), modelled ILO estimate, World Bank; http://data.worldbank.org/indicator/SL.UEM.TOTL.ZS
17 Report on Employment–Unemployment Survey, Volume 1, 2015–16, Government of India, Ministry of Labour and Employment, Labour Bureau, Chandigarh; pp. vi-vii. http://labourbureau.nic.in/EUS_5th_Vol_1.pdf
18 Ibid. pp. vii-viii.
19 The Quarterly Employment Surveys cover eight employment-intensive sectors—textiles, metals, automobiles, IT/BPO, handloom/powerloom, gems and jewellery, transport and leather.
20 "Gem and Jewellery Sector has Direct Impact on Job Creation: Nirmala Sitharaman." http://www.newkerala.com/news/2016/fullnews-150796.html
21 'This is the Most Dangerous Time for our Planet', *The Guardian*, December 1, 2016. https://www.theguardian.com/commentisfree/2016/dec/01/stephen-hawking-dangerous-time-planet-inequality
22 Ibid.
23 "Impact of Automation on Developing Countries Puts up to 85% of Jobs at Risk." Oxford Martin School, University of Oxford, January 27, 2016. http://www.oxfordmartin.ox.ac.uk/news/201601_Technology_at_Work_2
24 Quarterly Report on Changes in Employment in Selected Sectors (July 2015–September 2015); Government of India, Ministry of Labour and Employment, Labour Bureau, Chandigarh, March 2016, Table 2.1, p. 12.
25 "L&T Sacks 14,000 Staff Due to Digitization, Slowdown in One of India's Biggest Ever Layoffs." *Financial Express*, November 23, 2016. http://www.financialexpress.com/industry/jobs/lt-sacks-14000-staff-due-to-digitisation-slowdown-in-one-of-indias-biggest-ever-layoffs/453392/
26 "Where are the Jobs?" *India Today*, April 20, 2016. http://indiatoday.intoday.in/story/employment-scenario-job-crunch-jobless-growth-economy/1/647573.html
27 "Automation to Replace Lakhs of Entry, Mid-level IT Execs: TV Mohandas Pai." *The Economic Times*, July 31, 2016. http://economictimes.indiatimes.com/tech/ites/automation-to-replace-lakhs-of-entry-mid-level-it-execs-tv-mohandas-pai/articleshow/53475940.cms
28 "Automation will Wipe Out 50% of All IT Jobs in India; But Digital Start-Ups Increase Hiring Activity." http://trak.in/tags/business/2015/10/06/automation-wipe-50-all-it-jobs-india-digital-startups-hiring-activity/

29 http://www.makeinindia.com/sectors
30 India–EU FTA negotiations have been going on since 2007 and are yet to conclude. The RCEP includes sixteen countries—Australia, Brunei, Cambodia, China, India, Indonesia, Japan, Korea, Lao PDR, Malaysia, Myanmar, New Zealand, Philippines, Thailand, Singapore and Vietnam. The talks began in 2013 and are at an advanced stage.
31 "Where are the Jobs?" *India Today*, April 20, 2016. http://indiatoday.intoday.in/story/employment-scenario-job-crunch-jobless-growth-economy/1/647573.html.
32 "Retail Industry in India." India Brand Equity Foundation. http://www.ibef.org/industry/retail-india.aspx
33 Paytm is one of the fastest mobile wallet service providers in India and is already being challenged by competitors like MobiKwik.
34 Author interviews.
35 "Now Demonetization Set to Cost 400,000 Jobs." *Financial Express*, November 24, 2016. http://www.financialexpress.com/jobs/now-demonetisation-set-to-cost-400000-jobs/454305/
36 The Budget for FY2017 increased the allocation for MGNREGA by almost 25 per cent from the previous year by allocating Rs. 48,500 crore (Rs. 485,000 million), which is the highest allocation for the scheme since its inception. Budget speech; http://indiabudget.nic.in/ub2017-18/bs/bs.pdf.
37 "Government Hikes Minimum Wages for Workers, Announces 2 Years' Bonus." *The Times of India*, August 30, 2016. http://timesofindia.indiatimes.com/india/Two-years-bonus-for-central-government-staff-Arun-Jaitley/articleshow/53927794.cms

References

Afridi, Farzana, Taryn Dinkelman and Kanika Mahajan. 2016. "Why Are Fewer Married Women Joining the Work Force in India? A Decomposition Analysis over Two Decades." IZA DP 9722, February. http://ftp.iza.org/dp9722.pdf

Basu, Kaushik. 2016. *Globalization of Labor Markets and the Growth Prospects of Nations*. [Policy Research Working Paper 7590] Washington DC: World Bank Group. http://documents.worldbank.org/curated/en/290261468194944594/Globalization-of-labor-markets-and-the-growth-prospects-of-nations

Chatterjee, Urmila, Rinku Murgai and Rama Martin. 2015. *Job Opportunities along the Rural–Urban Gradation and Female Labor Force Participation in India*. [Policy Research Working Paper 7412]. Washington DC: World Bank Group. http://documents.worldbank.org/curated/en/732961468189870923/pdf/WPS7412.pdf

Mehta, Pradeep and Amol Kulkarni. 2016. "It is Time to Address India's Abysmal Job Creation Record." *The Wire*, November 25. http://thewire.in/82017/india-abysmal-job-creation-record/

Narayana, M.R. 2016. "Robots to Take our Jobs: For India what Matters is Not Technological Unemployment but Unemployability." *Financial Express*, Delhi, 6 December. http://www.financialexpress.com/opinion/robots-to-take-our-jobs-for-india-what-matters-is-not-technological-unemployment-but-unemployability/465397/

World Bank. 2016. *Digital Dividends*. [World Development Report 2016]. Washington DC: World Bank. http://documents.worldbank.org/curated/en/896971468194972881/pdf/102725-PUB-Replacement-PUBLIC.pdf

Index

Note: Page numbers in bold refer to tables; those in italic refer to figures.

For Product Safety Concerns and Information please contact our EU representative GPSR@taylorandfrancis.com
Taylor & Francis Verlag GmbH, Kaufingerstraße 24, 80331 München, Germany

www.ingramcontent.com/pod-product-compliance
Ingram Content Group UK Ltd.
Pitfield, Milton Keynes, MK11 3LW, UK
UKHW020950180425
457613UK00019B/614

9780367873530